The Value of Events

The Value of Events fills an important niche in the literature on events, being the first book to comprehensively deal with the subject of value creation and measurement, as opposed to impact assessment and programme evaluation. Value creation and measurement is often done routinely from specific perspectives such as tourism, event management, corporate marketing, or customer satisfaction. However, there exist a number of discourses on value and evaluation that have not yet received adequate attention, including the justification of governmental intervention and the costs and benefits of hosting major events.

This edited book, written by an international group of academics with expertise in the relevant fields of events, tourism, sport and culture, offers new insight into events and their relationship to sustainability, social responsibility, cultural and social value. Fostering debate in the context of conceptual thinking, philosophising, multiple stakeholder perspectives and interdisciplinary approaches, it challenges the events industry, students, policy-makers and strategists with new perspectives on value, with implications for impact forecasting and assessment.

This is a book for all students pursuing degrees in fields where planned events are important topics, while being of great interest to researchers, policy-makers, evaluators and organisers/managers of planned events. Within a subject in need of further attention, *The Value of Events* offers the most comprehensive overview of event value to date.

Erik Lundberg, PhD, is a researcher and lecturer at the Centre for Tourism in the School of Economics, Business and Law at the University of Gothenburg, Sweden. He received his PhD in 2014. In his thesis, he describes and analyses tourism and event impacts from a sustainable development perspective. He has published in journals such as *Tourism Management*, *Scandinavian Journal of Hospitality and Tourism Management* and *International Journal of Event and Festival Management*.

John Armbrecht, PhD, is Head of the Centre for Tourism and Researcher at the School of Business, Economics and Law at the University of Gothenburg, Sweden. He received his PhD in marketing and has mainly published research on experiential and non-use values within areas like cultural tourism, cultural economics and event and festival economics.

Tommy D. Andersson, PhD, is Senior Professor in Tourism and Hospitality Management at the University of Gothenburg, Sweden and Professor II at Molde University College, Norway. He received his PhD in managerial economics and has been interested in economic impact analysis, event management and cost–benefit analysis. Most of his publications are in the area of event research and food tourism research.

Donald Getz is Professor Emeritus, the University of Calgary, Canada, and is affiliated with Linnaeus University in Sweden. He is author of numerous articles on events, and the books *Event Tourism* (2013) and *Event Studies* (Routledge, 3rd edn, 2016, co-authored with Stephen Page). Professor Getz acts as a management consultant to universities, cities and destinations in the fields of tourism and events, and participates in major research and development projects.

Routledge Advances in Event Research Series
Edited by Warwick Frost and Jennifer Laing
Department of Marketing, Tourism and
Hospitality, La Trobe University, Australia

The Future of Events and Festivals
*Edited by Ian Yeoman, Martin Robertson, Una McMahon-Beattie, Elisa Backer
and Karen A. Smith*

Exploring Community Events and Festivals
Edited by Allan Jepson and Alan Clarke

Event Design: Social perspectives and practices
Edited by Greg Richards, Lénia Marques and Karen Mein

Rituals and Traditional Events in the Modern World
Edited by Warwick Frost and Jennifer Laing

Battlefield Events: Landscape, commemoration and heritage
*Edited by Keir Reeves, Geoffrey Bird, Laura James, Birger Stichelbaut and Jean
Bourgeois*

Events in the City: Using public spaces as event venues
Andrew Smith

Event Mobilities: Politics, place and performance
Edited by Kevin Hannam, Mary Mostafanezhad and Jillian Rickly-Boyd

Approaches and Methods in Events Studies
Edited by Tomas Pernecky

Visitor Attractions and Events: Locations and linkages
Adi Weidenfeld, Richard Butler and Allan Williams

Critical Event Studies: A guide for critical thinkers
Karl Spracklen and Ian R. Lamond

The Value of Events
Edited by Erik Lundberg, John Armbrecht, Tommy D. Andersson and Donald Getz

The Value of Events

Edited by Erik Lundberg,
John Armbrecht, Tommy D. Andersson
and Donald Getz

Routledge
Taylor & Francis Group

LONDON AND NEW YORK

First published 2017
by Routledge

2 Park Square, Milton Park, Abingdon, Oxfordshire OX14 4RN
52 Vanderbilt Avenue, New York, NY 10017

Routledge is an imprint of the Taylor & Francis Group, an informa business

First issued in paperback 2020

British Library Cataloguing in Publication Data
A catalogue record for this book is available from the British Library

Library of Congress Cataloging in Publication Data
A catalog record for this book has been requested

ISBN: 978-1-138-67841-5 (hbk)
ISBN: 978-0-367-66783-2 (pbk)

Typeset in Times New Roman
by Cenveo Publisher Services

Contents

List of figures   ix
List of tables   x
Notes on contributors   xi
Preface   xvi

1. **Definitions and meanings of value**   1
    DONALD GETZ, TOMMY D. ANDERSSON,
    JOHN ARMBRECHT AND ERIK LUNDBERG

2. **The value of events and festivals in the age of austerity**   10
    EMMA WOOD

PART I
Value creation of events   37

3. **Exploring consumers' value co-creation in a festival context
    using a socio-cultural lens**   39
    SANDHIYA GOOLAUP AND LENA MOSSBERG

4. **Successful event–destination collaboration through
    superior experience value for visitors**   58
    NINA K. PREBENSEN

5. **Creating network value: the Barcelona Sónar Festival
    as a global events hub**   73
    GREG RICHARDS AND ALBA COLOMBO

PART II
Assessing the value of events 87

6. **The use and non-use values of events: a conceptual framework** 89
   TOMMY D. ANDERSSON, JOHN ARMBRECHT AND ERIK LUNDBERG

7. **Event evaluation: approaches and new challenges** 105
   LARRY DWYER AND PETER FORSYTH

8. **Economic valuation of events: combining methods based on revealed, stated and subjective preference data** 124
   REZA MORTAZAVI AND TOBIAS HELDT

9. **Valuing the inspirational impacts of major sports events** 136
   GIRISH RAMCHANDANI, RICHARD COLEMAN, LARISSA DAVIES, SIMON SHIBLI AND JERRY BINGHAM

10. **Understanding the value of events for families, and the impact upon their quality of life** 159
    RAPHAELA STADLER AND ALLAN JEPSON

PART III
Conclusions 179

11. **A synthesis, summaries and some ontological propositions** 181
    DONALD GETZ, TOMMY D. ANDERSSON, JOHN ARMBRECHT AND ERIK LUNDBERG

Index 200

Figures

1.1	Definitions of 'value' and related terms	4
1.2	A four-dimensional approach to event values	7
2.1	Diminishing returns and the triangle of engagement	18
2.2	Local government reasons for event involvement	20
2.3	Department with main responsibility for events (2012 data)	21
2.4	Local government and community involvement in festivals	23
2.5	How events are valued	30
3.1	Participants purchasing oysters and drinks	49
3.2	Learning how to open oysters	49
3.3	Musical entertainment	50
3.4	Participants enjoying their oysters and drinks	50
4.1	Collaboration for enhanced experience value for customers	66
6.1	A description of sub-categories of use and non-use values for cultural events	100
6.2	A summary chart of relevant measures of use and non-use values of events	100
7.1	Total economic value	112
7.2	A measurement model describing the total festival impact from a sustainability perspective	113
8.1	Example of choice set for the Peace and Love choice experiment	129
9.1	Ansoff Matrix	138
9.2	Stages of change (TTM)	140
9.3	Processes of change (TTM)	141
9.4	"I am inspired to do sport or recreational physical activity more frequently than I normally do": by event	144
9.5	"I am inspired to do sport or recreational physical activity more frequently than I normally do": by respondents' age and participation levels	145
9.6	Net changes in sport-specific and other participation by respondent clusters	154
9.7	Influence of other factors on participation increases	155
10.1	QOL research methods diagram	165
10.2	Festival and event value creation and the impact upon family QOL	167

Tables

6.1 How use and non-use values of cultural institutions
    are described by respondents   93
6.2 Event studies describing use and/or non-use values   97
8.1 Attributes and levels used for the choice experiment   129
8.2 Results from the conditional logit based on the
    choice experiment data   131
8.3 Results from a regression of willingness to pay to avoid more
    attendees on subjective well-being and some other
    independent variables   132
9.1 The events   142
9.2 Drivers of inspiration as indicated by spectators   147
9.3 Potential levers to participation   148
9.4 Derivation of net changes in post-event participation   151
9.5 Gross and net changes in sport-specific and other participation 152
9.6 Net changes by respondent clusters   153
10.A1 Example questions to stimulate focus group discussions
    and test theory to better understand the relationship
    between festivals/events and QOL   172

Contributors

Tommy D. Andersson, PhD, is Senior Professor in Tourism and Hospitality Management at University of Gothenburg, Sweden and Professor II at Molde University College, Norway. He received his PhD in managerial economics and has been interested in economic impact analysis, event management and cost–benefit analysis. Most of his publications are in the area of event research and food tourism research.

John Armbrecht, PhD, is Head of the Centre for Tourism and Researcher at the School of Business, Economics and Law at the University of Gothenburg, Sweden. He received his PhD in marketing and has mainly published research on experiential and non-use values within areas like cultural tourism, cultural economics and event and festival economics.

Jerry Bingham manages the research and evaluation programmes for UK Sport, the high-performance sports agency in the UK, seeking to ensure that policy decisions are based on sound evidence. He contributed to a number of studies around London 2012 and commissioned the research examining the inspiration effects of major sporting events. Jerry has also examined elite sport systems to identify the pillars underpinning international sporting success and is currently leading UK Sport's attempts to demonstrate the broader impacts of British medal success and the major events that take place in the UK.

Richard Coleman is a Principal Research Fellow at Sheffield Hallam University's Sport Industry Research Centre. His research interests include major events and their impacts. He was instrumental in the development of the eventIMPACTS online toolkit on behalf of UK Sport and its research partners. Richard has also managed and reported on event impact studies for: London Marathon Limited; Transport for London (on the Tour de France); All England Lawn Tennis Club (Wimbledon); the R&A (The Open); the ATP (World Tour Finals); and MCC (Lord's Ashes Test).

Alba Colombo is Lecturer and Researcher at the Open University of Catalunya (UOC), in Barcelona, and has experiences in events research and education. She holds a PhD in Social Sciences (2012) from the University of Girona. Her main research areas are cultural and creative industries, the relationship between those industries and events and youth tourism. She is involved in research projects related to events and their effects, management, policy and economy perspectives such as the EURO-FESTIVAL Project Arts Festivals and European Public Culture, financed by the Seventh Framework Programme, and the ATLAS Events Monitoring Project.

Larissa Davies is a Reader in Sport Management at Sport Industry Research Centre, Sheffield Hallam University. She has over 15 years' experience teaching and researching in the discipline areas of sport management and geography. Larissa has a PhD in the field of sports economics and specialises in the area of sport, events and urban regeneration. Her research interests include: Olympic legacies and regeneration; the economic importance of sport and major events; sports stadia and property regeneration; and the social impacts of sport. She has published widely around these themes in various international journals. Larissa is currently working on research relating to measuring and valuing the social impact of sport for the national government and a charitable organisation.

Larry Dwyer (University of Ljubljana, Slovenia; Griffith University, Australia; and University of NSW, Australia) publishes widely in the areas of tourism economics, management and policy, with 200 publications in international journals, government reports, books, book chapters and monographs. He has a special research interest in issues of event evaluation and has published many papers on this topic.

Peter Forsyth (Monash University, Melbourne, Australia; and Southern Cross University, Australia) publishes widely in the areas of microeconomics, tourism economics and air transport economics. He has published numerous papers on event evaluation. In this area he has a special research interest in combining the use of computable general equilibrium modelling and cost–benefit analysis

Donald Getz is Professor Emeritus, the University of Calgary, Canada, and is affiliated with Linnaeus University in Sweden. He is author of numerous articles on events, and the books *Event Tourism* (2013) and *Event Studies* (Routledge, 3rd edn, 2016, co-authored with Stephen Page). Professor Getz acts as a management consultant to universities, cities and destinations in the fields of tourism and events, and participates in major research and development projects.

Sandhiya Goolaup is currently a PhD candidate at the University of Gothenburg. She received a Bachelor's degree in Tourism, Leisure and Recreational Management from the University of Mauritius in 2007 and a Master's degree in Management, with specialisation in Marketing in 2012, from Umeå University, Sweden. Her research interest revolves around food tourism, tourist experience, consumer identity and value creation.

Tobias Heldt is Assistant Professor of Economics, specialising in Tourism, at Dalarna University, Sweden. Tobias received his PhD from Uppsala University, Sweden, in 2005. He has published in journals such as *Current Issues in Tourism, Ecological Economics, Transportation Research* and *Scandinavian Journal of Hospitality and Tourism.*

Allan Jepson, PhD, is a Senior Lecturer and researcher in critical event studies (CES) at the University of Hertfordshire. Allan has contributed to event studies literature within the realm of community festivals and events and has two key texts in this area (*Exploring Community Festivals and Events* and *Managing and Developing Communities, Festivals and Events*, both with Alan Clarke, University of Pannonia, Hungary). Allan's current research interests include: the role of inclusive/exclusive cultures and sub-cultures within festivals and events, the cultural relationships of festival stakeholders and, in particular, local community/ies, the role of stakeholders in event production/construction. He studies how the latter impact upon the consumption of cultural events and festivals, power and decision-making in local community festivals and events, the role of festivals and events as a catalyst for integrating culturally diverse communities, psychology and events; self- and group efficacy and how this affects community engagement in event planning and consumption; knowledge management in events, community festivals and events; and their impact on the quality of life (QOL) of individuals and families.

Erik Lundberg, PhD, is a researcher and lecturer at the Centre for Tourism in the School of Economics, Business and Law at the University of Gothenburg, Sweden. He received his PhD in 2014. In his thesis, he describes and analyses tourism and event impacts from a sustainable development perspective. He has published in journals such as *Tourism Management, Scandinavian Journal of Hospitality and Tourism Management* and *International Journal of Event and Festival Management.*

Reza Mortazavi is a Senior Lecturer in Economics at Dalarna University, Sweden. Reza received his PhD from Umeå University in 1999. He has done research in tourism and transportation economics and published in journals such as *Annals of Tourism Research, Tourism Economics* and *Journal of Transport Economics and Policy.*

Lena Mossberg is Professor of Marketing at the School of Business, Economics and Law at Gothenburg University, Sweden, and also Professor II at Nord University in Bodö, Norway. She holds a PhD in Business Administration and has interests in consumer behaviour and consumption, consumer experiences, service encounters and destination image. She has published several articles and books related to event marketing, food tourism, restaurant management and concept development (related to events, destinations, restaurants and hotels).

Nina K. Prebensen, PhD, is Professor at Buskerud and Vestfold University College. She holds a shared position as Professor at University of Tromso. She has published papers in various tourism marketing and management journals. Her research focuses, in particular, on the tourist decision and experience processes, especially co-creation of values for hosts and guests. Her teaching experiences include marketing, tourism marketing and management, service quality and branding strategies. Professor Prebensen has been part of 25 business boards, and has a long history in cooperating with the tourism industry.

Girish Ramchandani is a Reader in Sport Management at Sheffield Hallam University's Sport Industry Research Centre. His principal area of research is the evaluation of major sports events and he has published widely on their economic, sport development and elite performance outcomes. Girish is also a Social Return on Investment (SROI) trained practitioner. He is currently engaged by UK Sport to evaluate around 40 international sporting events till 2019.

Greg Richards is Professor of Placemaking and Events at NHTV Breda University of Applied Sciences and Professor of Leisure Studies at the University of Tilburg in the Netherlands. He has worked on projects for numerous national governments, national tourism organisations and municipalities, and he has extensive experience in tourism research and education in different European countries.

Simon Shibli (Sheffield Hallam University) is a qualified management accountant (ACMA) who specialises in the finance and economics of the sport industry. Simon has a long track record of conducting financial and economic evaluation exercises for Sport England, UK Sport, national governing bodies and private sector clients. He has a detailed knowledge of major sport and cultural events and has conducted research in this area for national agencies and local authorities.

Raphaela Stadler, PhD, is a Lecturer and Researcher in Event Studies at the University of Hertfordshire. Her PhD from Griffith University, Australia, investigated the issue of knowledge management within festival organisations, as well as knowledge transfer between festival organisations and other institutions and bodies. She has been involved in a range of research and work-related projects covering areas such as festivals and cultural policy; community cultural development; event social impacts; and community engagement and participation. Other research interests include knowledge management, transfer and creation, appreciative inquiry and appreciative leadership, community festivals and their impact on quality of life, as well as music history and music business.

Emma Wood is Reader in Festivals and Events Marketing within the International Centre for Research in Events, Tourism and Hospitality at Leeds

Beckett University. She is co-author of *Innovative Marketing Communication for Events* (Elsevier, 2005) and the European edition of Hoffman and Bateson's *Services Marketing* text (Cengage, 2008). Emma's current research interests are in the areas of experiential marketing, social marketing via festivals and events and the social impacts of events. Her doctorate included the development of an evaluation framework for local government-supported community events. Emma is joint editor of the *Journal of Policy Research in Tourism, Leisure and Events* and also chairs the Academy of Marketing special interest group in Sport and Event Experiential Marketing. Recent consultancy projects include festival impact studies for local government, the use of social media for events industry professional bodies and a longitudinal study of the changing role of local government in supporting events and festivals.

Preface

This is a book about the value of events – the definitions and meanings of value, terminology and, particularly, how to create and measure value from many perspectives. It is not a book specifically on evaluation concepts or methods, although some elements of evaluation are, of necessity, incorporated into the discussions.

The idea to write this book came out of two consecutive symposia on the subject of event evaluation (in 2014 and 2015), organized by the editors with help and financial support from BFUF (the R&D Fund of the Swedish Tourism & Hospitality Industry) and the Centre for Tourism at the University of Gothenburg. The centrality of the value concept was discussed at these meetings and the possibility to contribute to event literature and praxis by exploring the concept linked to planned events further. With the help of the attendees of the symposia and other colleagues, we have therefore gathered 11 chapters discussing value creation, definitions and the measurement of value in the event and festival context. Our objective has been to include state of the art research and to consider future challenges for stakeholders in the event industry.

In Chapter 1, we provide an overview of definitions, meanings and conceptualisations of value to set the stage for ensuing contributions. Frameworks to categorise and explore value in the context of planned events are illustrated. One major point is to stress the differences between extrinsic and intrinsic approaches of value. Another point is that studies investigating the value of events often implicitly or explicitly take the perspective of one or several stakeholders. This implies that the focus of the analysis can be on different types of objects of study, such as economic contribution, social inclusion or cultural diffusion. Other issues that are dealt with include whether the study interest is on an individual level or if a study focuses on an aggregated level such as *event participants* or *individuals of a society*. Thus the subject(s) of study are important to consider.

In Chapter 11, the editors provide a synthesis and draw conclusions both for theory and praxis. Implications are drawn for researchers, policy-makers, evaluators and organisers/managers of planned events.

1 Definitions and meanings of value

Donald Getz, Tommy D. Andersson,
John Armbrecht and Erik Lundberg

This chapter gives an introduction to *The Value of Events* and sets the stage for subsequent contributions by providing an overview of the most fundamental concepts. We start with definitions that can be found in most dictionaries, including examples of how terms are used in the context of events. This is followed by a general discussion of extrinsic versus intrinsic approaches to assigning value, drawing on economics and other disciplinary perspectives. Particular attention is given to planned events and a model for exploring extrinsic and intrinsic values is presented. Building on this model, the chapter elaborates on the important objects and subjects of study.

Introduction

Events have been studied from many disciplinary perspectives, including history, psychology, health, anthropology, sociology, heritage studies, economics and cultural studies. Looking upon events as representing institutionalised cultural phenomena, for example, allows us to apply theories of value from these disciplines to enrich the discourse on planned events and their contemporary roles (Armbrecht, 2014). The point is that value is not restricted to one or a few disciplines, even though economic approaches have been paramount in the event-specific literature.

The editors and contributors understand that valuing events (as in determining their overall or cumulative worth) is inherently subjective. These subjective evaluations may have the character of both qualitative and explorative descriptions and quantitative inputs. And we take a multi-stakeholder approach, looking at event value through the eyes of producers, consumers, residents, destinations and others involved in event production or those who are impacted by events.

Impact assessment, which is a major theme in the events literature, is in itself not evaluation but rather a method, or group of techniques, intended to reveal important information about the outcomes of events such as the economic contribution of event tourism or the social impacts of holding a festival. Impact assessments can be used to assess, compare or discuss different aspects of value. The exercise of impact assessment therefore has implications for event strategy formulation, public and private policies, as well as public planning. A better understanding of the impacts of events will improve the forecasting and evaluation of potential impacts, which are necessary when, for example, taking decisions about whether or not to bid on or support an event.

While understanding and describing value of one particular event is desirable, an even more urgent and complicated issue is to understand the value of portfolios of events that are important within many policy fields and industry strategies, and whole populations of events within cities and countries. The continuing expansion of the events sector, and of all types of events in terms of size and significance, reflects their legitimation in terms of government policies and industry strategies. As well, people expect their cities and countries to be eventful, offering many choices. There is, therefore, no question about how valuable planned events are in general terms – they are clearly highly valued all around the world. That observation, however, does not detract from the need to examine perspectives on value, its measurement and related discourses, in order to secure that public and private resources are invested carefully.

Definitions

In this section we start with dictionary definitions and terminology, including examples of how value-related terms are used in the events field. But this provides only superficial understanding of the issues, so it is followed by an exploration of meanings. It is clear that two inter-related streams of meaning exist, often referred to as "intrinsic" versus "extrinsic" approaches, and they are underpinned by philosophical as well as practical considerations.

According to Ng and Smith (2012), there are two relevant distinct meanings of 'value'. The first pertains to a person's or group's values, based on culture and ethics, influencing what a person becomes and does. In this sense, values determine (at least in part) attitudes towards events or tourism, and values influence what a group or society does by way of organising and facilitating (or regulating) planned events. Several definitions and usages of the concept of value in the events context have been explored (Brown *et al.*, 2015). However, Brown *et al.* mainly examined evaluation theory and praxis rather than value concepts in general.

In surge for synonyms for the noun 'value', one may think of terms such as 'worth', 'utility', 'advantage', 'benefit', 'profit', 'merit' and 'usefulness'. These suggest how the value of an event might be determined, but raise the question 'by whom' or 'from whose perspective'? Closely related to the noun 'value' is the term 'evaluation'. Robson (2000) observed: "Dictionary definitions refer to evaluation as assessing the value (or worth, or merit) of something. The 'something' focused on here is some kind of innovation, or intervention, or project, or service" (p. 8).

The 'something' in our case would be an event. Thus the definition of evaluation is proposed to be the assessment of the value of an event. However, the term 'evaluation' is not generally used in that way. Professional event managers, tourism strategists and policy-makers using events instrumentally are frequently concerned with evaluating policies, programmes and events in terms of proving cause and effect (e.g. did an event attract tourists or foster social integration?), or are preoccupied with the evaluation of management functions and personnel within an organisation, as that is essential for improving efficiency and effectiveness. Much of the literature concerns these forms of evaluation, but we argue that they serve to generate inputs to the broader determination of worth or merit.

Allen *et al.* (2011) offer a definition of event evaluation that encompasses the main aims of programme evaluation and management-system evaluation: "Event evaluation is the process of critically observing, measuring and monitoring the implementation of an event in order to assess its outcomes accurately" (p. 492). The authors of this definition said it is a continuous process that embodies pre-event feasibility studies, monitoring and control of event operations, and post-event evaluation that focuses on measuring outcomes and determining ways to improve the event.

The verbal form is 'evaluate'. To evaluate signifies the process of actually assigning and measuring the value of events. This process may include qualitative descriptions, but often focuses on how to measure the value of events.

In its adverbial form, it is common practice to refer to an event as being operated profitably, usefully, or valuably. As an adjective, we can call an event 'valuable' as a business or tourist asset, or worthy of public support. Employing any of these terms can greatly influence one's perception of an event, as illustrated in Figure 1.1.

Discourse on the value of events, or the worthwhileness of public support, is common around the world. In recent years, we have witnessed protests against the huge expenditure associated with mega events, riots surrounding political events (the event in these cases is a platform) and considerable debate regarding the relative merits of government intervention. The populations of Munich and Hamburg have even voted against using public resources for staging the Olympic games.

A major aim of this book is to advance discourse on the value, worth or merit of events from multiple perspectives. This has implications for research, which has traditionally been dominated by a positivistic paradigm stressing the measurement of impacts, with economics, management and marketing concerns being predominant.

Conceptualisation of value within an event context

A number of disciplinary approaches are relevant when conceptualising the value of events. For example, religious or spiritual value refers to the context in which events are perceived. Indigenous events may represent specific religious traditions for particular tribes or cultural groupings. Spiritual-specific outcomes are enlightenment or deeper inner insight and understanding. Pilgrimage, in this light, has value that enters the realm of the transcendental. To many people the religious rites, rituals and symbols incorporated into events (or constituting the event) cannot be challenged without committing sacrilege, which can give rise to tension and conflict between groups with different value systems.

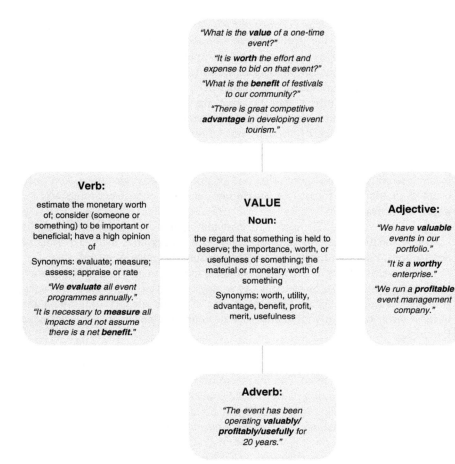

Figure 1.1 Definitions of 'value' and related terms.
Source: Brown *et al.* (2015).

An alternative to taking a religious stance is to base values on philosophical positions, such as secular humanism. This ties in with ethics and beliefs about what is inherently right or wrong. For example, many people believe in 'live and let live' or tolerance, which gives rise to acceptance of many other opinions and values. Aesthetics, and notions of what is beautiful or what art is, can be based on a philosophical position or world view.

Principles of sustainability are, at least in part, based on philosophical or religious positions, such as the necessity for stewardship of the planet's natural resources and its diverse life forms. When it comes to discourse on sustainable development and green events, underlying values cannot be ignored. An event might be judged to be inherently good or bad according to one's belief in the precautionary principle or a blanket condemnation of blatant consumption and revelry. Alternatively, an event might be valued for its stance on environmentalism, regardless of its programme and setting.

From a sociological perspective, value or bundles of values are capital (Bourdieu, 1973; Bourdieu and Passeron, 1990). Events can be regarded as facilitating and catalysing social interaction and social networks among individuals as well as groups of people. This development represents what some authors would describe as social capital. Throsby (2001) describes social value as "the sense of connection with others" (p. 29) that an experience may create. While some researchers consider the number of contacts to be most important, other researchers point to the significance of the strength of the ties (Granovetter, 1983; Lin, 2001).

Another outcome of events is their educational benefit. Both knowledge and skills can be results of events and festivals. Lipe (1984) refers to the learning effect as informational value, whereas the Burra Charter (ICOMOS, 1999) and English Heritage (1997) describe them as educational and academic value. Mykletun (2009), in a festival context, refers to the same phenomenon as building human capital.

Historical value is primarily related to historical and cultural events. The historical significance represents events' connection to the past, affecting individuals' identity today. While historical value represents the connection to the past, symbolic value is the ability of an event to reflect conditions of life in the past and the extent to which they throw light on the present. The stronger the connection, the stronger is the sense of continuity. Throsby discusses symbolic value and its ability to conveying "cultural meaning" (Throsby, 2001, p. 112).

To anthropologists and cultural sociologists events can be read as a text that illuminates cultural values and social structures. The concept of anthropological exchange is relevant, as it emphasises the power of symbolism as opposed to tangible, economic exchanges. Cultural capital is described as obtained knowledge and competence to interpret and make sense of cultural representations (Mahar *et al.*, 1990). Cultural capital is, for example, a vehicle to decode works of art (Bourdieu, 1968); it is the result of repeated, learned consumption, formal education or inheritance from parents. Throsby (2010) also used the term 'cultural capital' to represent "an asset which embodies, stores or provides cultural value in addition to whatever economic value" (p. 46) a cultural service or product may possess.

To understand the value of heritage, Mason (2002) developed a typology which has relevance within an event context. The typology is inspired by previous research by, for example, Lipe (1984), Riegl (1982), ICOMOS (1999), Frey (2003) and de la Torre (1997). In the typology Mason (2002) distinguishes between two broad categories of value: socio-cultural and economic values. Socio-cultural values may cover historical values, cultural/symbolic values, social values, spiritual/religious values and aesthetic values – a grouping also supported by Throsby (2001). The Burra Charter (ICOMOS, 1999) has a similar distinction and emphasises aesthetic, historic, scientific, social and spiritual value for past, present or future generations in describing cultural significance or value.

Intrinsic and extrinsic value

McCarthy *et al.* (2004) go further and use four dimensions to categorise value of culture and distinguish between private and public benefits and the *extrinsic* and *intrinsic value* dimensions. Intrinsic value is caused by intellectual, emotional and spiritual experiences and relates to the notion that something is valuable in itself. This perception differs from an economic logic and also from theories arguing that value is socially constructed (Mirowski, 1990). Extrinsic value stems from theories of utility and exchanges and provides tangible benefits to either individuals or society as a whole. This categorisation has been applied in previous event research (cf. Andersson *et al.*, 2012) and is elaborated on here for the purpose of understanding different approaches to value in this book.

Many value typologies, in one way or another, reflect the intrinsic–extrinsic dichotomy of value. Again it is helpful to refer to dictionary definitions (Oxforddictionaries.com):

> Intrinsic: Belonging naturally; essential. As in "access to the arts is **intrinsic to** a high quality of life".

> Extrinsic: Not part of the essential nature of someone or something; coming or operating from outside. As in "**extrinsic factors** that might affect time budgets; the idea that power is **extrinsic** to production and profits".

By saying that something like the arts or a festival is intrinsic to a high quality of life really implies a value judgement, and it might very well be disputed. Persons or groups might invoke the term to preclude opposition (which represents a form of political correctness), or groups might proclaim that certain traditions are intrinsic to their culture (which represents a form of identity building, and might be interpreted as defining boundaries). Conflicts between different event stakeholders, with opposing or different value sets, might occur. In planning for events with multiple goals common ground can be found between stakeholders. It is easier to consider intrinsic value at the individual level, and at the level of interest groups, social worlds or sub-cultures where values are shared.

Extrinsic benefits reflect value that is in focus for governments and policy decisions. Extrinsic value is commonly expressed in figures or statistics. An example is financial effects. Social, educational (Deasy, 2002) and health-related effects (Fiske, 1999) are other measurable extrinsic benefits of culture (Holden, 2006; McCarthy *et al.*, 2004) that could be applied in an event context.

The extrinsic and intrinsic values of planned events

Andersson *et al.* (2012) provided a model (Figure 1.2) which distinguishes between intrinsic and extrinsic value on the vertical axis and individual versus

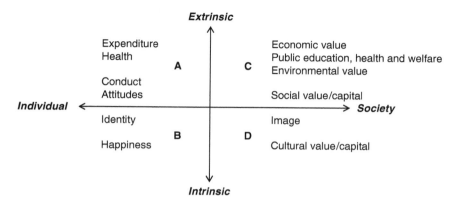

Figure 1.2 A four-dimensional approach to event values.
Source: Adapted from Andersson *et al.* (2012), Armbrecht (2014) and McCarthy *et al.* (2004).

societal value on the horizontal. The resulting categorisation can be viewed as a range of values assigned to planned events and/or values derived from planned events.

As discussed above, extrinsic value stems from utility and exchanges that provide tangible benefits or value to either individuals (including social groups and sub-cultures) or society as a whole (including the economy and environment).

Intrinsic value is largely intangible and stems from value-based positions held by persons and groups. The perceived worth of an event (or any of its components or outcomes) relates to how individuals or society judge them, without regard to utility.

The four quadrants defined by these axes separate value into these general categories:

A (top left): defined by utility; tangible value perceived by individuals or groups
B (bottom left): intrinsic value assigned by individuals
C (top right): defined by utility; tangible value accruing to society as a whole, including to the economy and the environment
D (bottom right): intrinsic value assigned by society

The horizontal axis from individual to society is, to a large extent, a reflection of how value on the individual level is aggregated into concepts on the society level, such as when health, identity, attitudes and conduct on the individual level are reflected in concepts such as public welfare, cultural capital and social capital (Andersson *et al.*, 2012). This axis also points at the need for a clearly defined subject of analysis: from whose perspective is an analysis being made – that is, is the focus of value for the individual, the family, the company, the region, the state or the entire society?

The subjects and objects of studies

Figure 1.2 indicates the vast number of potential focus areas for the value of events. Although limited to only two dimensions, each of these dimensions covers a range of situations.

The dimension spanning from the individual to society accommodates a large number of stakeholders and stakeholder groups as subjects of analysis, in the sense that they are affected and might have different perspectives on value. Local industry, particularly the local tourism industry, for example, is the typical subject of a standard economic impact analysis.

In regards to socio-cultural value, local residents are typically the subject of analysis, although a similar reasoning can be applied to stakeholder groups within the local society that are affected in different ways. Young local residents may constitute a stakeholder group that is affected quite differently than a stakeholder group composed of old local residents. Similarly, stakeholder groups differentiated after residence area may have quite different perceptions of the socio-cultural value of an event.

The second dimension in Figure 1.2 maps the type of value, from intrinsic to extrinsic. Whereas stakeholder groups ranging from the individual to the society can be characterised as the subject, the type of value should be characterised as the object. Standard economic impact studies thus describe how the subject "local tourism industry" is affected in terms of the object of study, which typically includes changes in terms of turnover, number of guest-nights, travel expenditure, shopping and ticket sales (i.e. extrinsic values). The range of study objects in the context of event value is wide, including psychological, social, cultural, environmental, political and economic values. Each one merits being the object in a study on value creation or value assessment.

The following chapters explore, describe, discuss, conceptualise and analyse a range of different objects and subjects in an event context. The book is divided into three parts where all chapters, with two exceptions (Chapters 2 and 11), are found. Chapters 3–5 are concerned with the *Value Creation of Events* (Part I) and Chapters 6–10 deal with *Assessing the Value of Events* (Part II). Chapter 2 sets the stage for the ensuing chapters. It discusses the changing rhetoric surrounding events and their value in the age of austerity. With cuts in public expenditure, events are affected directly, with more tensions between, for example, economic and social values (at least in Western societies). Chapter 11 (in Part III) includes a concluding discussion on the topic of value and events, a summary of each chapter and their highlights, and an ontological mapping of key concepts and terms.

References

Allen, J., O'Toole, W., Harris, R. and McDonnell, I. (2011). *Festival and Special Event Management*. Chichester: John Wiley and Sons.
Andersson, T.D., Armbrecht, J. and Lundberg, E. (2012). Estimating use and non-use values of a music festival. *Scandinavian Journal of Hospitality and Tourism*, 12(3), 215–31.
Armbrecht, J. (2014). Developing a scale for measuring the perceived value of cultural institutions. *Cultural Trends*, 1–21. doi:10.1080/09548963.2014.912041

Bourdieu, P. (1968). Outline of a sociological theory of art perception. *International Social Science Journal*, 20(4), 589–612.

Bourdieu, P. (1973). Cultural reproduction and social reproduction. In R. Brown (ed.), *Knowledge, Education and Cultural Change*. London: Kegan Paul, pp. 71–112.

Bourdieu, P. and Passeron, J.C. (1990). *Reproduction in Education, Society and Culture*. London: Sage.

Brown, S., Getz, D., Pettersson, R. and Wallstam, M. (2015). Event evaluation: definitions, concepts and a state of the art review. *International Journal of Event and Festival Management*, 6(2), 135–57.

de la Torre, M. (1997). *The Conservation of Archaeological Sites in the Mediterranean Region: An International Conference Organized by the Getty Conservation Institute and the J. Paul Getty Museum*. Los Angeles: Getty Conservation Institute.

Deasy, R.J. (2002). *Critical Links: Learning in the Arts and Student Academic and Social Development*. Washington, DC: Arts Education Partnership.

English Heritage (1997). Sustaining the Historic Environment: New Perspectives on the Future *English Heritage Discussion Document*. London: English Heritage.

Fiske, E.B. (1999). *Champions of Change: The Impact of the Arts on Learning*. Washington, DC: GE Fund.

Frey, B.S. (2003). *Arts and Economics: Analysis and Cultural Policy* (2nd edn). Berlin: Springer Verlag.

Granovetter, M. (1983). The strength of weak ties: a network theory revisited. *Sociological Theory*, 1(1), 201–33.

Holden, J. (2006). *Cultural Value and the Crisis of Legitimacy: Why Culture Needs a Democratic Mandate*. London: Demos.

ICOMOS (1999). The Burra Charter: The Australian ICOMOS Charter for the Conservation of Places of Cultural Significance *Australia ICOMOS*. Burwood, Victoria, Australia: Deakin University.

Lin, N. (2001). *Social Capital: A Theory of Social Structure and Action*. Cambridge: Cambridge University Press.

Lipe, W. (1984). Value and meaning in cultural resources. In H. Cleere (ed.), *Approaches to the Archaeological Heritage*. Cambridge: Cambridge University Press, pp. 1–11.

Mahar, C., Harker, R. and Wilkes, C. (1990). *An Introduction to the Work of Pierre Bourdieu: The Practice of Theory*. New York: St Martin's Press.

Mason, R. (2002). Assessing values in conservation planning: methodological issues and choices. In M. de la Torre (ed.), *Assessing the Values of Cultural Heritage: Research Report*. Los Angeles: Getty Conservation Institute, pp. 5–31.

McCarthy, K.F., Ondaatje, E.H., Laura, Z. and Brooks, A.C. (2004). *Gifts of the Muse: Reframing the Debate About the Benefits of the Arts*. Santa Monica, CA: RAND.

Mirowski, P. (1990). Learning the meaning of a dollar: conservation principles and the social theory of value in economic theory. *Social Research*, 689–717.

Mykletun, R.J. (2009). Celebration of extreme playfulness: Ekstremsportveko at Voss. *Scandinavian Journal of Hospitality and Tourism*, 9(2), 146–76.

Ng, I. and Smith, I. (2012), An integrated framework for value. *Review of Marketing Research*, 9, 207–43.

Riegl, A. (1982). The modern cult of monuments: its character and its origin. *Oppositions*, 25, 21–51.

Robson, C. (ed.) (2000). *Small-Scale Evaluation: Principles and Practice*. London: Sage.

Throsby, C.D. (2001). *Economics and Culture*. Cambridge: Cambridge University Press.

Throsby, C.D. (2010). *The Economics of Cultural Policy*. Cambridge: Cambridge University Press.

2 The value of events and festivals in the age of austerity

Emma Wood

Introduction

Events and festivals, within leisure policy, have seen marked changes over the last 50 years. In the UK, leisure first became recognised as something that was worthy of state funding as part of the development of the Welfare State in the 1950s, increasing in importance and culminating in a white paper in 1975 suggesting the need for leisure for its own sake and the citizen's right to recreation (Coalter, 1990). Although focused on sport and physical exercise, this notion slowly developed to encompass wider leisure activities. With a change of government in the late 1970s and a move to market-led economic policy, this view shifted to become leisure and recreation as a means to other ends (ibid.). This approach to leisure remains, with central and local government funding, as well as funding from other bodies such as arts councils, sports bodies and lotteries, allocated according to what the activity or event will achieve (health benefits, civic pride or economic return, for example). The need to evidence, or at least argue the case for, the value of such externalities has become further embedded in policy over the years (Foley *et al.*, 2012) and has been reinforced as the dominant rhetoric with the more recent cuts in public expenditure.

It can be argued that this view of leisure and recreation has affected both the funding and format of events and festivals, with a move away from the spontaneous, sometimes edgy and uncontrolled celebrations of the past (Gotham, 2002) to more formalised 'tools' of purported social good (Coalter, 1990); a move from "ritual to regeneration", as Foley *et al.* (2012, p. 27) summarise, at least within many Western societies. Here, a focus on market economies and competitiveness has created an environment where events and festivals have often become commoditised in order for cities and regions to compete in a global tourism market or to attract investment to a seemingly culturally diverse and vibrant area (Hassan *et al.*, 2007). They therefore attempt to provide social good, but are, according to Rojek (2012), hijacked by a capitalist ideology that perhaps uses events and festivals to placate rather than to change. Rojek's critique, although controversial, does highlight the need to view the value of events within the changing political landscape and to be more circumspect about their value to communities and society as a whole.

This chapter picks up on this theme of the changing approach to the value of festivals and events and focuses on how these activities are perceived at the level of local government. The discussion is supported by data gathered from three national (UK) surveys sent to identified local authority employees involved with events at both a strategic and operational level and taken at different points in time over the last eight years (2004, 2009 and 2012). The 56 responses from the 2012 survey are the main dataset drawn upon here, although these are compared with responses from 2009 (51 responses) and 2004 (58 responses) when appropriate (although similar in content and structure, the survey undertaken in 2004 is not directly statistically comparable with the 2009 and 2012 surveys). The survey data is enhanced by comments from interviews with five heads of strategic development in this area undertaken in 2013.

The picture that emerges is of the major changes in how local authorities (at least in the UK) view events within their remit. The survey data, along with interviews with policy-makers and planners, explore these changes under four main themes: expectations and the perceived benefits of events; level of community and local government involvement; funding sources and models; and value and evaluation.

Background and context

The political environment

Events with any level of public sector involvement are influenced by wider government policy and, in particular in the UK, by the £80 billion reduction in spending which began in 2011 (Mullard, 2011). Many other nations are seeing similar austerity measures. With this drastically reduced level of funding there are clearly challenges in maintaining the level of public services on offer, with local authorities concerned about how to continue supporting mandatory social welfare projects, let alone non-mandatory provision such as events and festivals. Indeed, those with differing economic viewpoints would argue that reduced spending leads to greater inequalities and it is these inequalities in wealth distribution that have led to economic recession or stagnation. However, austerity is here to stay, for a number of years at least, and its impact on the support for festivals and events is now beginning to become apparent.

In this climate, Shaw and Theobald (2011) argue that resilience (bouncing forward), as opposed to recovery (bouncing back), is needed and that this requires local creativity, innovation and risk-taking. However, these traits are themselves difficult to achieve within current economic and political constraints. In their recommendations for resilience, albeit related to climate change issues rather than events, they state that "one of the key dimensions of promoting a resilient local government is ensuring that all sectors of a local community are informed of and have the opportunities to engage with the [climate change] agenda" (p. 13). This is likely to be just as relevant for community festivals and events, where the ideal is to have little or no reliance on central government funding or policy-making and therefore to develop a far greater locally based adaptive capacity.

Originating in Canada, the BID (business improvement district) model is now being adopted in varying forms across many countries and all continents (Hoyt and Gopal-Agge, 2007). This form of private sector funding of 'public good' activities involves local businesses drawing up plans for projects in the locality, which, if agreed upon, are funded by an increase in the business rates they pay. This creates a form of public realm management arrangement designed to give greater power to local decision-making. Although developed in buoyant times, they have grown further in more difficult economic conditions as they are one way to plug the shortfall created by public sector cuts. However, straitened times do mean that private sector businesses are now more carefully weighing up the costs and benefits of being involved. Within the ongoing localism agenda, BID-type forms of local governance are likely to increase not decrease (De Magalhaes, 2012). Although they argue for an extended evaluation frame-work, in order to fully understand the success or otherwise of BIDs, Donaghy *et al.* (2013, p. 27) conclude that BIDs have the "ability to inculcate a new culture which is proactive and 'can do',... which goes on to enhance social and entrepreneurial capital at the local level and establish new forms of public/ private partnership". Others argue that the system puts too much power in the hands of local businesses, taking it away from local residents and, effectively, privatising the high street.

There are many examples in the UK and beyond where the BID model has been used to support events and festivals within towns and cities as part of a wider 'downtown revitalisation' strategy. For example, according to the festival's director,

> the continuing support of the Lancaster Music Festival by BID has enabled it to not only just survive, but also thrive, expand and start on the journey towards greater self-sufficiency and we look forward to partnering with Lancaster BID through 2016–21 on the many exciting projects we are currently planning.
>
> Ruth, 2015

The 'Big Society' philosophy of increased volunteerism and community respon-sibility has also created greater dialogue, if not action, in relation to empowering community-level decisions. The aim was to increase levels of social activism and volunteering as an alternative to central state provision, using terms such as 'social virtue', 'civil society' and 'collective and community action' (Williams, 2012). However, a recent audit concludes that "The Big Society project to hand power back to the people has largely failed against its own measures, leaving the country more divided, with less influence over decisions and receiving less accountable services" (Civil Exchange, 2015). There is clearly a tension between the desire to devolve power and ongoing funding cuts. Where devolved power is seen by some as a cost-saving rather than empowerment exercise, with a shifting of the funding problem from central government to local government and communities. Furthermore, Massey (2010) believes that the 'Big Society' rhetoric is a mere continuation of a political zeitgeist which has created elites in the financial sector and geographical inequalities through reduced state intervention.

The Civil Exchange (2015) audit of the Big Society goes on to recommend that we:

> continue to look for ways to give power back to people, to make services more responsive and to encourage local action. To do this successfully requires much better collaboration with local and voluntary groups, giving people a genuine stake in local decision making, targeting resources on those who have least, reviewing the way we contract companies to deliver public services and making sure major businesses give back.

This has clear implications for community events and festivals, which often rely on partnerships between the local government, businesses, volunteers and residents.

Influencing society for the good is often the purpose (even if unstated) of many community events. The social and cultural value can outweigh the negligible or even negative economic return. In order to continue funding and support needs to be maintained – however, as discussed above, the sources of this support could well be shifting.

Community events and festivals

Events and festivals are worthy of study in their own right due to their ubiquitous nature and recent exponential growth in both size and number; however, they also provide a context within which relations of power in broader culture can be studied (Sharpe, 2008). For example, the value gained from community events is clearly dependent upon the nature of the event and the players involved within it. A festival can be done to a community rather being done for or by that community and therefore has the potential to merely reinforce the views of existing social and political dominant groups (ibid.) and the values of the elite (Waterman, 1998). They can be seen, therefore, as reinforcing the status quo and providing a distraction from real change policy (Rojek, 2012).

The ability to foster social change may also be compromised by increasing commercialisation. Events that are created by private and public sector bodies to develop the economy, prolong the tourist season and encourage inward investment are unlikely to have as positive an impact on society as those designed primarily for social good. Squeezed budgets mean that most local authorities are now looking for private funding for the majority of events and festivals but may not have considered the impact that this change of emphasis and control may have on public embeddedness, inclusion and social change. Social change, therefore, will no longer (if it ever did) just happen, but is likely to "demand an active and intentional effort" (Sharpe, 2008, p. 220). Leisure events are inherently political; we need to consider the power embedded in practices, messages and commitments that can both expand and reduce opportunities for social and political emancipation (Rojek, 2012). This suggests that value gained through contributions to community well-being and positive social change will happen only if these are inclusive and planned into each stage of the event, from inception, through design and planning, to delivery and post-event activities (Quinn and Wilks, 2013).

The tension between the economic and cultural value of festivals was debated nearly two decades ago by Waterman (1998) and in particular the 'economic' use of arts/cultural festivals as place marketing tools. The need to consider the dichotomies of festival as 'art or economics', 'culture or cultural politics', 'celebration versus enterprise' highlights the often opposing agendas which need to be reconciled within community events. In many cases it is the funders who control form and content, potentially leading to commercial interest above social need and artistic freedom, and the creation of elitist festivals. In fact, it is impossible to separate the 'art' from the 'consumer' from the 'place'. Culture is created and culture is consumed at a festival and at the same time the place is consumed by the audience, whose presence is necessary for the festival to take place.

However, it is the balance of power that is shifting as "reduced public subsidy demands an increase in the search for private or corporate sponsorship and the festival becomes a medium for business image-making as well as an arena characterised by less adventurous and less expensive programming" (Waterman, 1998, p. 69). In developing festivals that meet the needs of local firms and the local community it could be seen by purists (or elites) that culture or authenticity is in some way being compromised and, due largely to population size and economic forces, this is most likely to happen within cities. However, this does not appear to have been the case so far. Indeed, the opposite may well be true in that arts and culture are surviving in cities where there is a diminishing, but still comparably greater pool of resources to be drawn upon (Wood and Kornilaki, 2010).

Different political goals can lead to tensions within a variety of events – for example, when a cultural festival has a more overt political role in that it is planned as part of image making, place marketing, or civic boosterism (McClinchey, 2008). Even within smaller-scale community festivals, which rarely attract out of town visitors, there is an increasing divergence between place marketing goals and the meanings of place and belonging for the community. This complexity of the 'festival place' needs to be recognised within local and national government support, alongside a meaningful reflection upon whose festivals are encouraged and whose are discouraged. McClinchey's study of festivals in ethnically diverse Toronto concludes that "place marketing that includes festival promotion should be able to answer questions pertaining to image, political influences and agendas, authenticity, social identity and cultural representation" (ibid., p. 261). Even for small-scale community events "the multiple realities of places of festivals, neighbourhood and city need to be acknowledged in order to address deeper meanings and the complexities that exist" (ibid., p. 262).

The debate suggests that community festivals may struggle to maintain a social purpose and survive as the pressure to deliver on commercial or place marketing objectives grows. This is alongside the shift in funding sources which potentially puts power and ownership further outside the reach of the community.

Analysis and discussion

Expectations and blind belief

Over the years of event impact research there has been a focus on quantifying the legacy of events through economic impact studies (Andersson and Lundberg, 2013), cost–benefit analysis and, more recently, social benefits in terms of social capital (Wood *et al.*, 2009; Wilks, 2011; Quinn and Wilks, 2013; Richards *et al.*, 2013). Many event programmes have been justified through reference to the economic good that will ensue alongside the more intangible benefits to the local community (civic pride, community cohesion, feel-good factor). This has occurred in times where money was available from central government, from private investors (sponsors and philanthropists) and from participants willing to pay. Many event programmes have been developed and become a part of the traditions of that town, city or community with the ensuing expectation of continuity. Many are a 'looked forward to', part of the local calendar and others are a much needed attractor of tourist income in off-seasons. The previous decades of exponential growth in local events with some level of public sector involvement has created expectations and a reliance upon them which may no longer be sustainable.

From the national surveys very little appears to have changed in terms of the belief in what events can achieve. Although the respondents may be prone to bias in their opinion (due to the nature of their role within the local authority), the overwhelming perception is that events have a positive impact on the social, cultural and economic activities in their region. In the most recent survey there is some disagreement on environmental impacts, although even here the majority see the impacts as positive, with only 6 per cent viewing events as having a negative impact on the environment.

One aspect of the economic value discussion around events and festivals is the suggestion that they can create employment within the local economy, either directly through skills development, volunteering, workforce increases or indirectly through tourism, increased local business etc. In the 2012 sample responses were mixed, although the majority believed that they did make some contribution and only 7 per cent felt they made no contribution to employment. Investigating these responses further showed that the benefit to employment was assumed to arise as a result of increased tourism and town centre footfall. Only a few respondents mentioned any direct impact on employment through employing local people at the event and through event-related training initiatives and volunteerism.

The responses explaining how they make a contribution show both direct and indirect impacts through the creation of temporary jobs and the knock-on effect on related businesses such as printers and equipment suppliers and the accommodation sector, and the further knock-on effect for laundry services, food suppliers, transport – all requiring additional staff in the busy seasons. As these are based on perceptions, and may be wishful thinking rather than evidence-based, respondents were also asked how they 'know' these are the outcomes of events. As expected, most evaluation measures focus on visitor number and satisfaction surveys and were unlikely, therefore, to provide evidence of the assumed impacts. Extracts from the 2012 interviews illustrate these points:

> Reduced resources mean we are less able to properly assess and evaluate the impact of events. We have reduced manpower to undertake this ourselves and reduced funding means we can rarely fund consultants to assess and evaluate.

> Limited evaluation on these matters at the moment. Success is judged on numbers through the door.

> Unclear except anecdotal and visitor numbers by assessment.

However, some did indicate more sophisticated assessment of impact, with many at least gathering feedback from local businesses and sponsors and others tracking media coverage.

Several suggest more sophisticated evaluation, including economic impact assessment, and it seems that this is usually undertaken by external consultants. However, many also state that the budget for evaluation has always been small and will be cut further.

It appears that those that do more than visitor or attendee surveys tend to focus on the economic, with only one respondent alluding to social impact assessment where research had been done with residents about how they feel about where they live. Wishful thinking rather than evidence seems to be the basis for belief – certainly for value other than the economic. This also even appears to be the case for larger national and international events, where social impact is detailed as an outcome but is still not evaluated (Lin, 2012).

Despite the largely positive answers regarding the impacts of events, most participants did also mention disadvantages. These related both to the local authority in terms of being time consuming and generally resource intensive, and to the local community in causing disruption and issues with parking, litter and anti-social behaviour. A few of those interviewed also mentioned the concern at being seen to be spending public money on partying or frivolities in straitened times. Linked to this, and mentioned by several in 2012 (example quotes below), was the opportunity cost or redirection of funds that could be 'better' spent elsewhere. This did not seem to be an issue in 2004 and was only mentioned by one respondent in 2009.

> There is an opportunity cost associated with events. The money could be better spent on direct intervention in other areas of the local economy (skills programmes, business networking).

Events divert attention from other aspects of community engagement (and their sustainability) and are often resource intense.

Many respondents felt that the intensity of event involvement led to overstretched departments and budgets. As well as the financial risk, others also recognised the risk to reputation if something were to go wrong, as well as the increasing bureaucracy (and cost) needed in terms of health and safety, road closures, clean-up and policing.

In conclusion, over the eight years, the perceived value of events has changed little. It could be argued that this is largely due to the continuing lack of robust methods of evaluation beyond the basic – that is, a blind belief or at least a lack of evidence-based decision-making. An alternative explanation is self-protectionism, in that those questioned have a vested interest in maintaining events programmes within their regions. What does appear to have changed is the notion of opportunity cost – an increasing consideration of whether that same value could be achieved more efficiently through other means. Funding pressures are leading some, but still a minority, to re-evaluate the purpose of events and allocate funding to other interventions if deemed a better return on investment. Again, those that undertake meaningful evaluations also tend to be the ones who then reconsider the choice of events as the tool to deliver the required value (Wood *et al.*, 2009).

The value of involvement

In considering the value of events it is important to consider the recipients of that value. Although community members were not surveyed directly, 'community involvement' as both process and goal was explored with the local government respondents. The 'community' is often used as the basis for judgements on the value of events and community members are seen as the beneficiaries of public service provision and support. In terms of public sector provision, community is defined both by geography (within the statutory boundaries) and by economic, cultural and social factors and shared interests, traditions and backgrounds (Jepson and Clarke, 2014).

The benefits that events and festivals can bring to communities have been well researched over the years (e.g. Picard and Robinson, 2006; Derrett, 2003; Sharpe, 2008; Arcodia and Whitford, 2006; Quinn and Wilks, 2013), as have some of the negative consequences of events done to a community or in spite of the community for other benefits (economic, tourism, boosterism) (Rojek, 2012). A look at the wider literature on public engagement and participation is useful in understanding the processes and support mechanisms that need to be in place for the community to benefit in a meaningful and longer-term way.

The boom years in events and festivals arose due to the 'imperative of competition' in local government policies and the idea that a city's 'soft assets' (which include events and festivals as well as visual spaces) can be the means to attract financial investment and tourism (Pollock and Paddison, 2010) leading to a justification of local government support structured largely around purported economic benefits. In 2010 there was a discernible shift towards an increased reference to the social and community value of events and their potential in providing a catalyst for community engagement (Wood and Kornilaki, 2010). However, there is also continuing controversy regarding public art and public festivals in terms of how public or participatory they really are (Belfiore, 2002; Jermyn, 2001). It is argued that those involved in determining a local event strategy need to view these activities as a process in which the local community (the public) have a stake, rather than as a product to be acquired by the local authority on their behalf (or not). Waterman (1998, p. 354) also argues against viewing festivals as 'artefacts' as this creates "a denial of the multiple voices comprising community and contradicts its publicness", suggesting the importance of community embeddedness in any local authority event strategy.

May (2006) also emphasises the importance of involvement as a process rather than merely passive inclusion. The festival, therefore, needs to be seen as a series of activities rather than merely as an object or product to be consumed at a single point in time. Encouraging public participation in festivals and events at a meaningful level is a challenge. In many spheres of public life we see the 'triangle of engagement', with fewer people the further up the participation spectrum you go (ibid.). Figure 2.1 demonstrates this for community festivals.

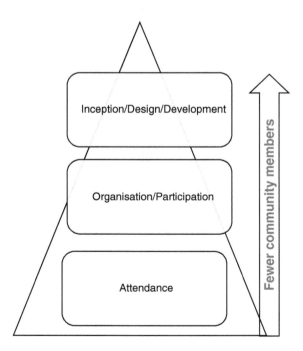

Figure 2.1 Diminishing returns and the triangle of engagement.

There is a kind of Catch 22 in operation here: public services want to engage with you if you are "ordinary", but if you show interest in engaging with them then you must be "extraordinary"... and therefore they needn't listen to you.

Ibid., p. 4

Although Arnstein's (1969) ladder of participation is a useful starting point for explaining the value of community involvement, others, such as May (2006) and Tritter and McCallum (2006), argue that, in fact, all points or rungs are equally valuable. These help us to see public participation from the participant's view with beneficial activities including transferring information, consultation, supporting, acting together and deciding together.

A social capital checklist for public participation initiatives (May, 2006)

1. Which citizens are the focus of the activity?
2. What practical support is offered to citizens as individuals to enable their involvement?
3. What practical support is being offered to groups of citizens to enable their involvement?
4. What training will the agency provide to enable the participants to interact with it more effectively?
5. How far will any training be transferable to other situations in the participants' lives or their communities?
6. In short: how will the initiative contribute to the creation of social capital?

May's social capital checklist (see box) can be usefully applied in assessing the likelihood of social capital gains from involvement in a festival or event and ensuring that, if this is one of the objectives, the event is designed to maximise social capital-building opportunities. Quinn and Wilks (2013) also provide a useful analysis of social capital through festivals and, in particular, provide a map of the festival in terms of geographic reach, stakeholders and the connections within.

Wider policies have the ability to greatly affect the types and levels of public engagement, participation and embeddedness. For example, proponents would argue that the localism agenda has put more power in the hands of local communities and in so doing has increased participation. Therefore, they argue, the broader ideas within the Big Society have encouraged this further, giving the desired resilience through engagement, discussed by Shaw and Theobald (2011). However, it can also be argued that the increased participation is by the 'same old faces' and often the social or business elite (May, 2006; Waterman, 1998; Rojek, 2012).

For example, the BID model encourages involvement, but puts the power within the hands of the business community.

To counteract this, Murray (2009, p. 433) calls for the mandatory use of 'social clauses' to ensure that all public sector contracts during a time of recession, maximise public value and create greater opportunities for inclusion and involvement. Indeed, in several countries this has been enshrined in policy. For example, in the UK, the Public Services (Social Value) Act requires those who commission public services to detail how they can also secure wider social, economic and environmental benefits (Cabinet Office, 2015). Any event or festival drawing upon public sector funding or support must therefore have the social and environmental impacts considered alongside the economic from the start of the process, rather than as a by-product. The need for these to be community focused is not stipulated.

Involvement also needs to be considered from a local government perspective. In Europe and beyond, national and local governments have long histories of involvement in the development, support and funding of various types of events, ranging from small-scale community festivals to larger income-generating hallmark events (Mintel, 2015). This involvement has seen a steady increase, with a marked bandwagon effect started in the late 1990s and continuing over the next two decades (Woodward *et al.*, 2014). This has culminated in local, regional and national events policies being formulated; however, their efficacy is yet to be proven. For example, an analysis of event policy documents in Australia concluded that they contain "redundant rhetoric, are ad hoc and reactive… and are developed by an insular policy community" (Whitford, 2009).

Looking at the data from surveys of local authorities in the UK, we can see that there are varied and multiple reasons for their involvement with events. The reasons show little change between 2009 and 2012 (Figure 2.2), although there is

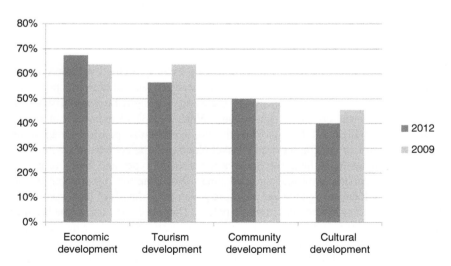

Figure 2.2 Local government reasons for event involvement.

an emerging greater emphasis on economic development. The change from 2004 was more marked, where the majority of respondents stated that 'attracting day visitors' and encouraging 'community involvement' were the main reasons for hosting events. Attracting tourists was the least important reason. There therefore appears to have been a slight movement towards economic reasons (e.g. regeneration, tourism), although development of community is still of importance.

This may be a reflection of the economic climate, with a greater emphasis on being able to show an economic return as well as social benefits. The emphasis on the economic is also not surprising when it is noted that most local government event responsibility is situated within departments with economic focus (Figure 2.3) and is in line with the more ubiquitous 'economy' narrative noted by Massey (2010).

However, governments have also begun to recognise that festivals provide more than just economic benefit. For example, a variety of national arts organisations promote programmes of events and projects with wider outcomes, including support for cultural diversity, uniting communities, opportunities for young and old community groups, creative learning and development, and promoting and sustaining the environment (Bunting, 2007). And, of course, the claims for mega events such as the 2012 Olympics encompass many of these views, with the tagline 'inspire a generation' and the underlying aims of increasing participation, inclusion, national pride and civic boosterism, as well as greater levels of sport participation. High hopes are all well and good, but the evidence for what is actually achieved is contradictory and often sketchy due largely to inconsistent and inaccurate evaluation (Getz, 2012; Foley *et al.*, 2012; Lin, 2012; Agha and Taks, 2015).

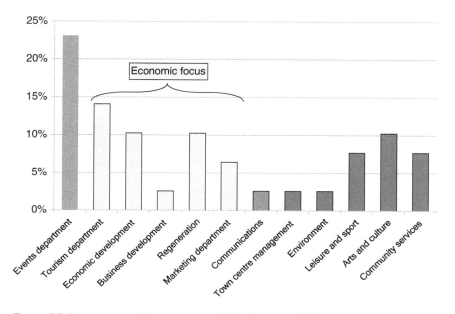

Figure 2.3 Department with main responsibility for events (2012 data).

The growth in the number of local authorities with an 'events department' seen between 2004 and 2012 suggests that the size, number and importance of events has led to the need for a separate area of responsibility. This has positive implications for the strategic planning of events within the regions, although the 'mixed' responsibility across departments also indicates that this is not an easy task.

Strategic planning is necessary if the aimed-for objectives are to be achieved (O'Sullivan *et al.*, 2009; Pugh and Wood, 2004; Getz, 2009). Positive benefits do not just happen and are lesser and shorter-lived if limited to single events (Wood *et al.*, 2009; Wood, 2004). However, research suggests that involvement at a strategic level in leisure, entertainment, culture and the arts has been first to be cut in times of local government budget tightening (Wood, 2004).

Short-term festivals and special events are increasingly considered to be important factors in a location's portfolio of tourism products (Ryan, 1998), claiming a significant contribution to driving the economic development and cultural diversity of a region (Long and Perdue, 1990). Since the mid-1980s, events have consciously been used as a form of economic development and regeneration, but gradually there has been recognition that such activity also often carries social, dis-benefits, which need to be mitigated, or at least accounted for (Hall and Jenkins, 1995; Jones, 2012). As well as the potential negative social effects, there is also a growing recognition and concern about the contribution of events and festivals to environmental issues (Getz, 2009), whether this is directly (within the location of the event) or on a global scale through the increased tourism and hence travel that so many events are staged to achieve. The overall value therefore needs to consider the wider impacts of the event and, as discussed earlier, the alternative approaches to generating similar outcomes.

Despite these concerns, the lack of evidence-based policy and the continuing financial constraints, it is clear that the belief in the worth of events and festivals continues. The level and type of both local government and community involvement, however, is shifting, which, in turn, will lead to changes in who benefits and to what extent. 'Involvement' is therefore worthy of consideration and leads to a number of different event models illustrated as a two-dimensional continuum in Figure 2.4 (Wood, 2009).

The responses to the national survey of local authorities in the UK suggests that local communities have a say in most events and are actively involved in their production, marketing and evaluation, as well as attendance. Although this is less often the case in the decision whether or not to host, there was still a higher than expected reporting of involvement. However, the level of community involvement as reported by the local authority events department does not necessarily equate to the level of involvement experienced by the community. It may also refer to a small number being involved, elites or the same old faces (Rojek, 2012). Some of the open comments on involvement from the 2012 survey illustrate the varying perspectives on involvement:

> It is often the role of the local authority to raise interest and engagement levels. Different events have varying degrees of the above. Some are community

Level of involvement	Community located	Community attendance	Community participation	Community organised	Community created
Local government permitted	Little or no involvement either party				High community involvement
Local government supported/ endorsed		Increasing level of partnership and involvement			
Local government resourced /funded					
Local government created	High local government involvement				High involvement both parties

Figure 2.4 Local government and community involvement in festivals.

Source: Wood (2009), p. 3.

led, some trade led and their level of involvement is influenced by their role within the event either as co-organisers or as audience/attendees.

As the local community, both residents and businesses can be participants, beneficiaries and hosts; it is always important to gather input from them.

We want residents to be involved in and enjoy events in the area. We want to minimise risk and disruption to businesses, and give them maximum opportunities to promote themselves.

The comments suggest that the diversity of events within the remit of the local authority require a variety of community involvement practices. Most recognise the importance of community involvement for event success, but others interpret this and put it into practice in very different ways, with several viewing attendance as involvement. This is clearly out of kilter with current thinking on public participation, engagement and the embeddedness of events and festivals and the added value this generates.

Their ability to involve communities is also being impacted by austerity measures. Local authorities have moved from being the source of funding for local festivals to being the conduit for funding from other sources and to playing a supportive rather than leading role in the development and management of the event, giving them less control over community engagement.

Policy and funding

Direct funding will decrease, but efforts to maintain or improve on current levels are being focused on sponsorship and grant income as well as shared services.

Local Authority Head of Arts, Culture and
Regeneration, interview 2013

Over the last five years, economic recession, political policy and social changes have started to affect this non-statutory aspect of local authority provision at both a strategic and operational level. The extent to which these changes are affecting event provision and support is not yet well understood, although there are a growing number of studies that consider events and festivals within the age of austerity (Papadimitriou, 2014; Lee and Goldblatt, 2012; Lyck and Long, 2012; Bonet and Donat, 2011) alongside wider studies into the impact of changes in the public sector on leisure and culture (Bertelli *et al.*, 2014; Dalle Nogare and Bertachinni, 2015).

Mermiri (2012) discusses the changes in the funding tripod for arts and heritage, which consists of the public sector, the private sector and earned income. Unsurprisingly, the balance in the tripod is changing within many countries, with a decrease in public sector funds, a slight decrease in private sector and an increase in earned income. This leads us to again consider what the mix should be and the implications for provision if more is paid for by attendees and supported by commercial organisations. Analysis shows that there is a strong lagged correlation between private investment and earned income (ibid.); however, this may be merely due to investors favouring events that have potential for earned income rather than their investment creating higher earned income. We could also conclude that in times when the public need free or lower-cost leisure activities fewer of these will exist. Furthermore, although private investment is more resilient in recession it is unevenly distributed, creating a geographic divide with smaller regional organisations losing out to larger city-based ones (Arts and Business, 2013; Massey, 2010).

It is unlikely that the private sector will be able or willing to make up the shortfall in public sector funding as tougher economic times also squeeze the corporate sector and therefore affect all revenue sources (Lee and Goldblatt, 2012). There are a growing number of events being cancelled due to sponsor withdrawal as it could be viewed as tactless to be seen to sponsor *partying* when cutting back on staff. However, on the positive side, there are also plenty of examples of festivals being born during tough times, perhaps because their importance to the community increases in times of hardship (Grzeskowiak, 2009).

The insight box illustrates how even the most successful festival cities are struggling to find new patterns of support and funding to maintain their cultural offer.

Insight: funds shake-up looms for Edinburgh's arts sector

Festivals, theatres, art galleries, concert halls and literary bodies may be stripped of long-term funding or find current deals dramatically cut under a shake-up proposed by the local authority as it grapples with a spending squeeze.

Dozens of groups have already been warned to brace themselves for a 10 per cent cut over the next four years – while a recent 'financial health check' carried out on all those currently supported found many are at risk of going bankrupt or defaulting on financial obligations.

It is not yet clear if the city's festivals, which are estimated to be worth more than £260 million to the economy, will be particularly targeted. A major study into their long-term future, published in May, included a warning that Edinburgh faces "relegation from the premier division" of world-class programming if finances are not maintained.

The review by the council – which has a £5.2 million arts funding pot at present – has emerged months after a separate vision for the future of culture in Edinburgh called for more help to be offered to the grassroots scene.

The 'Edinburgh Cultural Promise' was drawn up following the city's biggest survey of artists, venue operators, promoters and producers.

That report stated: "It was felt strongly that [they] should not have to brand themselves as part of a festival to receive investment and support. It should be made financially easier for local presenters and producers to participate in the festivals, but the work of those who actively avoid this period should not be deemed inferior or less valued by the city."

Richard Lewis, the council's culture leader, said: "We want to make sure our support is as effective as it can be. We're proposing a renewed process for handling applications, including the creation of a new open fund to support emerging talent. Collaborative working between Edinburgh's organisations and with the council would be at the heart of this approach. Promoting stronger partnerships is something the sector has called for."

Adapted from Ferguson (2015)

Clearly, the changing funding structures and availability are affecting how events are seen in terms of success. The focus on financial benefits is undoubtedly encouraged by the current economic situation and resulting government policies. When asked about funding for events the majority of the survey respondents saw this as an area that would be hit by local government cutbacks and austerity measures affecting private sector investment. In 2012 85 per cent predicted a decrease over the next five years, with 48 per cent of respondents predicting substantial decreases. This compares with only 29 per cent in 2009 (and 3 per cent in 2004). There is also evidence of a widening gap between the haves and have-nots. Perhaps, as indicated by some of the interviewees, this is down to the relative prosperity of their region, local philanthropy and, in some cases, guaranteed commitment to strategies put in place before the funding cuts.

An analysis of the many comments on funding obtained shows that all three legs of the tripod (Mermiri, 2012) were being weakened, with a reduction in funding from central government and greater difficulties in securing private sector investment combined with a greater need for free or low-cost events. However, it is public sector cuts that are biting hardest at the moment, as one respondent stated: "Eighty per cent of our funding is from central government and 30 per cent of this is being cut next year."

These are particularly difficult times for events programmes as, despite their previous lauding as catalysts for economic and social regeneration, they have remained a non-statutory area of local government service and are therefore relatively easy to cut back. As the interviewee below suggests, the need to save money can lead to short-term decisions, where events are an easy hit.

> The austerity and rebalancing agenda effectively removes the mandate to weigh up long-run cost–benefit decisions which can and do show the importance of cultural services and events in generating competitive economies. Instead, the short-run imperative to reduce spending has impacted disproportionately on the non-statutory areas which underpin strong economic development in the future.
>
> Borough Council Head of Leisure and Economic Regeneration

And similarly, "Events are not statutory, therefore the council will not fund events, the community will be encouraged to find their own funding" (District Council Head of Events Department).

A fairly common response to reduced direct funding is a withdrawal from local authority-run events and a more 'backseat' role in supporting (non-financially) and promoting events organised by others in the community: "We are moving away from delivery of events but will still enable where possible" (Head of Tourism), as well as a move to charging for the services they provide: "Promoting of festivals and events will become the responsibility of the promoter and not the [local authority] – we will continue to promote very actively, but the activity will be charged the going rate as opposed to free" (District Council Head of Arts and Culture).

Others are relying on increased funding from the private sector and self-funding opportunities, but recognise the challenges in this approach.

> Generally we are seeking greater private sector support against a backdrop of falling public sector funding – we are seeking greater opportunities for commercialisation of activity.
>
> Manager within and Events Department

Events appear to remain popular, but budgetary pressures may limit the council's capacity to maintain this level of support. In an economy with very few large businesses, private sector sponsorship is also extremely hard to come by.

City Council Head of Tourism and Leisure

When questioned further about the specific sources of funding it becomes clear that, although there is a great degree of variation in the responses, it does appear that private sector funding plays a small part in the supporting of events at present. This is despite the recognition shown earlier that this is where financial resources must come from as budgets are cut. Self-funding through income generation appears to be more successful and may lead to fewer free events to the detriment of community engagement.

From the 2012 survey responses a variety of funding models exist, with funding directly from the local authority ranging from 10 per cent to 95 per cent, but still with the greatest proportion largely coming from local government. This is despite an increased drive to secure funds from private investors and grant funders.

Many of the 2012 survey comments reflected a frustration with funding issues and the resulting effects of these:

Raising private sector sponsorship has been difficult. Public sector funding for events and festivals has been cut, so is more difficult to win; we are having to look for additional funding through local business sponsorship. These businesses in general have less money to spend on events and sponsorship, so the number of events per year has been reduced.

Budgets have been reduced year on year, resulting in an inability to support community-led events. We have had to turn down applications for assistance from newly developed and promoted events.

In one case it was felt that the funding cuts were having a direct impact upon inclusivity:

For the first time, the local festival following the annual parade has had to charge. Rather than furthering integration, it presents a financial barrier to inclusivity. There have traditionally been large costs in terms of policing and clean-up operations, which could not be justified this year due to budget constraints. Another local festival, which sees us collaborate with our twin town in France, has been cancelled entirely due to the inability of the [local authority] to bridge funding gaps. This represents a serious setback to the development of local art and cultural production, and potentially harms the future cultural output of the city.

Others continue bravely on in the face of adversity, exemplified by comments such as: "We are continuously looking to deliver more for less." Still others recognise the value of events within the community and the increased importance of this when residents are feeling financially vulnerable: "Residents and visitors are looking for alternative low-cost leisure activities, so city-led events are welcomed." There is a two-pronged difficulty in that, "more and more events are relying on local authority support" in a time when that support is being cut.

The outcome is clear: events are being squeezed from all directions in that budgets are being cut, there is increased difficulty in obtaining private sector sponsorship, attendees are less willing or unable to pay, alongside, an increased demand from community-organised events for local government support.

The interviews with strategy heads within local government highlight three differing responses to this '*squeeze*', dependent upon the 'resilience' of the local authority:

- Creative funding – exemplified by focusing on "development of a greater number of partnerships", "encouraging events/festivals to look at alternative ways of raising funds" and "examining the potential for increasing prices or adding value in event programming – or creating more 'popular' programmes (in order to create more earned income)". Those that are taking more of an indirect role in events are now "seeking to help event organisers find funds and be self-supporting rather than offering cash support".
- Cost saving – for example, "more conservative with bookings and made cost savings where possible (e.g. combined two events over one weekend). The number of events has been reduced and others cut back." Several respondents were conscious that cutbacks would negatively affect the economy through reduced tourism, viewing some cuts as ill thought through, "a knee jerk reaction without consideration for the consequences".
- Caution – this manifests itself through "a more bureaucratic line on administration of events and audit trails" and a reluctance to "spend on the 'feel-good' events that cannot give strong evidenced outcomes". An increased pressure "not to be wasting money on frivolities over core functions" and a more selective approach, "priority being given to better-quality events and sustainable events over number of events".

As funding becomes more dependent upon outcomes, then it follows that the objectives of events need to be more explicitly formulated and that these are then evaluated and compared to what could be achieved through other means.

Value and evaluation

Despite the ongoing calls for systematic, holistic and robust evaluation of the economic, socio-cultural and environmental impacts (Andersson and Lundberg, 2013; Getz, 2012; Wood, 2009; Small *et al.*, 2005), it appears that, within local government at least, this is rarely happening. The wide variety of events that local authorities are involved in and the reasons for being involved would suggest that a range of criteria need to be applied to ascertain the value of each type of event. When asked in the survey to describe the three main criteria for judging the success of an event, the largest response indicated attendance numbers or footfall as the main determinant of success. Several other criteria were mentioned, including economic benefit, inward investment, profile raising and PR, alongside attendee enjoyment/satisfaction. A very small percentage of respondents also indicated community involvement and engagement. The majority of responses (other than attendance) related to economic benefit (to local businesses, inward investment) and financial benefit (cost recovery, ticket sales, funding). Another common response focused on the event itself, rather than what could be achieved through it, in terms of attendee satisfaction, feedback from stakeholders and the 'feel-good' factor. Profile raising, PR and media coverage clearly include elements of both event success and economic benefit.

From the 2004 survey to the one undertaken in 2009 there was an increase in the number gathering feedback and measuring customer satisfaction as opposed to mainly attendance figures, visitor numbers and town centre footfall, which were the most common responses in 2004. Between 2009 and 2012 the most marked change is in the use of economic or financial criteria for success and, specifically, a significant increase in those looking for a financial return or at least cost recovery. This, perhaps surprisingly, seems to be at the expense of consideration of attendee satisfaction, which has declined in importance over the time period covered by the three surveys.

Although, again, a small number mentioned community/social benefits, there has not been a marked change in this as a criteria for success. There is still, therefore, a possible mismatch between the stated objectives or reasons for involvement in events and the criteria by which success is judged. This tallies with O'Sullivan *et al.*'s (2009) findings that even when events were being justified on socio-cultural grounds they were being evaluated on economic outputs.

Figure 2.5 shows the changes from 2009–12, with the centrally grouped bars representing the economic focus.

The simplicity of attendance numbers as a measure explains its frequency in the responses. However, beyond that, the apparent focus on the economic and/or financial fits with the current political emphasis and the acceptance within the public sector of 'economic' as the dominant discourse. An 'audit' mentality exists, which means that the social, community or cultural aspects of what are largely community and/or cultural events are not a high priority in terms of criteria for success. There are a number of possible reasons for this and previous research (Wood, 2009) shows that this may be linked to the lack of understanding of these values and of practical ways to identify and assess them. It is also likely to be driven, to a large extent, by other stakeholders (national government, private sector funders, grant awarding bodies) and their audit or 'return on investment' requirements. Taxpayers will want to know what their money is buying, corporates will want a measure of media coverage and grant-givers will have a variety of post-event evaluation requirements, many of which are likely to include community participation, involvement and inclusion. Value therefore needs to be

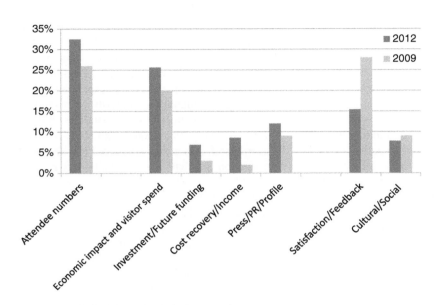

Figure 2.5 How events are valued

recognised and evaluated in a much wider sense than merely economic benefit or financial return.

Conclusions

It appears that the global economic crisis is having a marked effect on local government involvement in community events. Concern has previously been shown regarding 'festivalisation' and globally undifferentiated festivals (Getz, 2009; Britton, 1991; Urry, 1995), with debates around the homogenisation of cities. Their ability to differentiate a city/region has declined through overuse and therefore their economic benefit is also likely to have dwindled. Perhaps, therefore, austerity is a wake-up call to local, and national, government. A time to take stock of the true value of events (both economic and social) – which might well lead to further cutbacks in the creation and funding of such events, but at least this will be an informed evidence-based decision.

Back to roots, culturally authentic festivals, where public involvement is embedded in the process, would seem to be the way forward, eliciting social change when economic benefit is less achievable and fitting with the current political ethos of community involvement (or at least localism), back to basics and less spending on 'frivolities'.

If arguments were once made, and apparently evidence provided to support them, that the value of events lay in the prosperity they brought to deprived areas, the bringing together of communities and improved quality of life of residents, then surely this would suggest that they are a vital part of most local government services and should be maintained in difficult times. Indeed, are they not needed more than ever? However, if they were only ever 'spare money spent on party-ing', then surely this is an area that should be cut in order for more effective interventions to be funded.

Changing social and economic perspectives have impacted markedly on atti-tudes to events and this is reflected in the views gathered from those involved in local authority events at all levels, including events officers, regeneration manag-ers, cultural strategists and heads of economic development. The most pronounced changes relate to funding models and the changing rhetoric, with an even greater tension emerging between the economic and social benefits arguments. The views expressed vary in terms of outlook, with some identifying positive consequences brought about by political, economic and social changes and a forced re-address-ing of the reasons for being involved in events. This may be leading to a greater use of evaluation, higher level of 'real' community involvement and a move away from the boosterism and bandwagon activities seen in the earlier surveys.

There is some evidence to suggest that harder times lead to more creativity, thoughtfulness and a return to grassroots, which could create benefits at a local community level. The alternative view is that an increasing dependence on private sector funding will negatively impact the cultural integrity of some events and limit accessibility and inclusivity due to the need to generate income, often through admission charges. Although local government funding cuts do not appear to have directly affected event programmes (as many drew down funding from other bodies), they have affected the level of support they receive in that consultancy positions and advisory roles within local authorities were some of the first to be cut. It is, perhaps, here where the greatest tension lies. With an increased need to engage communities and support events which are community led and free to attend, but with less expertise to guide and encourage this type of activity, the funded positions that remain tend to be those with a clear economic remit and this may be to the detriment of social needs.

Finally, the challenges for event evaluation lie in the changing and increasing funder demands, with even greater emphasis on audit-style outcomes. Unfortunately, continuing austerity measures will pull much needed evaluation in two ways: first, by creating a need for greater evidence to prove value and justify expenditure and, second, by providing fewer resources for that evaluation to take place.

We appear to be at a critical point in terms of the effect of austerity – as policies and cuts are bedded in; the impetus may be towards community and social or may fall towards the economic or commercial. But without meaningful evaluation it will be difficult to know what has been lost (or gained). It will be interesting to see what the picture is in another ten years.

References

Agha, N. and Taks, M. (2015). A theoretical comparison of the economic impact of large and small events. *International Journal of Sport Finance*, 10(3), 199–216.

Andersson, T.D. and Lundberg, E. (2013). Commensurability and sustainability: triple impact assessments of a tourism event. *Tourism Management*, 37, 99–109.

Arcodia, C. and Whitford, M. (2006). Festival attendance and the development of social capital. *Journal of Convention and Event Tourism*, 8(2), 1–18.

Arnstein, S. (1969). A ladder of citizen participation. *Journal of the American Planning Association*, 35(4), 216–24.

Arts and Business (2013). *Private Investment in Culture Survey 2011/12*. Available from http://artsandbusiness.bitc.org.uk/research/private-investment-culture-survey-201112, accessed 1 May 2015.

Beck, A. (2015). Raising a glass to Assets of Community Value. *Walker Morris Business Insights*. Available from https://www.walkermorris.co.uk/business-insights/raising-glass-assets-community-value, accessed 1 May 2015.

Belfiore, E. (2002). Arts as a means of alleviating social exclusion: does it really work? A critique of instrumental cultural policies and social impact studies in the UK. *International Journal of Cultural Policy*, 8, 91–106

Bertelli, A.M., Connolly, J.M., Mason, D.P. and Conover, L.C. (2014). Politics, management, and the allocation of arts funding: evidence from public support for the arts in the UK. *International Journal of Cultural Policy*, 20(3), 341–59.

Bonet, L. and Donato, F. (2011). The financial crisis and its impact on the current models of governance and management of the cultural sector in Europe. *ENCATC Journal of Cultural Management and Policy*, 1(1), 4–11.

Britton, S. (1991). Tourism, capital, and place: towards a critical geography of tourism. *Environment and Planning D: Society and Space*, 9(4), 451–78.

Bunting, C. (2007). Public value and the arts in England: discussion and conclusions of the arts debate. Arts Council England.

Cabinet Office (2015). Guidance: Social Value Act: information and resources. Available from https://www.gov.uk/government/publications/social-value-act-information-and-resources/social-value-act-information-and-resources, accessed 1 August 2015.

Civil Exchange (2015). Whose Society? The Final Big Society Audit. 20 January 2015. Available from http://www.civilexchange.org.uk/wp-content/uploads/2015/01/Whose-Society_The-Final-Big-Society-Audit_final.pdf, accessed 1 August 2015.

Coalter, F. (1990). Analysing leisure policy. In I.P. Henry (ed.), *Management and Planning in the Leisure Industries*. Basingstoke: Macmillan.

Dalle Nogare, C. and Bertacchini, E. (2015). Emerging modes of public cultural spending: direct support through production delegation. *Poetics*, 49, 5–19.

Datamonitor (2011). Country analysis report: the UK. *In-depth PESTLE Insights*. July.

DCLG (2011). A plain English guide to the Localism Act – update. Overview of the main measures of the Localism Act 2011. Available from https://www.gov.uk/government/publications/localism-act-2011-overview

De Magalhaes, C. (2012). Business improvement districts and the recession: implications for public realm governance and management in England. *Progress in Planning*, 77, 143–77.

Derrett, R. (2003). Making sense of how festivals demonstrate a community's sense of place. *Event Management*, 8, 49–58.

Donaghy, M., Findlay, A. and Sparks, L. (2013). The evaluation of business improvement districts: questions and issues from the Scottish experience. *Local Economy*, 28: 471–87.

Ferguson, B. (2015). Funds shake-up looms for Edinburgh's arts sector. *The Scotsman*, 17 October. Available from http://www.scotsman.com/what-s-on/theatre-comedy-dance/funds-shake-up-looms-for-edinburgh-s-arts-sector-1-3920151#axzz3queIcw8N, accessed 1 February 2016.

Foley, M., McGillivray, D. and McPherson, G. (2012). *Event Policy: From Theory to Strategy*. Abingdon: Routledge.

Getz, D. (2009). Policy for sustainable and responsible festivals and events: institutionalization of a new paradigm. *Journal of Policy Research in Tourism, Leisure and Events*, 1(1), 61–78.

Getz, D. (2012). Event studies: discourses and future directions. *Event Management*, 16(2), 171–87.

Gibb, D., Longhurst, J. and Braithwaite, C. (1996). Moving towards sustainable development? Integrating economic development and the environment in local authorities. *Journal of Environmental Planning and Management*, 39(3), 317–32.

Gotham, K.F. (2002). Marketing Mardi Gras: commodification, spectacle and the political economy of tourism in New Orleans. *Urban Studies*, 39(10), 1735–56.

Grzeskowiak, J. (2009). Cause for celebration? Local festivals feel the strain of the down economy. *American City and County*. Available from http://americancityandcounty.com/administration/economic_dev/local-festivals-feel-down-economy-200906, accessed 1 August 2015.

Hall, C.M. and Jenkins, J.M. (1995). *Tourism and Public Policy*. London: Routledge.

Hassan, G., Mean, M. and Tims, C. (2007). The dreaming city and the power of mass imagination. *Demos Report*.

House of Commons Communities and Local Government Committee Community Rights (2015). Sixth Report of Session 2014–15. Available from http://www.publications.parliament.uk/pa/cm201415/cmselect/cmcomloc/262/262.pdf, accessed 1 May 2016.

Hoyt, L. and Gopal-Agge, D. (2007). The business improvement district model: a balanced review of contemporary debates. *Geography Compass*, 1(4), 946–58.

Jepson, A. and Clarke, A. (2014). *Exploring Community Festivals and Events*. Abingdon: Routledge.

Jermyn, H. (2001). *The Arts and Social Exclusion: a Review Prepared for the Arts Council of England*. London: Arts Council of England.

Jones, C. (2012). Events and festivals: fit for the future? *Event Management*, 16(2), 107–18.

Lee, S. and Goldblatt, J. (2012). The current and future impacts of the 2007–2009 economic recession on the festival and event industry. *International Journal of Event and Festival Management*, 3(2), 137–48.

Lin, Y. (2012). A critical review of social impacts of mega-events. *International Journal of Sport and Society*, 3(3), 57–64.

Loaf (2015). The Lifford BID (business improvement district) Vote. Available from http://www.loafonline.co.uk/2015/07/the-lifford-bid-business-improvement-district-vote/, accessed 1 May 2016.

Long, P.T. and Perdue, R. (1990). The economic impact of rural festivals and special events: assessing the spatial distribution of expenditures. *Journal of Travel Research*, 28(4), 10–14.

Lyck, L. and Long, P. (eds) (2012). *Tourism, Festivals and Cultural Events in Times of Crisis*. Copenhagen: Copenhagen Business School.

Massey, D. (2010). The political struggle ahead. *Soundings*, 45, 6–18.

May, J. (2006). Ladders, stars and triangles: old and new theory for the practice of public participation. *International Journal of Market Research*, 48(3), 305–19.

McClinchey, K.A. (2008). Urban ethnic festivals, neighborhoods, and the multiple realities of marketing place. *Journal of Travel and Tourism Marketing*, 25(3–4), 251–64.

Mermiri, T. (2011). Private investment in culture: the sector in and post recession. *Cultural Trends*, 20(3–4), 257–69.

Mintel (2015). Music Concerts and Festivals – UK – August.

Mullard, M. (2011). Explanations of the financial meltdown and the present recession. *The Political Quarterly*, 82(2), 204–21.

Murray, J.G. (2009). Public procurement strategy for accelerating the economic recovery. *Supply Chain Management: An International Journal*, 14(6), 429–34.

O'Sullivan, D., Pickernell, D. and Senyard, J. (2009). Public sector evaluation of festivals and special events. *Journal of Policy Research in Tourism, Leisure and Events*, 1(1), 19–36.

Papadimitriou, L. (2015). Weathering the crisis: Sixteenth Thessaloniki Documentary Festival (14–23 March 2014). *Journal of Greek Media and Culture*, 1(1), 169–76.

Picard, D. and Robinson, M. (2006). *Festivals, Tourism and Social Change*. Cleveland: Channel View.

Pipe, J. (2013). Two years on, what has the Localism Act achieved? *The Guardian Public Leaders Network*, 2 November. Available from http://www.theguardian.com/local-government-network/2013/nov/02/localism-act-devolution-uk-local-authorities, accessed 1 August 2015.

Pollock, V.L. and Paddison, R. (2010). Embedding public art: practice, policy and problems. *Journal of Urban Design*, 15(3), 335–56.

Pugh, C. and Wood, E. (2004). The strategic use of events within local government: a study of London borough councils. *Event Management*, 9(1), 61–71.

Pumar, E. (2005). Social networks and the institutionalization of the idea of sustainable development. *International Journal of Sociology and Social Policy*, 25, 63–86.

Quinn, B. and Wilks, L. (2013). Festival connections: people, place and social capital. In G Richards, M. De Brito and L. Wilks (eds), *Exploring the Social Impacts of Events*. Abingdon: Routledge, pp. 15–30.

Richards, G., Brito, M.P. and Wilks, L. (2013). *Exploring the Social Impacts of Events*. Abingdon: Routledge.

Rojek, C. (2012). Global event management: a critique. *Leisure Studies*. 1–16 ifirst article.

Ruth, B. (2015). BID supports local festival. *Lancashire Evening Post*, Friday, 30 October.

Ryan, C. (1998). Economic impacts of small events: estimates and determinants: a New Zealand example. *Tourism Economics*, 4, 339–52.

Sharpe, E.K. (2008). Festivals and social change: intersections of pleasure and politics at a community music festival. *Leisure Sciences*, 30, 217–34.

Shaw, K. and Theobald, K. (2011). Resilient local government and climate change interventions in the UK. *Local Environment*, 16(1), 1–15.

Small, K., Edwards, D. and Sheridan, L. (2005). A flexible framework for evaluating the socio-cultural impacts of a (small) festival. *International Journal of Event Management Research*, 1(1), 66–77.

Thomas, R. and Wood, E. (2004). Event-based tourism: a survey of local authority strategies in the UK. *Local Governance*, 29(2), 127–36.

Tritter, J.Q. and McCallum, A. (2006). The snakes and ladders of user involvement: moving beyond Arnstein. *Health Policy*, 76(2), 156–68.

Urry, J. (1995). *Consuming Places*. London: Psychology Press.

Ward, K. and Cook, I.R. (2014). Business improvement districts in the UK: territorialising a 'global' model? Imagining urban futures. Working Paper 13. Available from http://research.northumbria.ac.uk/urbanfutures/wp-content/uploads/2012/03/Ward-and-Cook-2014-BIDs-in-the-UK.pdf, accessed 28 August 2014.

Waterman, S. (1998). Carnivals for elites? The cultural politics of arts festivals. *Progress in Human Geography*, 22(1), 54–74.

Whitaker, R. (2010). United Kingdom. *European Journal of Political Research*, 49, 1193–202.

Whitford, M. (2009). A framework for the development of event public policy: facilitating regional development. *Tourism Management*, 30, 674–82.

Wilcox, D. (2006). Summary of the Guide to Effective Participation. Available from http://www.globenet.org/archives/web/2006/www.globenet.org/horizon-local/partnership/wilcox.html, accessed 1 August 2015.

Wilks, L. (2011). Social capital in the music festival experience. In S. Page and J. Connell (eds), *The Routledge Handbook of Events*. Abingdon: Routledge, pp. 260–72.

Williams, B. (2012). The Big Society: post-bureaucratic social policy in the twenty-first century? *The Political Quarterly*, 82(1), 120–32.

Wood, E.H. (2004). Measuring the economic and social impacts of local authority events. *International Journal of Public Sector Management*, 18(1), 37–53.

Wood, E.H. (2009). An impact evaluation framework: local government community festivals. *Event Management*, 12, 1–17.

Wood, E.H. and Kornilaki, M. (2010). Then and now: the changing landscape of local authority events. Global Events Congress. Leeds Metropolitan University, Leeds. 14–16 July.

Wood, E.H. and Long, P. (2009). Great Yorkshire shows: event tourism in Yorkshire. In R. Thomas (ed.), *Managing Regional Tourism: A Case Study of Yorkshire, England*. Bradford: Great Northern.

Wood, E.H. and Syson, F. (2006). Local authority arts events and the South Asian community: unmet needs. *Managing Leisure*, 11, 245–58.

Wood, E.H. and Thomas, R. (2006). Measuring cultural values: the case of residents' attitudes to the Saltaire Festival. *Journal of Tourism Economics*, 12(1), 137–45.

Wood, E.H. and Thomas, R. (2008) Festivals and tourism in rural economies. In J. Ali-Knight, M. Robertson, A. Fyall and A. Ladkin (eds), *International Perspectives of Festivals and Events*. Oxford: Elsevier.

Wood, E.H., Robinson, L. and Bowdin, G. (2006). Evaluating the social impacts of community and local government events: a practical overview of research methods and measurement tools. In S. Fleming and F. Jordan (eds), *Events and Festivals: Education, Impacts and Experiences*. Eastbourne: Leisure Studies Association, pp. 81–92.

Wood, E.H., Smith, B. and Thomas, R. (2009) Linking community festivals to social change: trial and tribulation. The Australian Centre for Event Management 5th International Event Management Research Conference. Gold Coast, Australia, July.

Woodward, I., Taylor, J. and Bennett, A. (eds) (2014). *The Festivalisation of Culture*. Farnham: Ashgate.

Part I

Value creation of events

3 Exploring consumers' value co-creation in a festival context using a socio-cultural lens

Sandhiya Goolaup and Lena Mossberg

Introduction

The concept value is central to the consumer experience. Value has been represented in different ways; (1) as what is perceived by the consumers; (2) attached to a product or service and; (3) as well as a trade-off between what a consumer gives in order to receive something (Woodruff, 1997). Research on value outcome explores how consumers make value assessments and has mainly been discussed in terms of what the consumer gives and receives (Gummerus, 2013). From this perspective, economic and cognitive reasoning is traditionally used to assess the benefits and costs involved (e.g. Zeithaml, 1988). In principle, these 'get' and 'give' components have focused on transforming use value into exchange value. Within the context of those studies, the value-in-use reflects the utility of a commodity, whereas value-in-exchange is the goodness of exchange with something else (Ng and Smith, 2012). Using a similar line of thought, Holbrook sees consumer value as an evaluation of an object by the subject and defined it as "an *interactive, relativistic preference experience*" (1999, p. 5, italics original). Instead of viewing 'economic' value as being at the core of a consumer experience, he categorised it as a subspecies of more general value. Holbrook (1999) proposed a typology of consumer value based on three dichotomies: extrinsic versus intrinsic; self-oriented versus other-oriented; and active versus reactive. The typology of consumer value is further categorised as comprising of eight value dimensions: efficiency, excellence, status, esteem, play, aesthetics, ethics and spirituality. Likewise, Sheth *et al.* (1991) portrayed consumer choice as comprising of multiple consumption value: functional, social, conditional, emotional and epistemic. This perspective of value has also been applied in event studies. For instance, utilising a two-dimensional consumer attitude scale, Gursoy *et al.* (2006) found that both hedonic and utilitarian value are useful indicators explaining festival attendance. Lee *et al.*'s (2010) study of the Boryeong Mud Festival provides further support for the multi-dimensional nature of value by demonstrating that the festival programme (comprising unique, funny and exciting moments) and the natural environment are associated with the emotional value, while the convenient facility is associated with functional value.

Within marketing and consumer research, value has also been studied as a value creation process. This is a stream of research focusing on the activities, resources and interactions occurring in the creation of value (Gummerus, 2013). Unlike the value outcome perspective, value is seen not as residing in an object but rather as being inherently conceived in an experience. This perspective supports a phenomenological stance suggesting that individuals give meaning to their existence through actions and projects (Ng and Smith, 2012). Philosophically, it provides support for the increasingly subjective and interpretative orientation present within consumer research (Levy, 2005). An underlying aspect of the value creation process is the interaction occurring between consumers and the other actors. For Grönroos (2011), value creation through interaction occurs when mutual or reciprocal actions between two or more parties have an effect upon one another.

In line with this perspective, Vargo and Lusch (2004, 2008) advocated a service-dominant logic, which conceptualises the consumer as a co-creator of value through active engagement in an experience. This perspective emphasised value as being "idiosyncratic, experiential, contextual and meaning laden" (Vargo and Lusch, 2008, p. 7). The service-dominant logic is underpinned by ten fundamental premises, one of which suggests that value is always co-created and is uniquely and phenomenologically determined by the beneficiary. Essentially, Vargo and Lusch (2008) stated that value is created as a result of joint integration of resources by multiple actors being associated with an exchange. In the co-creation of value, the different actors integrate both the operant and operand resources they have at their disposal. For Vargo and Lusch (2004), the operant resources comprise the invisible and intangible resources such as skills, knowledge, cultural and social resources that the consumers possess. The operand resources are the tangible and economic resources that require some actions by the different actors in order to create value. In short, this perspective visualises the market as comprising a network of actors who co-create value through interaction and integration and application of various resources. This perspective of value has also been applied in tourism and hospitality research. In particular, the co-creation of value has greatly focused on the role of the tourist as consumer and the service company as producer or provider (Binkhorst and Den Dekker, 2009; Prebensen *et al.*, 2014; Prebensen and Foss, 2011; Shaw *et al.*, 2011). The tourists are perceived as active agents, who are involved in the creation of their experiences by acting as operant resources and the provider as facilitator. Prebensen and Foss (2011), for instance, explore how tourists on vacation co-create their experiences with other people/participants.

To further explore the process of consumer co-creation of value, we follow Graeber (2001) and Karababa and Kjeldgaard's (2013) socio-cultural conceptualisation of value. Such a perspective is focused on the "cultural meanings, sociohistoric influences, and social dynamics that shape consumer experiences and identities in the myriad messy contexts of everyday life" (Arnould and Thompson, 2005, p. 875). It also entails positioning consumer value as an outcome of the socio-cultural contexts and processes that an individual has been exposed to. To understand the consumer value co-creation process, there is a need to focus on consumption experiences (Holbrook, 2006) in various contexts. Festivals, in particular, are interesting as they provide consumers with leisure and social opportunity (Jago and Shaw, 1998), where value and extraordinary experiences can be created and shared (Morgan, 2008). Within the context of festival/event, considerable research has been dedicated to what Gummerus (2013) called the value outcome, by exploring consumers'/participants' perceived value (e.g. Andersson and Armbrecht, 2014; Andersson *et al.*, 2012; Lee *et al.*, 2010; Yang *et al.*, 2011). However, this perspective is not enough if we want to learn more about festival participants' experiences and the consumer value co-creation process. Arguing in a similar vein, Arnould made a call for further studies to explore "how value is created rather than what kinds of value are created" (2013, p. 4). Applying a socio-cultural perspective in the study of consumer value in festivals involves looking at value being co-created, not on an intra-subjective level (individual), but rather in an intersubjective sphere – that is, subjectively determined on a shared level (Heinonen *et al.*, 2013). More precisely, we highlight the socio-cultural construction of three abstract but inter-related ways of talking about value – social, semiotic or economic value – that the existing literature has given little explicit attention (Karababa and Kjeldgaard, 2013).

A socio-cultural conceptualisation of consumer value

This study enunciates a socio-cultural perspective on consumer value. The perspective of consumer value co-creation we used in this study converges with work on 'meaning' production in consumer culture theory (hereafter CCT). In principle, CCT theorises cultural discourses and practices as structuring socio-cultural life in ways that produce meanings for individuals (Slater, 2002). Under the CCT lens, the market is seen as a site where consumers negotiate meanings and value collectively (Arnould and Thompson, 2005). Therefore, rather than viewing the market as a form of exchange of products/services and capital, the market is perceived as being socially and culturally constructed. Likewise, Peñaloza and Mish (2011) portray the markets as comprising of value and mean-ings that are co-produced by marketers and consumers.

Value is not only limited to the market; it is also what really matters for an indi-vidual (Miller, 2000). For Peñaloza and Venkatesh (2006) and Edvardsson *et al.* (2011) value is a socially constructed phenomenon and it gains meaning when individuals interact within a socio-cultural context. In principle, the socio-cultural contexts represent criteria that people use to judge what they consider as legiti-mate and worthwhile and what they do not. Under this perspective, value is embedded in the experience and increases when the experience is relived through discussion in related socio-cultural groups (McAlexander *et al.*, 2002). However, given that different socio-cultural groups exhibit different meanings, they are also more likely to be contested in contexts that do not embrace similar ideologies. Graeber (2001), in particular, sees value in terms of actions and interactions that are capable of creating meaningful differences. He argues that value is likely to emerge as a result of action, and what an individual considers as most meaningful. As Graeber puts it:

> Value emerges in action; it is the process by which a person's invisible potency – their capacity to act – is transformed into concrete, perceptible form… If one sees value as a matter of the relative distribution of that, then one has a common denominator. One invests one's energies in those things one considers most meaningful.
>
> Ibid., p. 45

Therefore, it can be posited that value emerges as a result of action and interaction, with consumers engaging in experiences that they consider to be of value. In order to develop a socio-cultural perspective of consumer value, we refer to Graeber (2001) and Karababa and Kjeldgaard (2013), who advance three inter-related value types: social, semiotic and economic value. Venkatesh and Peñaloza (2014) also suggest that environmental value should be included. However, within the context of this study, we position environmental value as being represented by the semiotic value, as it is an ideology/belief, which is embraced by certain socio-cultural groups. Graeber (2001) defined social value as a conception of what is ultimately good, proper or desirable in human life. He derived the semiotic value from structural linguistics, as 'meaningful difference', and economic value as the degree to which objects are desired, measured by how much others are willing to give up to get them. When associated with an experience or object, these three value types cannot be disentangled and treated in isolation as they are inter-related and co-generative (Karababa and Kjeldgaard, 2013).

In the next section, we proceed towards elaborating on the three dimensions of socio-cultural constructed value: social, semiotic and economic. We also develop subsequent propositions for each of them and, where possible, connections are made to studies conducted within the festival and/or event context.

Social value

Social value is likely to occur when an individual associates himself/herself with a specific social group, socio-economic or cultural-ethnic group (Sheth *et al.*, 1991). The individuals associating themselves with a group usually comprise what scholars have called a consumption community (e.g. Muniz and O'Guinn, 2001), consumer tribes (e.g. Cova and Cova, 2002; Maffesoli, 1995), cultures of consumption (e.g. Kozinets, 2002), or a sub-culture of consumption (e.g. Schouten and McAlexander, 1995; Thompson and Troester, 2002). Within these consumption communities, there are networks of meanings, values, outlook and lifestyle practices that are shared by specific socio-economic milieus (Thornton, 1997). Each consumption community tends to exhibit distinct patterns of socially shared meanings and practices. In the words of Unruh (1980), this is reflective of the social world where people are united as a result of shared 'world views' and interactional characteristics. The behaviours of people who gather in such communities are generally influenced by their social links rather than by outside forces such as formal institutions, marketing and media (Cova and Cova, 2002).

However, a group of studies has demonstrated that the consumption community is not only related to gender, ethnicity, regionality or socio-economic standings, but is also tied to a shared avocational interest and the consumption experience (e.g. Celsi *et al.*, 1993; Kozinets, 2002; Schouten and McAlexander, 1995). The shared interest usually constitutes a social consensus that shapes the perceptions and interaction of individuals within a context. By interacting with those having a shared interest in an object or experience, Muniz and O'Guinn (2001) noted that consumers are more likely to derive value, as it helps in strengthening interpersonal ties. They identified three traditional markers of community that bind individuals together: (1) shared consciousness, (2) rituals and traditions and (3) a sense of moral responsibility. Likewise, Rihova *et al.* (2015) argue that when festivals and events are conceptualised as socially constructed, it provides further insight on the bonding, communing and belongingness occurring. More specifically, the meanings of those experiences are shaped and reinforced through the socialisation that comes from participation in the shared activities (Richins, 1994). These collective experiences also create heightened social interaction, where members learn and generate further meanings. Schouten and McAlexander (1995), for instance, demonstrated how Harley Davidson riders derive value (i.e. allow them to express their patriotism and manliness) by associating themselves with people having similar interests. Similarly, *Celsi et al.* (1993) found that skydivers sharing transcendent information, experience and technical language felt together as members of one cultural community. It can also be argued that the social value realised conveys a sense of connection with others, identity and belonging. Previous studies have noted that the social value derived relates to what is considered to be socially acceptable or unacceptable within the specific context. Hence, the social context is crucial as it has certain norms, values and ethical standards that facilitate the value co-creation process (Edvardsson *et al.*, 2011).

The act of social belonging and the social value derived also play an important role in informing the consumer skills and capabilities. Consumers acting as operant resources bring intangible skills, knowledge and competencies that influence the co-creation of value (Vargo and Lusch, 2004). Inspired by this, Arnould *et al.* (2006) presented three types of operant resources: physical (i.e. energy, emotions, strength), social (i.e. family relationship, brand communities, consumer tribes) and cultural (i.e. specialised knowledge and skills). They further argued that the operant resources are linked with the cultural schemas that are applied in the enactment of social life. Notably, a number of studies have showed that the operant resources of the consumers play an important role in influencing the experience of others, the dynamics of the group experience and the value co-creation process (e.g. Arnould *et al.*, 2006; Baron and Harris, 2008; Celsi *et al.*, 1993;

Yngfalk, 2013). Yngfalk (2013), for instance, demonstrated how football supporters – through their cheering, screaming and singing – provide the 'wow' atmosphere and enhance the attractiveness of attending a match. Hence, through their operant resources, they create preferred cultural schemas that fit the ideology of the community. However, possessing insufficient operant resources influences not only the value co-creation process negatively, but also how an individual is perceived within the community. Following a similar line of thought, Celsi *et al.* (1993) demonstrated how skydivers were judged, based on their perceived competences, and how the less experienced (students and novices) had to struggle and further develop their skills in order to gain acceptance within the skydiving community. Nevertheless, each consumption community also offers access to a wide range of learning resources, which an individual can benefit from by playing an active and independent role in his or her learning, hence facilitating the value co-creation process (Hibbert *et al.*, 2012). Within the context of a folk festival in rural Australia, Begg (2011) illustrated how participants use the festival as a platform to perfect their instruments and performance, learn tunes and have the best knowledge of all the songs.

To summarise, we argue that, within a socio-cultural context such as a festival, the social value derived by consumers/participants is linked with their feeling of belongingness within the particular community. It is also influenced by the prevailing social forces that have a major impact on the development of their operant resources and ability to use operand resources, therefore having implications for the process of value co-creation. Hence, in relation to the above discussion, we propose that:

> P1: The extent of social value derived is linked to the consumers' belongingness to a consumption community.

Semiotic value

Value, in the semiotic sense, refers to the sign value or meaning attributed to a product or experience (Baudrillard, 1993; Graeber, 2001). Referring to the seminal work of Sydney Levy, dating back to the mid- to late 1900s, it has been acknowledged that consumers buy products or participate in an experience not only for their functional benefit, but also for what they mean. Following a similar line of thought, various studies have acknowledged that consumers are more likely to engage in experiences that they deem valuable and have symbolic meanings for them (e.g. Schouten 1991; Larsen *et al.*, 2010; Ulusoy 2016). The use of signs and symbols have also moved the perception from a good-production to a more image-production perspective (Venkatesh *et al.*, 2006). The image associated with an experience usually becomes a central driver for consumption. In a general sense, semiotics analyses the structures of meaning-producing events and deals with how an experience becomes meaningful for the consumer. Within a consumption community, the shared meanings, rituals, myths, signs and beliefs are vital in making the experience more meaningful. Kozinets' (2002) study of the Burning Man Festival, for instance, illustrated how different sub-cultural groups became one as a result of the widely and deeply shared ideologies, artistic meaning and communal ethos of the event. The shared meanings and symbols also allow them to synchronise together, thus heightening their experience and facilitating the co-creation of value. Arguing in a similar vein, Akaka *et al.* (2014) demonstrated how shared symbols facilitate the effective coordination of interaction, integration of resources and communication of information within a particular consumption community.

Festivals are representative of platforms known for celebrating community values, ideologies and identities (Getz, 2010). Each festival, depending on the theme, size and location, conveys different symbolic meanings and ideologies. Ideology refers to the world view or value-and-belief system of a particular group or class of people (Eagleton, 1991). The collections of symbols used by festivals usually define the participant community and represent it to the outside world. For example, iconic carnivalesque festivals such as Sydney Gay and Lesbian Mardi Gras are known to embrace various symbolic practices and meanings such as sexual freedom, self-esteem, equality, self-disclosure to gay and straight others (Kates, 2003). Similarly, the 'slow food' movement, which embraces locally sourced ingredients, reinvigorating traditional recipes and causing less harm to the environment and health (Hall and Sharples, 2008), has attracted a lot of attention. This has eventually led to a number of food festivals following these ideologies, such as the Salone del gusto in Turin, Italy. Likewise, individuals identifying with those communities are likely to endorse ideologies, which are consistent with the group belief. As a result, it can be argued that, through symbolisation, festivals communicate messages that endorse values that are consistent with the beliefs of the consumption community.

Symbolisation is a central component that supports both personal and collective identities of consumers (e.g. Goulding and Saren, 2009; Luedicke *et al.*, 2010; Maffesoli, 1995). In his conceptualisation of neo-tribes, Maffesoli (1995) highlighted the importance of collective consumption for the maintenance of group solidarity and identity. Similarly, various scholars within the area of festivals studies, have acknowledged the importance of symbols and sign value by illustrating how they help in maintaining, reinforcing or constructing sense of self (e.g. Eder *et al.*, 1995; Goulding and Saren, 2009; Hannam and Halewood, 2006). The different signs and symbols associated with festivals also comprised multiple layers of meanings that are rendered intelligible within the social groups. In particular, festivals act as liminal space by nurturing and upgrading the symbolic capital of the group members and enable them to lean towards what they consider to be an authentic and desired sense of self. In their study of the Viking Heritage festivals, Hannam and Halewood (2006), for example, demonstrated how members constructed their identities around forms of collective consumption by engaging in the globalised communication of meanings, socialisation, authenticity, consumption and regulation. In a similar vein, Goulding and Saren (2009) described how Goths used the Whitby festival and its associated symbols, signs and codes for self-expression and extension of their Goth identities. In line with that, it can be argued that the participants of festivals find some relief from structured life through participation in activities that allow them to thrive, engage in some kind of fulfilment and help in defining their belongingness to a social group.

Symbolisation also plays an important role in highlighting the social image of individuals or groups of people attending particular festivals. Depending on the ideologies adopted, the participants become associated with the image projected by the festivals. Particular signs linked with a festival can manifest the operationalisation of certain skills and knowledge needed to be part of a festival. For instance, participants of the Australian Wintersun Festival, who participated in workshops and contests such as classic car restoration, showed that they have the skills and knowledge to fix and maintain their own cars, which they have gained through networking with other car owners and years of reading (Mackellar, 2009). Prestigious festivals provide a platform for the participants to engage in some form of conspicuous consumption and enhance their status by interacting with like-minded people and, at the same time, distancing themselves from those not sharing the same kinds of values or ideologies. In a similar vein, Mackellar (ibid.) illustrated how the Australian Wintersun Festival provided a platform for the participants to show off their vintage cars and connect with other owners, hence reinforcing both their self- and group identities. Mackellar framed her analysis by referring to Ego Involvement Theory, which has been employed to explain event tourist travel careers.

Hence, in relation to the above discussion, it is postulated that the different meanings and symbols associated with a consumption community are useful not only to enhance the group's desired image, but also to play a significant role in transmitting information about the community (social image). In short, consumers are most likely to participate in those festivals and activities that provide them with the opportunity to construct their desired self-identities. The shared understanding among members of the consumption communities also renders intelligible their interaction with others. This is an important element in the branding of events, especially branding of iconic events that appeal to specific communities of interest.

> P2: The semiotic value derived is linked to the extent to which participants can engage in festival activities that facilitate their identity creation process.

Economic value

Derived from a traditional producer perspective, economic value is primarily based on the notion of exchange – that is, the act of giving in order to get something in return. However, from a consumer perspective, exchange is a much more complex phenomenon. Predominantly, the market is seen as a mechanism that involves the exchange of different meanings and value for money. For Østergaard *et al.* (1999), exchange transcends the economic and market relations between buyer and seller to include both the social and affective exchange taking place. Similarly, Miller (2000) emphasised the social context, arguing that the exchange of commodities in the market is a socio-culturally derived phenomenon and can be contextualised as the act of gift-giving. Gift-giving, originating from the seminal work of Marcel Mauss in 1954, considers this kind of transaction as a social activity aimed at integrating society by engaging in reciprocity. Belk (1979) further highlighted the complexity of gift-giving by elaborating on its four functions: communication (e.g. to celebrate life events); social exchange (to maintain and establish interpersonal relationship); as a form of economic exchange; and socialisation. The act of gift-giving also conveys different symbolic meanings. Goodwin *et al.* (1990), for instance, demonstrated how gift-giving can represent a specific relationship, expression of affection or it may be used to symbolise the identities of the receiver or giver.

Likewise, Venkatesh *et al.* (2006) suggest that both 'value-in-use' and 'value-in-exchange' are derivations of sign value. From their perspectives, the market is a culturally constituted economic system where exchanges occur according to mutually negotiated systems of language and meanings. In short, this implies that the co-creation of value by consumers and producers includes both meanings in exchange and use. Using a similar perspective, Clarke (2000), illustrated how second-hand baby clothes comprised various symbolic values – such as history, prior social life and personality of the garments – adding value in the eye of the buyer, thereby also creating the willingness to pay a higher price for it. Furthermore, Sherry (1983) argued that transaction/exchange should be understood as expressive statements in the management of meaning. That is, exchange is the basic expressive act by which symbols mediate their cultural meanings. Therefore, it is exchange itself that is used for the creation of value, with value standing as the normative basis of culture (Slater, 2002).

What is considered as valuable and worthy of exchange will also differ from culture to culture. For instance, engaging in an experience that might not be of value for the community unless it is gaining something out of it or it can help in enhancing its collective image. This is in line with Graeber (2001), who argued that people try to obtain certain things because it makes them happy or gratifies them in some way. This notion can be related to what Østergaard *et al.* (1999) refer to as social exchange. For them, social exchange is the exchange occurring between groups of individuals within a social space for the purpose of social integration and differentiation. This aspect also relates to the fact that consumers are more likely to engage in activities or festivals where they can reinforce their self-identities. The act of choosing to attend a particular festival and willingness to engage in some kind of exchange signifies that it has a certain value for the participants. Hence, by engaging in an exchange, individuals or consumption communities are trying to maximise their social standing, or the prestige that accrues to them by doing so (Graeber, 2001).

Therefore, in relation to the above discussion, it is postulated that consumers derive economic value in an experience when it offers both semiotic and social value. It is summarised with the following proposition:

> P3: The extent of economic value derived by consumers is linked to both the social and semiotic value of the experience.

To summarise, we argue that consumers co-create three different types of value: social, semiotic and economic. Although the three types of consumer value are rather abstract, we have demonstrated that they are also inter-related and co-generative in nature. The next section provides an overview of how consumer value can be studied and an illustrative case is used to explore consumer value co-creation.

Methodological consideration

Using a socio-cultural perspective to study consumer value co-creation pertains to the adoption of the social constructionism approach, which sees reality as being socially constructed and is based on the notion that the experience of self is one developed in meaningful interaction with others (Berger and Luckmann, 1991). Qualitative approaches and methodologies such as participant observation and interview-based methods grounded in ethnographic and interpretive traditions are useful to study such a perspective (Rihova *et al.*, 2015). For Holloway *et al.* (2010), ethnography is useful in providing an overview of what participants at the festival are actually doing (e.g. bodily interactions, actions), as well as what is happening to the participants (their lived experiences). Through this approach, we can gain insight into the different types of meanings and emerging values (Rihova *et al.*, 2015).

Therefore, to understand how consumers co-create value, the first author carried out participant observation for three consecutive years (2013, 2014 and 2015) at an oyster festival. Participant observation is suitable as it can offer an understanding of the festival and the people. During those visits, notes were made on the different activities undertaken by the participants, how they were interacting with others and how the festival was presented. In short, descriptive notes with the general question in mind of 'What is going on here?' were made. Photographs were taken at the festival to try to capture the wider socio-cultural scene and make reliable observations that were useful during the analysis. However, one limitation of the study is that interviews were not conducted to have a more in-depth understanding of the participants' value co-creation process. Therefore, we do not consider the study as a case, rather as an illustrative example and a starting point to explore consumer value co-creation during a festival.

The Oyster Festival in Grebbestad, Sweden: an illustrative example

The Oyster Festival is an annual one-day event held during the first week of September in Grebbestad, a picturesque fishing village in Sweden, to celebrate the oyster day. The festival provides an engaging platform through which people can celebrate the locally grown oysters. The festival was initiated and is organised annually by the local Oyster Academy. Each year, it attracts a number of middle-aged visitors, who stay in the village and nearby areas. The festival offers its participants the opportunity to taste the local Swedish oysters (European flat oysters, *Ostrea Edulis*), together with champagne and the locally brewed porter (all branded by the local Oyster Academy). It also offers a range of other oyster-related activities, such as opportunity to learn how to open oysters, information on the different types of oysters, information regarding membership at the local Oyster Academy, the possibility to purchase oyster-opening knives, fishing equipment and other related accessories, plus musical entertainment. In particular, the festival provides a platform for oyster lovers, allowing them to enjoy the local speciality and socialise with people having a similar interest. Figures 3.1–3.4 illustrate some of the activities taking place during the Oyster Festival held on 5 September 2015. Using this festival at Grebbestad as an illustrative example, we provide a preliminary descriptive analysis of how consumers co-create value. In particular, we analyse the festival in terms of the three inter-related consumer value perspectives discussed above: social, semiotic and economic value.

Figure 3.1 Participants purchasing oysters and drinks.

Figure 3.2 Learning how to open oysters.

Figure 3.3 Musical entertainment.

Figure 3.4 Participants enjoying their oysters and drinks.

Social value

The Oyster Festival held in Grebbestad facilitates the co-creation of social value by providing a platform where both aficionados and the merely curious can interact. In particular, the opportunity to mingle and socialise with those interested in oysters provides a sense of community, where attendees can bond and have an enjoyable experience together. For instance, the participants enjoy their oysters and champagne and/or porter sitting across tables and sharing the experience not only with their friends and relatives, but also with strangers. Thereby, this provides an opportunity for them to discuss oysters and the festival, and to widen and strengthen their social groups and create friendships with other participants. In addition, the aficionados use the festival as an occasion to show off their competencies by demonstrating to their friends, relatives or other participants, for instance, how to best eat the oysters. The festival is also representative of a liminal world, where they become bonded together in the shared atmosphere of festivity, laughter, celebration of the local produce, identity of the place (Grebbestad is known for its special oysters) and appreciation of fresh produce.

Further, within the context of this study, social value arises as a result of the participants getting to further develop their skills and knowledge by engaging in a number of oyster-related activities. For instance, oyster-opening lessons, becoming a member of the Oyster Academy to legitimise their support for the community, participating in lectures related to different types of oysters, the farming of oysters and learning about its beneficial effect on the marine environment. The opportunity to interact with distinguished personalities and experts in oysters also facilitates the co-creation of social value.

Semiotic value

The festival provides an important social context for oyster lovers to meet in one place and celebrate shared values and ideas. For instance, community togetherness, reinvigoration and appreciation of local produce and celebrations of environmentally friendly oysters are some of the symbolic values embraced by the Oyster Festival. The first author has also observed that the shared joy and enthusiasm expressed by the participants was an important sign used to acknowledge their presence within the wider social context and with those having the same values and beliefs. In particular, the festival offers a range of activities for both aficionados and amateur participants to engage in, to reinforce both their personal and social identities. The amateur participants, for instance, had the opportunity to reinforce their identities through participation in oyster-opening classes, learning about different oysters, becoming a member of the Oyster Academy and mingling and interacting with members sharing the same values as them. The aficionados further affirm their identities by showing off their skills when it comes to the opening of oysters, being cheered by other members for successfully opening the oysters, showing to others how to best eat the oysters and interacting with distinguished personalities at the festival, such as key members of the Oyster Academy. The Swedish European flat oysters and champagne that are served at the festival are considered to be luxurious, expensive and a product known to be appreciated by gourmets. Therefore, the festival provides participants with a social image where they are perceived as engaging in a form of conspicuous consumption.

Economic value

The derived economic value is linked to both the social and semiotic value. As the Oyster Festival is representative of a form of conspicuous consumption, for most visitors it is also a relevant context for gift-giving. Some use the festival to invite family, friends and colleagues to participate on their account. To eat oysters and drink champagne with them can mark who they are or who they aspire to be. In addition, objects bought at the event, like oyster knives, can be used as a symbolic gift to signal skills and prestige. Other participants who do not buy oysters for different reasons (e.g. do not like, allergic or cannot afford) are also part of this festival. For them, it reflects an opportunity to be around when the activities go on; they might hope to meet some old friends, just to socialise, have a good time and get entertainment for free. Finally, those who are members of the Oyster Academy and take part in various duties as volunteers also affect other visitors' experiences by transmitting their enthusiasm, passion and interest in oysters and the area. Therefore, it can be argued that all actors are involved in the process of co-creating value as they enjoy being there and like to share the experience with others. In addition, the enthusiasm and joy demonstrated by the participants are signs that the Oyster Festival is perceived to be of value, a meaningful experience and worthy of attendance.

Discussion and conclusion

Festivals are typically social happenings, where people with similar interests gather to share activities and experiences. They represent opportunities for the participants to engage in activities that contrast with their daily life and provide them with feelings of fantasy and fun. Festivals are also arenas where people can engage in activities that allow them to maintain or construct their identities (e.g. Goulding and Saren, 2009), socialise and bond with people sharing their interests (e.g. Arcodia and Whitford, 2007) or even support certain ideologies and beliefs (e.g. Kates, 2003). In this chapter, we argue for the applicability of a socio-cultural perspective as we positioned consumer value as being a culturally and socially constructed phenomenon. Such a perspective specifically portrays consumer value as emerging in action and interactions. Value is co-created when consumers or participants of the festival are actively involved in interacting with each other and sharing meanings. It contrasts with previous studies within the festivals context that have mainly focused on consumer value as being subjectively perceived by the consumer and provided by the organisers or service providers (e.g. Andersson *et al.*, 2012; Lee *et al.*, 2011; Gursoy *et al.*, 2006). Further, previous studies have mostly focused on portraying value as 'exchange value', 'perceived value', 'experiential value', 'value as co-created' and ' identity and linking value', without focusing on providing a more conceptually grounded synthesis of these different conceptions of value (Karababa and Kjelgaard, 2013).

Therefore, we present three abstract but inter-related types of consumer value that are relevant within the context of festival/events: social, semiotics and economic. Social value is derived when participants belonging to a consumption community and, having similar interests, use the festival as an opportunity to strengthen feelings of belongingness and further enhance their operant resources. The semiotic value, on the other hand, occurs when the different signs and symbols associated with the festival play an important role in enhancing the social image of the participants, reinforcing their self-identities or communicating certain messages about the participants' beliefs and ideologies. Finally, economic value is when the festival and the meanings associated with it are perceived to be of value and worthy of engagement in exchange. In principle, we also argued that economic value is likely to occur when it offers both social and semiotic value. Indeed, a number of scholars have acknowledged that participants are part of a festival not only for its functional/utilitarian benefits, but also due to the different meanings associated with it (e.g. Kates and Belk, 2001; Quinn, 2003). The different meanings associated with the festival are what the participants/consumers consider worthy justifications for attendance and interaction. The participants also play an active role by bringing cultural skills, knowledge and competencies. Specifically, through their operant resources, they influence the experience of others and the value co-creation process. Some participants also use the festival as a platform for improving their operant resources, while others use it to connect with other participants or to show off.

Unlike previous studies, we have showed that the proposed framework offers a more embracing and comprehensive approach to understanding the process of consumer value co-creation. In addition, previous studies have illustrated the different types of value as being separated, but, by using the socio-cultural perspective, we have demonstrated that they are related and cannot be separated. One limitation of this study is that the illustrative case is explorative in nature. It has just provided a snapshot using participant observation of one festival during three consecutive years. Future research should consider supplementing observation with consumer interviews in order to have a better understanding of their value co-creation process. We also believe that the proposed framework is applicable not only within the context of a festival, but also in other experiential contexts. Even though the focus of the illustrative case has been on consumers, it is equally applicable in explaining the value co-creation process among volunteers, as they are working for fun and free – therefore, they also perceive the festival as being meaningful.

References

Akaka, M.A., Corsaro, D., Kelleher, C., Maglio, P.P., Seo, Y., Lusch, R.F. and Vargo, S.L. (2014). The role of symbols in value cocreation. *Marketing Theory*, 14(3), 311–26. doi:10.1177/1470593114534344

Andersson, T.D. and Armbrecht, J. (2014). Factors explaining the use-value of sport event experiences. *International Journal of Event and Festival Management*, 5(3), 235–46.

Andersson, T.D., Armbrecht, J. and Lundberg, E. (2012). Estimating use and non-use values of a music festival. *Scandinavian Journal of Hospitality and Tourism*, 12(3), 215–31. doi:10.1080/15022250.2012.725276

Arcodia, C. and Whitford, M. (2007). Festival attendance and the development of social capital. *Journal of Convention and Event Tourism*, 8(2), 1–18.

Arnould, E.J. (2013). Rudiments of a value praxeology. *Marketing Theory*. doi:10.1177/1470593113500384

Arnould, E.J. and Thompson, C.J. (2005). Consumer culture theory (CCT): twenty years of research. *Journal of Consumer Research*, 31(4), 868–82. doi:10.1086/426626

Arnould, E.J., Price, L.L. and Malshe, A. (2006). Towards a cultural resource-based theory of the customer. In R.F. Lusch and S.L. Vargo (eds), *The Service-Dominant Logic of Marketing: Dialog, Debate, and Directions*. Armonk, NY: M.E. Sharpe, pp. 91–104.

Baron, S. and Harris, K. (2008). Consumers as resource integrators. *Journal of Marketing Management*, 24(1–2), 113–30.

Baudrillard, J. (1993). *Symbolic Exchange and Death*. London: Sage.

Begg, R. (2011). Culturing commitment: serious leisure and the folk festival experience. In C. Gibson and J. Connell (eds), *Festival Places: Revitalising Rural Australia*. Bristol: Channel View, pp. 248–64.

Belk, R.W. (1979). Gift-giving behaviour. In J. Sheth (ed.), *Research in Marketing*, vol. 2. Greenwich, CT: JAI Press, pp. 95–126.

Berger, P.L. and Luckmann, T. (1991). *The Social Construction of Reality: A Treatise in the Sociology of Knowledge*. London: Penguin.

Binkhorst, E. and Den Dekker, T. (2009). Agenda for co-creation tourism experience research. *Journal of Hospitality Marketing and Management*, 18(2–3), 311–27. doi:10.1080/19368620802594193

Celsi, R.L., Rose, R.L. and Leigh, T.W. (1993). An exploration of high-risk leisure consumption through skydiving. *Journal of Consumer Research*, 1–23.

Clarke, A. (2000). Mother swapping: the trafficking of nearly new children's wear. In P. Jackson, M. Lowe, D. Miller and F. Mort (Eds.), *Commercial Cultures: Economies, Practices, Spaces*. Oxford: Berg, pp. 85–100.

Cova, B. and Cova, V. (2002). Tribal marketing: the tribalisation of society and its impact on the conduct of marketing. *European Journal of Marketing*, 36(5/6), 595–620.

Eagleton, T. (1991). *Ideology: An Introduction* (Vol. 9). Cambridge: Cambridge University Press.

Eder, D., Staggenborg, S. and Sudderth, L. (1995). The National Women's Music Festival Collective: identity and diversity in a lesbian-feminist community. *Journal of Contemporary Ethnography*, 23(4), 485–515.

Edvardsson, B., Tronvoll, B. and Gruber, T. (2011). Expanding understanding of service exchange and value co-creation: a social construction approach. *Journal of the Academy of Marketing Science*, 39(2), 327-339.

Getz, D. (2010). The nature and scope of festival studies. *International Journal of Event Management Research*, 5(1), 1–47.

Goodwin, C., Smith, K.L. and Spiggle, S. (1990). Gift-giving: consumer motivation and the gift purchase process. In *Advances in Consumer Research*, 17, 690–8.

Goulding, C. and Saren, M. (2009). Performing identity: an analysis of gender expressions at the Whitby Goth festival. *Consumption, Markets and Culture*, 12(1), 27–46.

Graeber, D. (2001). *Toward an Anthropological Theory of Value: The False Coin of Our Own Dreams*. Basingstoke: Palgrave Macmillan.

Grönroos, C. (2011). A service perspective on business relationships: the value creation, interaction and marketing interface. *Industrial Marketing Management*, 40(2), 240–7. doi: http://dx.doi.org/10.1016/j.indmarman.2010.06.036

Gummerus, J. (2013). Value creation processes and value outcomes in marketing theory: strangers or siblings? *Marketing Theory*. doi:10.1177/1470593112467267

Gursoy, D., Spangenberg, E.R. and Rutherford, D.G. (2006). The hedonic and utilitarian dimensions of attendees' attitudes toward festivals. *Journal of Hospitality and Tourism Research*, 30(3), 279–94. doi:10.1177/1096348006287162

Hall, C.M. and Sharples, L. (2008). Future issues and trends: food events, festivals and farmers' markets. In C.M. Hall, L. Sharples and T. Emma (eds), *Food and Wine Festivals and Events Around the World: Development, Management and Markets [Elektronisk resurs]*. Oxford: Butterworth-Heinemann, pp. 331–46.

Hannam, K. and Halewood, C. (2006). European Viking themed festivals: an expression of identity. *Journal of Heritage Tourism*, 1(1), 17–31.

Heinonen, K., Strandvik, T. and Voima, P. (2013). Customer dominant value formation in servicenull. *European Business Review*, 25(2), 104–23. doi:10.1108/09555341311302639

Hibbert, S., Winklhofer, H. and Temerak, M.S. (2012). Customers as resource integrators: toward a model of customer learning. *Journal of Service Research*, 1094670512442805.

Holbrook, M.B. (1999). *Consumer Value: A Framework for Analysis and Research*. London: Routledge.

Holbrook, M.B. (2006). Consumption experience, customer value, and subjective personal introspection: an illustrative photographic essay. *Journal of Business Research*, 59(6), 714–25. doi: http://dx.doi.org/10.1016/j.jbusres.2006.01.008

Holloway, I., Brown, L. and Shipway, R. (2010). Meaning not measurement: using ethnography to bring a deeper understanding to the participant experience of festivals and events. *International Journal of Event and Festival Management*, 1(1), 74–85.

Jago, L.K. and Shaw, R.N. (1998). Special events: a conceptual and definitional framework. *Festival Management and Event Tourism*, 5(1–2), 21–32. doi:10.3727/106527098792186775

Karababa, E. and Kjeldgaard, D. (2013). Value in marketing: toward sociocultural perspectives. *Marketing Theory*. doi:10.1177/1470593113500385

Kates, S.M. (2003). Producing and consuming gendered representations: an interpretation of the Sydney Gay and Lesbian Mardi Gras. *Consumption Markets and Culture*, 6(1), 5–22. doi:10.1080/10253860302699

Kates, S.M. and Belk, R.W. (2001). The meanings of lesbian and gay pride day resistance through consumption and resistance to consumption. *Journal of Contemporary Ethnography*, 30(4), 392–429.

Kozinets, R.V. (2002). Can consumers escape the market? Emancipatory illuminations from Burning Man. *Journal of Consumer Research*, 29(1), 20–38. Retrieved from http://jcr.oxfordjournals.org/content/29/1/20.abstract

Larsen, G., Lawson, R. and Todd, S. (2010). The symbolic consumption of music. *Journal of Marketing Management*, 26(7–8), 671–85.

Lee, J.S., Lee, C.-K. and Choi, Y. (2010). Examining the role of emotional and functional values in festival evaluation. *Journal of Travel Research*. doi:10.1177/0047287510385465

Levy, S.J. (2005). The evolution of qualitative research in consumer behavior. *Journal of Business Research*, 58(3), 341–7. doi: http://dx.doi.org/10.1016/S0148-2963(03)00107-3

Luedicke, M.K., Thompson, C.J. and Giesler, M. (2010). Consumer identity work as moral protagonism: how myth and ideology animate a brand-mediated moral conflict. *Journal of Consumer Research*, 36(6), 1016–32.

Mackellar, J. (2009). An examination of serious participants at the Australian Wintersun Festival. *Leisure Studies*, 28(1), 85–104.

Maffesoli, M. (1995). *The Time of the Tribes: The Decline of Individualism in Mass Society* (Vol. 41). London: Sage.

Mauss, M. (1954). *The Gift: Forms and Reasons for Exchange in Archaic Societies*. London: Routledge Classics.

McAlexander, J.H., Schouten, J.W. and Koenig, H.F. (2002). Building brand community. *Journal of Marketing*, 66(1), 38–54.

Miller, D. (2000). Introduction: the birth of value. In P. Jackson, M. Lowe, D. Miller and F. Mort (eds), *Commercial Cultures: Economies, Practices, Spaces*. Oxford: Berg, pp. 77–83.

Morgan, M. (2008). What makes a good festival? Understanding the event experience. *Event Management*, 12(2), 81–93. doi:10.3727/152599509787992562

Muniz, A.M. and O'Guinn, T.C. (2001). Brand community. *Journal of Consumer Research*, 27(4), 412–32. doi:10.1086/319618

Ng, I.C.L. and Smith, L.A. (2012). An integrative framework of value. In S.L. Vargo and R.F. Lusch (eds), *Special Issue: Toward a Better Understanding of the Role of Value in Markets and Marketing* (Vol. 9). Bingley: Emerald, pp. 207–43.

Østergaard, P., Fittchet, J.A. and Jantzen, C. (1999). On appropriation and singularisation. *Advances in Consumer Research*, 26, 405–9.

Peñaloza, L. and Mish, J. (2011). The nature and processes of market co-creation in triple bottom line firms: leveraging insights from consumer culture theory and service dominant logic. *Marketing Theory*, 11(1), 9–34. doi:10.1177/1470593110393710

Peñaloza, L. and Venkatesh, A. (2006). Further evolving the new dominant logic of marketing: from services to the social construction of markets. *Marketing Theory*, 6(3), 299–316. doi:10.1177/1470593106066789

Prebensen, N.K. and Foss, L. (2011). Coping and co-creating in tourist experiences. *International Journal of Tourism Research*, 13(1), 54–67. doi:10.1002/jtr.799

Prebensen, N.K., Chen, J.S. and Uysal, M. (2014). *Creating Experience Value in Tourism*. Boston: CAB International.

Quinn, B. (2003). Symbols, practices and myth-making: cultural perspectives on the Wexford Festival Opera. *Tourism Geographies*, 5(3), 329–49.

Richins, M.L. (1994). Valuing things: the public and private meanings of possessions. *Journal of Consumer Research*, 21(3), 504–21. Retrieved from http://www.jstor.org/stable/2489689

Rihova, I., Buhalis, D., Moital, M. and Gouthro, M.-B. (2015). Social constructions of value: marketing considerations for the context of event and festival visitation. In O. Moufakkir and T. Pernecky (eds), *Ideological, Social and Cultural Aspects of Events [Elektronisk resurs]*. Wallingford: CABI, pp. 74–84.

Schouten, J.W. (1991). Selves in transition: symbolic consumption in personal rites of passage and identity reconstruction. *Journal of Consumer Research*, 412–25.

Schouten, J.W. and McAlexander, J.H. (1995). Subcultures of consumption: an ethnography of the new bikers. *Journal of Consumer Research*, 43–61.

Shaw, G., Bailey, A. and Williams, A. (2011). Aspects of service-dominant logic and its implications for tourism management: examples from the hotel industry. *Tourism Management*, 32(2), 207–14. doi: http://dx.doi.org/10.1016/j.tourman.2010.05.020

Sherry, J. F. (1983). Gift giving in anthropological perspective. *Journal of Consumer Research*, 157–68.

Sheth, J.N., Newman, B.I. and Gross, B.L. (1991). Why we buy what we buy: a theory of consumption values. *Journal of Business Research*, 22(2), 159–70. doi: http://dx.doi.org/10.1016/0148-2963(91)90050-8

Slater, D. (2002). Capturing markets from the economists. In P. Du Gay and M. Pryke (eds), *Cultural Economy: Cultural Analysis and Commercial Life*. London: Sage, pp. 59–77.

Thompson, C.J. and Troester, M. (2002). Consumer value systems in the age of postmodern fragmentation: the case of the natural health microculture. *Journal of Consumer Research*, 28(4), 550–71.

Thornton, S. (1997). General introduction. In K. Gelder and S. Thornton (eds), *The Subcultures Reader*. London: Routledge, pp. 1–6.

Ulusoy, E. (2016). Subcultural escapades via music consumption: identity transformations and extraordinary experiences in Dionysian music subcultures. *Journal of Business Research*, 69(1), 244–54.

Unruh, D.R. (1980). The nature of social worlds. *Sociological Perspectives*, 23(3), 271–96. doi:10.2307/1388823

Vargo, S.L. and Lusch, R.F. (2004). Evolving to a new dominant logic for marketing. *Journal of Marketing*, 68(1), 1–17. doi:10.1509/jmkg.68.1.1.24036

Vargo, S.L. and Lusch, R.F. (2008). Service-dominant logic: continuing the evolution. *Journal of the Academy of Marketing Science*, 36(1), 1–10.

Venkatesh, A. and Peñaloza, L. (2014). The value of value in CCT. *Marketing Theory*, 14(1), 135–8. doi:10.1177/1470593113500386

Venkatesh, A., Peñaloza, L. and Firat, A.F. (2006). The market as a sign system and the logic of the market. In R.F. Lusch and S.L. Vargo (eds), *The Service-Dominant Logic of Marketing: Dialog, Debate, and Directions*. Armonk, NY: M.E. Sharpe.

Woodruff, R.B. (1997). Customer value: the next source for competitive advantage. *Journal of the Academy of Marketing Science*, 25(2), 139–53.

Yang, J., Gu, Y. and Cen, J. (2011). Festival tourists' emotion, perceived value, and behavioral intentions: a test of the moderating effect of festivalscape. *Journal of Convention and Event Tourism*, 12(1), 25–44. doi:10.1080/15470148.2010.551292

Yngfalk, A. (2013). "It's not us, it's them!" – Rethinking value co-creation among multiple actors. *Journal of Marketing Management*, 29(9–10), 1163–81.

Zeithaml, V.A. (1988). Consumer perceptions of price, quality, and value: a means–end model and synthesis of evidence. *Journal of Marketing*, 52(3), 2–22. doi:10.2307/1251446

4 Successful event–destination collaboration through superior experience value for visitors

Nina K. Prebensen

Introduction

Events are value creation entities affecting individuals, firms and society in various ways (Andersson *et al.*, 2012; Andersson and Lundberg 2013). As a commercial business, the event creates revenues for its owners and stakeholders, and provides work and income for its employees. Because of events' ability to attract visitors, they have become a substantial element of destination branding. However, research claims that event marketers and destination marketers have not yet learned how to synergise their efforts (Jago *et al.*, 2003). This chapter aims to explore how destinations and events may benefit through collaboration. The idea is to show how this collaboration becomes successful through facilitating superior experience value for visitors.

The key for events and destinations is to create value to attract the customer to visit the event and the destination. In the attempt to attract locals and tourists to visit an event, the event develops, facilitates and communicates potential experience value – that is, emotional, social and epistemic value (Williams and Soutar, 2009). In a similar way, destination marketing management companies aim to attract tourists to visit the destination. Through this process, successful events and destinations create reputations, providing awareness and visitation for themselves and the collaborative partners.

Special events such as a music festival or a sporting competition are produced and consumed in a certain place, at a certain time – often once a year. This makes it challenging in terms of income and profits, despite the fact that it might be well known and liked. Even though many events are profitable and successful, the vast potential of their value resides in the prospect of exploiting the image and resources at the destination – that is, at place, region or country level. One of the major issues in destination management and marketing is to attract tourists to visit the place throughout the whole year. It is also recognised that repeat visitation will simplify marketing efforts and help enhance revenues. This is a major issue in tourism, in that loyalty, in terms of repeat purchase, is relatively low in tourism compared to other consumption. A number of studies show that even though tourists are satisfied and intend to recommend the place to others, they do not necessarily aim to return to the destination (e.g., Assaker *et al.*, 2011).

This phenomenon is about the individual need to experience novel experiences and destinations and is an important issue many destinations experience. So, while events have groups of special interest visitors, intending to visit the event repeatedly (once a year), destinations struggle to increase the number of repeat visitors. As such, the present work shows the imperative of a collaborative framework for events and destinations, in that events attract a relatively loyal customer group and that destination and its actors may benefit from this if they support and ensure an enriching and successful event. Events and destinations are both concerned with attracting the right customers. Attraction value can be delineated as value realised through recognition of the experience at the event and the destination, in which the inhabitants may benefit from the experience and the subsequent spill-over effects. The simple idea is that attraction value reflects the customer attitudes – that is, information and knowledge, emotions and liking, and buying intentions (Bagozzi and Burnkrant, 1978). Attraction value thus is about signalling the right values for the right customers, and doing so repeatedly in order to be recognised, liked and chosen.

Events attract local, regional, national and even international spectators, depending on uniqueness, status and promotion. Getz (1997, p. 338) depicts event tourism as "the systematic planning, development, and marketing of festivals and special events as investor attractions, development catalysts, and image builders for attractions and destination areas". As such, an event might supplement the tourism industry by functioning as an attraction for visitors.

Special events might function as a distinct type of attraction at a destination. They attract visitors and other stakeholders because the customers perceive them as unique and different from other types of attractions (Getz, 1989). Destinations and events, in particular those situated in rural areas, struggle with limited marketing budgets to communicate and promote themselves. Destinations might earn from events in that they attract people to visit, resulting in increased number of overnight stays. Many destination planners and promoters employ events to help "reinforce, consolidate, and assist the promotion" to increase visitation (Walsh-Heron and Stevens, 1990, p. 12). Destinations and events have many overlapping customers and stakeholders – that is, accommodation, transporters and restaurants. Events can provide destinations with enhanced publicity via media and national and international business tourism (sponsors), and offer the community and local inhabitants experience value. Destinations may also help enhance visitation to the event. The destination may offer the event a local network, infrastructure and branding network and tools. The destination may also help facilitate improved experience value for the eventgoers. Addressing the process of co-creating successful events helps tourism and destination managers and marketers in their attempt to attract visitors to the destination and, as such, adds value in positioning and branding destinations.

Two theoretical perspectives are utilised to explore value creation potentials for destinations and events: the collaborative value approach (Austin and Seitanidi, 2012a, 2012b) and the stakeholder experience value (e.g. Sheth *et al.*, 1991; Prebensen, 2010). The idea is that collaboration should benefit the core customers of the respective partners. This work thus shows how collaboration may create value for eventgoers and tourists and, subsequently, provide positive attraction value for destinations and events.

Austin and Seitanidi (2012a, 2012b) suggest value in terms of a collaborative value creation (CVC) framework. Austin and Seitanidi's articles reveal, in particular, value creation dynamics and effects in collaboration between non-profit makers and businesses, which often occurs in tourism – some destination marketing and management offices (DMMOs) include both private and public operations. Events may also include public as well as private ownership and interests. This chapter implements the CVC framework to show value creation potential for various stakeholders within the collaborating networks – that is, destination network and event network. By an event–destination collaboration, both actors are expected to acknowledge network value potentials, such as 'associative value', 'transferred resource value', 'interaction value' and 'synergistic value' (Austin and Seitanidi 2012a, pp. 5–6), which will help them in their effort to provide value propositions (Williams and Soutar, 2009) for enhanced customer experience value. These values are described below.

The chapter is structured as follows. First, a review of value and value co-creation literature from a marketing and management perspective is presented. Next, the idea that destinations and events are value-creating entities is discussed. Then, literature regarding collaborative networks is delineated, followed by a discussion of potential synergies of collaborative networks between destinations and events. Finally, impacts of collaboration between destination and events in enhancing visitors' experience value are demonstrated.

Theoretical perspectives

The value concept

Value as a business concept has received significant attention in marketing and management literatures. Zeithaml (1988, p. 14) defines value as "the consumer's overall assessment of the utility of a product based on perceptions of what is received and what is given". According to Ulaga (2003, cited in Smith and Colgate, 2007, p. 8): "Customer value is perceived uniquely by individual customers; it is conditional or contextual (dependent on the individual, situation, or product); it is relative (in comparison to known or imagined alternatives) and it is dynamic (changing within individuals over time)." The interactive facet of an experience value deals with the involvement of people and objects (Holbrook and Hirschman, 1982). In networks and between networks, the type of value that is appreciated by the various participants is expected to vary largely. According to these scholars, the main purpose of a business network should be to focus on defining who their customers or stakeholders are, and then to deliver expected value in the marketplace. However, a simple focus on value for customers or stakeholders might lose some important perspectives; value created in and within organisations and networks might be ignored. In particular, value creation as a result of sharing capabilities and competencies in networks might be neglected. The different stakeholder groups and individuals partaking in networks may also have different positions and roles inside and outside the network – that is, as a customer, as a firm, as individuals and as part of a group.

Customer (eventgoers and tourist) value

The conceptualisation of value as a trade-off between 'get' and 'give' has boosted a universal interest in the amalgamated nature of consumer value (e.g. Bradley and Sparks, 2012; Gallarza and Saura, 2006; Sweeney and Soutar, 2001; Woodruff, 1997). Perceived customer value is delineated as key to acknowledging consumer behaviour (Sheth *et al.*, 1991; Williams and Soutar, 2009). Woodruff (1997, p. 142) defines customer value as: "a customer's perceived preference for and evaluation of those product attributes, attribute performances, and consequences arising from use that facilitate (or block) achieving the customer's goals and purposes in use situations". Experiential consumption such as partaking and joining an event is described as an "interactive relativistic preference experience" (Holbrook, 1999, p. 5). Woodall (2003, p. 21), furthermore, claims the relevance of "personal perception of advantage arising out of a customer's association with an organization's offering".

Individuals visiting a destination and/or an event search for experience value (Prebensen *et al.*, 2013a, 2013b). Perceived value as a concept including specific dimensions was suggested by Sheth *et al.* (1991). This study suggests four distinct dimensions of perceived value: emotional, social, quality/performance and price/value for money. As these dimensions are tested for in various tourism contexts, they are adopted in the present work. Williams and Soutar (2009) test the Sheth *et al.* scale and suggest novelty/epistemic as a supplement to the former four dimensions, in particular in experiential consumption situations.

Value for events and destinations

Research demonstrates that cities and destinations more often utilise events to improve their image, stimulate urban development and attract visitors and investment (Richards and Wilson, 2004). The aim for many destinations has been to attract visitors and to stimulate consumption among residents, while at the same time positioning the destinations in the mind of existent and potential visitors.

An event embraces certain identities and images that both companies and individuals can identify with and even present themselves. Clearly, a successful event might function as instrument to fulfil other needs or goals than the core theme of the event. Subsequently, the event might function as an arena for meetings and social gatherings, as well as a place to communicate own products, brands, or organisation. In a similar way, events may be valuable for branding the place or region hosting the event. For destinations to attract and boost the number of visitors, ensure repeat visitors and brand equity, co-branding their destination together with an event is a potential strategy.

Value co-creation in networks

A number of different stakeholders collaborate to co-create value in events (e.g. Achrol and Kotler, 2006; Grönroos, 2006; Gummeson, 2006; Prebensen, 2010). Most stakeholders participate for economic and other instrumental reasons, such as building brand equity, in addition to enjoying the event. From an eventgoer's perspective, an event may be attractive to participate in and join for reasons such as fun, pleasure and good experiences. Research shows how customers and stakeholders (participants) create value for themselves and others by their presence and through their resources (Prebensen, 2010). The participants also co-create value. Identifying these actors and how value is created through collaboration is vital in order to further enhance value for all actors, including the customer (ibid.).

Destination organisations and events include many participants for whom participation resides in different needs, interest and purposes. Both groups therefore reflect a system or a network of stakeholders and customers. Additionally, the stakeholder groups may function as customers in the same network. For instance, a sponsor of an event is also often a customer for the media covering the same event. This shows the intricate system of participation and value creation for events and destinations. Even so, this work intends to discuss the main impacts for the destination and the event when collaborating to enhance experience value for their customers.

The Prebensen (ibid.) study explores how value is created through stakeholders' participation and involvement within a network framework. The study analyses seven various stakeholder groups (including audience) and their purposes for, and structures in, joining an event in northern Norway, situated in the Arctic. As such, the study is also a valid example of co-creation of value in events at remote places. This study defines stakeholders to include both organisations and individuals and both firms and customers. The findings reveal that the various stakeholders have numerous reasons for participating in the event, classified as autotelic and instrumental value experiences. Autotelic value experiences are those enjoyed in the moment – for example, sunbathing for the sake of an immediate feeling of well-being. Instrumental value experiences, are those consumed with other purposes or for reasons that may exist in the future – for example, sunbathing to get a nice tan. The stakeholders experience various types of value through their participation and involvement, dependent on their own or, in the case of representing a firm, the firm's motivation and participation in the event. The study explores value creation because of other stakeholders' participation as well. An example is that sponsors will get amplified value with increased media coverage. Media coverage and sponsors will also attract other and perhaps more qualified participants (the case is a sporting event), which is expected to attract more spectators to the event and the destination. When the best athletes are attracted to join the event, the media will give it more attention. A popular event would also be more attractive for volunteers to enjoy. This positive spiral would give the event potential to grow and ensure income and revenue. Positive reputations and images regarding a specific event may spread to the destination as well. The Prebensen (ibid.) study points to how destinations might gain value through networking and cooperation, exemplified by the stakeholders' involvement and participation in the event. Value-creating synergy effects are attained when organisations get access to each other's infrastructures, capabilities, knowledge, customers and opportunities for economies of scale and cost reduction (Austin and Seitanidi, 2012a; Ireland *et al.*, 2002).

An event strongly depends on all its actors and stakeholders to build a positive reputation and other value for its stakeholders. Interdependency and collaborations are core issues in arranging appealing events. As a result, the event becomes more attractive for all stakeholders by each and everyone's participation and interaction. The same logic is expected to amplify the value co-created by two networks collaborating, the destination and the event.

Relations and networks thus might facilitate or restrain the organisations' abilities to perform (Wilkinson, 2008). Relations and networks hence play basic roles in "assessing, combining, recombining and coordinating the activities, resources and outputs of people and firms" (ibid., p. 23), and "are the means by which the knowledge, skills and resources required to develop, exploit and commercialize new ideas are marshalled and coordinated" (ibid., p. 25). Consequently, networks are essential for most organisations – in particular, for events – in that they add value to the entity at stake, and consequently potentially add value to the destination as well.

Destinations and events as value co-creating entities

Tourism is an industry where organisations interact and collaborate comparatively closely. This collaboration is often a result of mutual interest to more efficiently communicate and facilitate the destination or its benefits to specified customers. Even if events represent their own network, they are also part of the destination network.

Destinations and countries reside in a situation of intense competition to attract customers to visit (Kim and Fesenmaier, 2008). As the world becomes increasingly globalized, destination marketing seems to be both the cause and the effect of increased competition (Cai, 2002; Konecnik and Gartner, 2007).

Customers visit events due to a variety of motivations and purposes. However, one key motivation, for most visitors, is specific interest in the activity – that is, a certain type of music or a certain type of sport event. Sport enthusiasts seem to visit sport events regularly. Even though some spectators or eventgoers visit fewer times than enthusiasts, repeat purchase is more common for events than for tourist attractions in general (Taks *et al.*, 2009). Eventgoers may, therefore, be defined as special interest customers, which are delineated in literature as searching for a serious leisure activity. Serious leisure is defined by Stebbins (1982, in Bartram, 2001, p. 5) as "the systematic pursuit of an amateur, hobbyist, or volunteer activity, that is sufficiently rewarding despite the costs, such that participants find a career in the acquisition and expression of its special skills and knowledge". Kelly and Godbey (1992) state that special interests often result in development of trust, sharing and intimacy. The shared social or cultural worlds of the visitors can influence the positive or negative perception of an experience (Arnould *et al.*, 1998).

Destinations are more complex and diverse than specific tourism products, such as an event (Ooi and Stoeber, 2010). The creation of a destination image has to address multiple groups of stakeholders and socio-cultural identities, and take into consideration the intangible and multiple facets of a destination. A destination's image and reputation includes tangible and positive outcomes of the realisation of unity and collaboration among its stakeholders (Prideaux and Cooper, 2002). In addition, research demonstrates the imperative of the intangible effects such as the image and the reputation (Balakrishnan, 2009). Therefore, collaboration and inter-relationships among stakeholders to enhance attraction value is key to success for destinations (Cai, 2002). One strong voice is delineated as essential to the creation of positive destination attraction value (Foley and Fahy, 2004; Konecnik and Gartner, 2007).

The collaborative value creation perspective

The collaborative value creation (CVC) perspective is defined as the "transitory and enduring benefits relative to the costs that are generated due to the interaction of the collaborators and that accrue to organizations, individuals, and society" (Austin and Seitanidi, 2012a, p. 3). The CVC framework components include: (1) the value creation spectrum, suggesting a new perspective in defining and analysing value creation, (2) collaboration stages, including how value creation diverges across different types of collaborative relationships, (3) partnering processes, delineating value creation dynamics in the formation and implementation stages and (4) collaboration outcomes fronting impacts at the micro, meso and macro levels. The authors show, by including important sources of value, different types of collaborative value reflecting different ways in which benefits arise in and between the various levels of value creation spectrum – that is, from solitary creation towards co-creation of value.

Austin and Seitanidi (ibid., pp. 4–5) develop four hypotheses regarding successful collaboration and delineate the following resources as fundamental in value co-creation processes:

1.   Organisational fit indicates that collaboration should be based on level of resource complementarity rather than the idea of collaboration to obtain access to resources.
2.   Resources may be generic, i.e. money or positive reputation, or organisational specific, i.e. knowledge, capabilities, infrastructure and relationships.
3.   The degree and type of interaction (e.g. one-way versus reciprocal) will affect value co-creation.
4.   Mutual interests and reciprocity in terms of value and perspectives of fair value exchange.

By combining these four resource sources, four different types of value (CVC) are suggested (Austin and Seitanidi, 2012a). Both networks, the destination and the event networks, may benefit from the collaboration in various ways, which will result in benefits for the respective customer groups:

1. *Associational value* is derived benefit accumulating from one organisation to another due to the collaborative relationship, which can be described in terms of synergy effects through collaborations. Synergy effects may be awareness formation and image building for both/all parties. As long as there are some sorts of fit between the stakeholders (e.g. images, identities), synergy effects through collaboration are expected. The notions of destination and event image are based on the "associative network memory model" (Anderson, 1983), where the memories and knowledge of a product (i.e. image) are built by the association of nodes connected. The more noticeable the nodes and the tighter the associations are, the more likely the information is to be processed by the consumers, which leads to stronger brand image and to competitiveness in the market.

2. *Transferred resource value* is the benefit derived through knowledge-sharing processes regarding use of resources. Transferred value might transpire through a systematic approach to attract various stakeholders to partake in the system. A central element in order to ensure transferred value would be through knowledge transfer. Knowledge transfer between stakeholders provides opportunities for mutual learning and cooperation that stimulate the creation of new knowledge and, at the same time, contribute to the organisations' or the stakeholders' ability to innovate (e.g. Kogut and Zander, 1992; Tsai and Ghoshal, 1998). Knowledge transfer happens in a shared social context in which different stakeholders are connected to one another. Dissimilar network positions represent different opportunities for a stakeholder to access new knowledge that is critical to developing new products or innovative ideas.

3. *Interaction value* derives from the intangibles created through collaboration. This reflects value co-creation through intangibles such as "reputation, trust, relational capital, learning, knowledge, joint problem-solving, communication, coordination, transparency, accountability, and conflict resolution" (Austin and Seitanidi, 2012a, p. 3). Interaction value is a function of the strength of the ties between the stakeholders in the network. The strength of ties is a function of frequency of interaction, duration, emotional intensity and reciprocity (Granovetter, 1973). To ensure interaction value within a network and a system of networks, the relevant or core actors could define formal task assignments (committees, training programmes) and informal activities. Within this work, the network leader should address and promote the effect of collaboration to all stakeholders.

4. *Synergistic value* is about synergies stemming from working together rather than solitarily. Outcome value or synergistic value is about results and evaluations. Synergistic value may be reached through an open process of

how to attract customers, reduce costs and enhance income and revenues. Working together will give opportunities to ensure cost effectiveness and to implement quality standards and measurements, which will benefit all stakeholders.

These effects of collaboration reflect the reasons for stakeholders and networks to participate in collaborative work. The networks and the respective stakeholders within the networks – that is, a destination and an event – have similar and different needs and purposes for their organisations. They also have the same or different types of customers that they want to accommodate. Nevertheless, both actors will benefit in various ways by sharing information, reducing costs and improving reputation (see the four collaborative value dimensions above); the major issue is if this collaborative value effects the visitors in a positive way. The success of the collaboration is consequently about the respective partners' ability to meet their own customers' needs better due to collaboration than if working alone (arrows from 'value for visitors' to 'value for destination and event') (see Figure 4.1). Figure 4.1 shows how collaborative efforts will succeed through meeting the respective customers' needs; the customers experience value, resulting in enhanced attraction value for the actors.

This work shows that tourists and eventgoers may benefit from destination- and event-management collaboration in various ways. Based on the work of Sheth *et al.* (1991), the present work adopts the idea that consumers perceive different values, such as perceived functional and social values, during consumption processes such as being on a vacation.

Functional value (see Figure 4.1) is about perceived quality and value for money and signifies "the perceived utility acquired from an alternative's capacity for functional or utilitarian performance" (ibid., p. 160). This dimension represents a more rational (rather than emotive) dimension to value

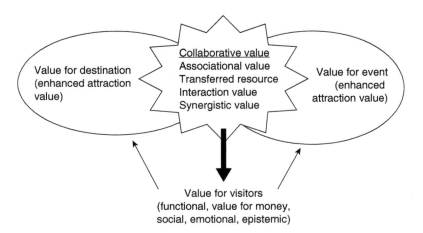

Figure 4.1 Collaboration for enhanced experience value for customers

determination. Functional value for a tourist is derived from product quality in the service setting. The service quality and the price are of particular importance and include two sub-dimensions: the value derived from the perceived performance (quality) of the offering and value for money. Collaboration between destinations and events may ensure quality standards, which will benefit the customers. Ensuring the right information to customers before and during travel may enhance the perception of experience value. Other functional elements may be parking, toilet facilities, maps, trails and roads. To be more efficient in terms of packaging and bundling single products and offerings to eventgoers and tourists, the partners may collaborate on selected media, including social media, which most likely will help enhance value for customers.

The social dimension is described in terms of two underlying factors: social image and reputation (Sheth *et al.*, 1991). Collaboration to enhance the customers' perceptions of the destination's and the event's activities and the manner in which it conducts its relationships is expected to improve the customers' experience value (Foil *et al.*, 2009). In line with Veblen (1899) and the idea of 'conspicuous consumption', in which a customer extends and supports their self-image through brands and experiences to signal wealth and infer power and status, the collaboration efforts should concentrate on creating and communicating a strong link between the tourist self and the image of the destination and the event. An image link between the collaborative partners will enhance this effect.

Collaborative activities may further reduce external search behaviours and result in reduced perceptions of risk among visitors, which will help improve repeat visitation (Mason, 1984, 2005; Moliner *et al.*, 2005). Furthermore, the present chapter argues that the collaborative partners may facilitate enhanced social value during the whole experience process. Before the visit, customers can actively provide value for themselves and others. During the visit, collaboration may help the partners provide sights, scenes and servicescapes (Bitner, 1992) for communication, relationships and socialisation. These stages may also function as arenas for teaching and involving people in the situation (situational involvement). Furthermore, the stage may include role-play and activities, ensuring social relationships, which could be part of such innovative propositions for co-creating enhanced customer value. After the trip, the actors could support existing and encourage new relationships by word of mouth. By facilitating communication strategies and tactics between service provider and guest, and between guests, the events and the destinations may work as platforms for relationships. To ensure social value, the event may invite different customer groups to come together, mingle and talk. As such, the event and the destination may be associated with a positive social interaction, which would affect stakeholders' interest in the event and the destination as well. The arenas will thus function as a positive value creation loop for both customers and stakeholders. An example could be inviting spectators to mingle and discuss a soccer game before the match.

Events are mainly about entertaining and/or educating various customer groups and stakeholders. In order to ensure the right associations, the event needs to understand which emotions the diverse stakeholder groups prefer. Emotions are considered to play a dominant role in the initiation, development and sustaining of relations (Andersen and Kumar, 2006). Positive emotions produce feelings of trust and reduce uncertainty in a relationship (Haakannson, 1987). Elements that help stimulate emotions throughout the whole tourist experience could include atmospherics, elements affecting one's senses (smell, sight, sound and touch) and exciting information and stories. In experience-based products and services, presenting the experiences through a medium is obligatory in that it is the customer who is transported to the destination; the way in which the offerings are presented is crucial. In order to motivate and involve the tourist to partake in value creation processes before the journey starts, the firm may utilise various strategies and tactics, focusing on creating awareness and triggering knowledge-seeking behaviour and further search behaviour. Providing the customers with maps and information regarding history, food and other local specialities may enhance involvement. After the visit, emotions may be activated through images and other products and communications that affect positive memories. Social media offer imperative tools for this work, including, for example, pictures of a certain place to enhance interest among customers.

Epistemic value materialises when a product, service or experience arouses curiosity, provides novelty and/or satisfies a desire for knowledge (Sheth *et al.*, 1991). Novelty and seeking new knowledge are significant motives in tourist experiences (Weber, 2001; Walle, 1997; Crompton, 1979). As tourists often want to experience something new, explore unknown territories and/or meet new people, tourism sets the scene for variety-seeking behaviour (Zuckerman, 1994). Tourist firms therefore have to acknowledge the need for change and adjust and develop their offerings accordingly. For instance, they should regularly ensure novel elements in their products and promote them accordingly, through elements such as developing new walking tracks near to the tourist destination and cooperating with other firms and even other destinations in order to provide new and exciting experiences. An example would be to provide maps with different difficulty levels, where the customer can buy a personal guide or trainer.

As eventgoers tend to revisit the event to a larger extent than tourists do, good opportunities occur to market other activities and new visits all seasons as well. Provision of learning aspects such as information and stories should be recognised and presented before, during and after the journey, for both tourists and eventgoers. By focusing on the right identity and image in the collaborative work – that is, authentic experience during the stay – both tourists and eventgoers will experience epistemic value. If the event and the destination agree to focus on one idea or image (message) in their communication strategy, the attraction effect will be stronger.

Summary

Destinations and events are likely to create value for their customers by collaborating. This will subsequently create value for the destinations and the events. This collaboration will, therefore, help ensure success for all parties. The underlying premise for success is that collaboration results in enhanced experience value for the customers of the collaborative partners. Both destinations and events will gain attraction value – that is, reputation and visitations – through enhancing their customers' experience value.

The idea is that events can enhance a positive image and increase visitation intentions through their value proposal linked to customers' special interest goals for partaking in the event. A positive and strong image and reputation for the event will result in positive attraction value for the destination, and vice versa.

Value-creating synergy effects occur when organisations get access to each other's infrastructures, capabilities, knowledge, customers and opportunities for economies of scale and cost reduction (Austin and Seitanidi, 2012a; Ireland *et al.*, 2002). Collaboration between destinations and events will benefit tourists and eventgoers in various ways. Both visitor groups travel to experience various values – that is, emotional, social, epistemic value, in addition to various functional values, including certain physical qualities and value for money. As visitors appreciate the various values differently, the destination and the event need to analyse and monitor their customer segments carefully, and develop communication, facilitation and co-creation strategies corresponding with their segments, as well as making a common effort to attract both customer groups to the destination and the event. A fit between the event and the destination will augment potential for value creation for the customer in the whole process of preparing, travelling and remembering a journey, which will enhance the experience value for the customers and, subsequently, have a positive effect on the destination and the event.

By utilising theories, perspectives and literature on experience value and collaboration value, the present chapter suggests a collaborative framework to ensure success for both destination and event through collaboration to enhance the customers' experience value. It has exemplified how these various experience value dimensions may be enhanced for customers. The present work argues that the success of collaboration will result in enhanced attraction value for collaborative partners.

However, research claims that event marketers and destination marketers have not yet learned how to synergise their efforts (Jago *et al.*, 2003). This chapter aims to explore how destinations and events may benefit through collaboration. The idea is to show how this collaboration becomes successful through facilitating superior experience value for visitors.

The key for events and destinations is to create value to attract the customer to visit the event and the destination. In the attempt to attract locals and tourists to visit an event, the event develops, facilitates and communicates potential experience value – that is, emotional, social and epistemic value (Williams and Soutar, 2009). In a similar way, destination marketing management companies aim to attract tourists to visit the destination. Through this process, successful events and destinations create reputations, providing awareness and visitation for themselves and the collaborative partners.

Building on the framework of the present chapter, future research should explore the success factors, such as visitation and sustainability (economic, ecological and social), of destination–events collaborations. Case studies of best–worst practices could be undertaken.

References

Achrol, A.V. and Kotler, P. (2006). The service dominant logic for marketing: a critique. In R.F. Lush and S.L. Vargo (eds). *The Service-Dominant Logic of Marketing: Dialog, Debate, and Directions*. Armonk, NY: M.E. Sharpe, pp. 320–33.

Andersen, P.H. and Kumar, R. (2006). Emotions, trust and relationship development in business relationships: a conceptual model for buyer–seller dyads. *Industrial Marketing Management*, 35(4), 522–35.

Anderson, J.R. (1983). A spreading activation theory of memory. *Journal of Verbal Learning and Verbal Behavior*, 22, 261–95.

Andersson, T.D. and Lundberg, E. (2013). Commensurability and sustainability: triple impact assessments of a tourism event. *Tourism Management*, 37, 99–109.

Andersson, T.D., Armbrecht, J. and Lundberg, E. (2012). Estimating use and non-use values of a music festival. *Scandinavian Journal of Hospitality and Tourism*, 12(3), 215–31.

Arnould, E.J., Price, L.L. and Tierney, P. (1998). Communicative staging of the wilderness experience. *The Service Industry*, 18(3), 90–115.

Assaker, G., Vinzi, V.E. and O'Connor, P. (2011). Examining the effect of novelty seeking, satisfaction, and destination image on tourists' return pattern: a two factor, non-linear latent growth model. *Tourism Management*, 32(4), 890–901.

Austin, J.E. and Seitanidi, M.M. (2012a). Collaborative value creation: a review of partnering between nonprofits and businesses: Part I. Value creation spectrum and collaboration stages. *Nonprofit and Voluntary Sector Quarterly*, 41(5), 726–58.

Austin, J.E. and Seitanidi, M.M. (2012b). Collaborative value creation: a review of partnering between nonprofits and businesses: Part 2: Partnership processes and outcomes. *Nonprofit and Voluntary Sector Quarterly*, 41(6), 929–68.

Bagozzi, R.P. and Burnkrant, R. (1978). Attitude measurement and behavioral change: a reconsideration of attitude organisation and its relationship to behavior. In W.L. Wilkie (ed.), *Advances in Consumer Research* (Vol. 6). Ann Arbor, MI: Association for Consumer Research.

Balakrishnan, M.S. (2009). Strategic branding of destinations. *European Journal of Marketing*, 43(5/6), 611–29.

Bartram, S.A. (2001). Serious leisure careers among whitewater kayakers: a feminist perspective. *World Leisure Journal*, 43(2), 4–11.

Bitner, M.J. (1992). Servicescapes: the impact of physical surroundings on customers and employees. *Journal of Marketing*, 56, 57–71.

Bradley, G.L. and Sparks, B.A. (2012). Antecedents and consequences of consumer value: a longitudinal study of timeshare owners. *Journal of Travel Research*, 51(2), 191–204.

Cai, L. (2002). Cooperative branding for rural destinations. *Annals of Tourism Research*, 29, 720–42.

Crompton, J.L. (1979). Motivations for pleasure vacations. *Annals of Tourism Research*, 6, 408–24.

Foil, C., Luis J., Alcaniz, E.B., Moliner, M.A. T. Sanchez García, T. and Sanchez García, J. (2009). Customer loyalty in clusters: perceived value and satisfaction as antecedents, *Journal of Business-to-Business Marketing*, 16, 276–31.

Foley, A. and Fahy, J. (2004). Incongruity between expression and experience: the role of imagery in supporting the positioning of a tourism destination brand. *Journal of Brand Management*, 11, 209–17.

Gallarza, M.G. and Saura, I.G. (2006). Value dimensions, perceived value, satisfaction and loyalty: an investigation of university students' travel behaviour. *Tourism Management*, 27(3), 437–52.

Getz, D. (1989). Special events: defining the product. *Tourism Management*, June.

Getz, D. (1997). *Event Management and Event Tourism*. New York: Cognizant.

Granovetter, M.S. (1973). The strength of weak ties. *American Journal of Sociology*, 6, 1360–80.

Grönroos, C. (2006). What can service logic offer marketing theory? In R.F. Lush and S.L. Vargo (eds). *The Service-Dominant Logic of Marketing: Dialog, Debate, and Directions*. Armonk, NY: M.E. Sharpe, pp. 354–464.

Gummeson, E. (2006). Many-to-many marketing as grand theory. In R.F. Lush and S.L. Vargo (eds). *The Service-Dominant Logic of Marketing: Dialog, Debate, and Directions*. Armonk, NY: M.E. Sharpe, pp. 339–53.

Haakansson, H. (1987). *Corporate Technological Behaviour: Co-operation and Networks*. London: Routledge.

Holbrook, M.B. (1999). Introduction to customer value. In M.B. Holbrook (ed.), *Consumer Value: A Framework for Analysis and Research*. New York: Routledge, pp. 1–29.

Holbrook, M.B. and Hirschman, E.C. (1982). The experiential aspects of consumption: fantasies, feelings and fun. *Journal of Consumer Research*, 9(2), 132–9.

Ireland, R., Hitt, M. and Vaidyanath, D. (2002). Alliance management as a source of competitive advantage. *Journal of Management*, 28, 413–46.

Jago, L., Chalip, L., Brown, G., Mules, T. and Ali, S. (2003). Building events into destination branding: insights from experts. *Event Management*, 8(1), 3–14.

Kelly, J.R. and Godbey, G. (1992). *Today's Leisure as a Market Commodity*. State College, PA: Venture.

Kim, H. and Fesenmaier, D.R. (2008). Persuasive design of destination websites: an analysis of first impression. *Journal of Travel Research*, 47(1), 3–13.

Kogut, B. and Zander, U. 1992. Knowledge of the firm, combinative capacities and the replication of technology. *Organization Science*, 3, 383–97.

Konecnik, M. and Gartner, W. (2007). Customer-based brand equity for a destination. *Annals of Tourism Research*, 34, 400–21.

Mason, R. (1984). Conspicuous consumption: a literature review. *European Journal of Marketing*, 18(3), 26–39.

Mason, R. (2005). Missing links: product classification theory and the social characteristics of goods. *Marketing Theory*, 5(3), 309–22.

Moliner, M.A., Sánchez, J., Rodríguez, R.M. and Callarisa, L. (2005). Perceived relationship quality and post-purchase perceived value. *European Journal of Marketing*, 41(11/12), 1392–42.

Ooi, C.S. (2004). Brand Singapore: the hub of 'New Asia'. In N. Morgan, A. Pritchard and R. Pride (eds), *Destination Branding: Creating the Unique Destination Proposition* (2nd edn). Oxford: Elsevier Butterworth-Heinemann, pp. 242–60.

Ooi, C.S. and Stoeber, B. (2010), Authenticity and place branding: the arts and culture in branding Berlin and Singapore, in B.T. Knudsen and A.M. Waade (eds), *Reinvesting Authenticity: Tourism, Places and Emotions*. Bristol: Channel View, pp. 66–79.

Prebensen, N.K. (2010). Value creation through stakeholder participation: a case study of an event in the High North. *Event Management*, 14, 37–52.

Prebensen, N.K., Uysal, M. and Woo, E. (2013a). Experience value: antecedents and consequences. *Current Issues in Tourism*, 17(10), 910–28.

72 *Nina K. Prebensen*

Prebensen, N.K., Woo, E., Chen, J. and Uysal, M. (2013b). Motivation and involvement as antecedents of the perceived value of the destination experience. *Journal of Travel Research*, 52(2), 253–64, first published 20 September 2012.

Prideaux, B. and Cooper, C. (2002). Marketing and destination growth: a symbiotic relationship or simple coincidence? *Journal of Vacation Marketing*, 9, 35–48.

Richards, G. and Wilson, J. (2004). The impact of cultural events on city image: Rotterdam, cultural capital of Europe. *Urban Studies*, 41(10), 1931–51.

Sheth, J.N., Newman, B.I. and Gross, B.L. (1991). Why we buy what we buy: a theory of consumption values. *Journal of Business Research*, 22(2), 159–70.

Smith, J.B. and Colgate, M. (2007). Customer value creation: a practical framework. *Journal of Marketing Theory and Practice*, 15(1), 7–23.

Stebbins, R.A. (1982). Serious leisure: a conceptual statement. *Pacific Sociology Review*, 25, 251–72.

Sweeney, J.C. and Soutar, G.N. (2001). Consumer perceived value: the development of a multiple item scale. *Journal of Retailing*, 77(2), 203–20.

Sweeney, J.C., Soutar, G.N. and Mazzarol, T. (2008). Factors influencing word of mouth effectiveness: receiver perspectives. *European Journal of Marketing*, 42(3/4), 344–64.

Taks, M., Chalip, L., Green, B.C. and Kesenne, S. (2009). Factors affecting repeat visitation and flow-on tourism as sources of event strategy sustainability. *Journal of Sport and Tourism*, 14(2–3), 121–42.

Tsai, W. and Ghoshal, S. 1998. Social capital and value creation: the role of intrafirm networks. *Academy of Management Journal*, 41, 464–76.

Ulaga, W. (2003). Capturing value creation in business relationships: a customer perspective. *Industrial Marketing Management*, 32(8), 677–93.

Veblen, T. (1899). *The Theory of the Leisure Class*. New York: New American Library.

Walle, A.H. (1997). Pursuing risk or insight: marketing adventures. *Annals of Tourism Research*, 24(2), 265–82.

Walsh-Heron, J. and Stevens, T. (1990). *The Management of Visitor Attractions and Events*. New Jersey: Prentice-Hall.

Weber, K. (2001). Outdoor adventure tourism: a review of research approach. *Annals of Tourism Research*, 28(2), 363–80.

Wilkinson, L. (2008). *Business Relating Business: Managing Organisational Relations and Networks*. London: Edward Elgar.

Williams, P. and Soutar, G.N. (2009). Value, satisfaction and behavioral intentions in an adventure tourism context. *Annals of Tourism Research*, 36(3), 413–38.

Woodall, T. (2003). Conceptualising value for the customer: an attributional, structural and dispositional analysis. *Academy of Marketing Science Review*, 12, 1–42.

Woodruff, R.B. (1997). Customer value: the next source for competitive advantage. *Journal of the Academy of Marketing Science*, 25(2), 139–53.

Zeithaml, V.A. (1988). Consumer perceptions of price, quality, and value: a means–end model and synthesis of evidence. *Journal of Marketing*, 52(3), 2–22.

Zuckerman, M. (1994). *Behavioral Expressions and Biosocial Bases of Sensation Seeking*. Cambridge: Cambridge University Press.

5 Creating network value

The Barcelona Sónar Festival as a global events hub

Greg Richards and Alba Colombo

Introduction

This chapter examines the different ways in which value is co-created between cities and events. We focus on the idea that value is generated through interactions between an event and the network of connections that it has around the world. In particular we consider the concept of 'network value' as one of the important benefits that events can generate. We focus our analysis on a specific case of a globalised cultural event, the Sónar International Festival of Advanced Music and New Media Art. This festival was founded in Barcelona in 1994 and, from the beginning, it has developed strong relationships with the music industry around the world. Sónar is both an event and a cultural form that has been deliberately globalised from a single original location, and it represents an interesting lens with which to examine processes of globalisation and localisation of culture, and how these processes create value for both the city of Barcelona and the event itself.

In the case of Barcelona, it is clear that the local context has had an important influence in shaping the Sónar Festival. The festival emerged after the 1992 Barcelona Olympics, helping to provide a contemporary cultural product for the city and also to animate the newly developed area around the cultural facilities of the Museu d'Art Contemporani de Barcelona (MACBA) and the Centre de Cultura Contemporània de Barcelona (CCCB). The event also fitted with the policy of the Municipality of Barcelona to globalise the culture of the city.

We argue here that the city of Barcelona obtains different forms of value from the Sónar event, and that the city, in turn, delivers different types of value to the event. In this study we try to expand the analysis of value creation from the traditional areas of economic, social and cultural value towards new sources of value that are particularly important in the 'knowledge economy' or the 'network society'. We focus, in particular, on the ways in which the Sónar Festival has generated 'network value' for Barcelona, which, in turn, provides the physical and symbolic hub around which Sónar has developed.

The concept of network value

Most previous studies of value creation related to festivals and events centre on their economic, cultural or social value. For example, numerous economic impact studies have emphasised the important outputs of employment, income and image change that can accrue to cities staging events (e.g. Richards and Wilson, 2004; Seaman, 2003; Smith, 2012). The economic impact is often seen as the most important and visible form of value, particularly by the host city or region and the sponsors of the event. Social forms of value include the development of social cohesion and social capital, which are often claimed as benefits of events (e.g. Fredline *et al.*, 2003) but which are rarely measured (Richards *et al.*, 2014). This is because the determination of social value is much more complex than measuring economic impacts (Colombo 2009) and often requires the use of qualitative research. As Colombo (2015) illustrates, the cultural value of events is usually related to support for cultural participation, personal and group identity, support for cultural and creative production and preserving cultural heritage. Again, measuring the cultural value of events is challenging, given the complexity of culture and the challenges in developing appropriate measures. The areas of economic, social and cultural value creation represent the bulk of previous research.

Much less attention has been paid the 'new' forms of value that relate to the recent major changes that have taken place in the economy and society. In particular, the rise of the 'knowledge economy' has created more attention for the 'soft factors' of development in cities and regions, such as the quality of public space or the 'atmosphere' of places. One of the important areas in which cities and regions increasingly need to compete is in the development and utilisation of networks. In the contemporary network society, Castells (2010) argues, the countervailing forces of globalisation and localisation increase the importance of networks that link people, locations and organisations. Events, like most other organisations, increasingly have to consider how to operate within networks of stakeholders, and how they can create value through these networks. The network can deliver value by attracting attention, resources and flows of power to specific actors who are able to attain a powerful and/or central position in the network (Richards, 2013). Events that are able to generate value from and with their networks will arguably be more successful than others.

In the network society, value is created through linking actors, or organisations and individuals. A value network facilitates exchange relationships among actors distributed in space and time. Network value is defined here as *the value that can be created through the linkages provided by a network, above the value created by the links available to individual network members alone* (or 'intrinsic value', as defined by Oestreicher-Singer *et al.*, 2013). As Stabell and Fjeldstad (1998) note, network value will tend to increase with the size of the network, as this provides more potential linkages, and therefore opportunities, for each member. In a traditional value chain, economic value is added in each successive level of the chain, in a linear fashion. In a value network, actors may increase the value they can extract not just by expanding the number of network links they have, but also by obtaining a more central role in the network. Actors in networks compete to establish a more central role by positioning themselves so that flows of resources and knowledge have to pass through them (hub function). Actors who are not able to establish themselves as a network 'hub' can only act as network nodes, capable of sending or receiving resource flows to other nodes they are connected to, but unable to direct flows across the network as a whole. The value that actors may accrue through the network may be economic, but it can also include social, cultural, reputational and other forms of value. One of the distinguishing features of network value is its dispersed quality. Unlike social capital, for example, network value is not dependent on membership of a physically located community, but is spread across the network between non-proximate actors.

This definition of network value has a number of implications:

1. Total network value will be positively related to network size.
2. Actors will compete to establish a more central position in the network, since this yields greater potential network value.
3. The actual network value available to each actor will depend on their ability to utilise their network linkages and position to extract value from the network.

Because the flows of resources and knowledge within a network may vary considerably in terms of quantity, quality and type, the sort of value extracted by network actors from the network may also differ. Actors will often seek to extract economic value, but they may also be interested in generating cultural, social or symbolic value through their network membership. Actors will also vary in terms of their networking abilities and strategies. Some may actively use the linkages provided by the network to generate value and may also be willing to help the network as a whole to grow in order to increase their own ability to extract value from it (altruistic strategy). Others may be content to profit from the network-building activities of others without contributing to the network themselves (free rider strategy).

This 'network approach' to events (Richards *et al.*, 2014) is now becoming evident in many studies of events and event networks. For example, Bærenholdt (2012) has considered the role played by the Roskilde Festival in Denmark in 'making things happen' in a small Danish city. He demonstrates how the network as a whole helps to stimulate and consolidate change, rather than individual actors. Sacco (2017) likens events to creative clusters in which different local and external actors can come together to create value at both local and global scale. Richards and Palmer (2010) also illustrate that for some 'eventful cities' one of the major benefits of organising events may by the development of 'orgware' (or administrative systems or operational structures) that enable further event-based or wider cultural-driven development to continue in the longer term. Crowther and Orefice (2014) summarise these different roles of events in terms of a 'value creation platform', in which an event functions as a vehicle for creating different forms of value for a group of stakeholders clustered around an event. The recent work on event networks therefore suggests there is a need to pay more attention to the network value being derived from the organisation and staging of events, both at local and global level. This chapter attempts to analyse the network value being generated by a specific event, the Sónar Festival, which operates both in a local and a global context.

Methodological approach

The methodological approach of this chapter is based on a combination of a case study approach (Yin, 2009) and different qualitative techniques. The case study relies on two main data sources: collection of primary data through semi-structured in-depth interviews and analysis of archival data. Data from different editions of the event around the world were collected from sources including festival programmes and other documents, such as reports, media coverage and websites; interviews undertaken between 2009 and 2013 (including interviews conducted for the European financed research project EURO Festivals Arts Festivals and European Public Culture – see Giorgi, 2010); personal presentations, discussions and panels; additional reports; and media reviews, among others.

Interviews were held with three main groups of actors: (1) location-related stakeholders, journalists, local artists and programmers; (2) international professionals, such as festival organisers, buyers and programmers; and (3) national and international festival consumers. A total of 34 interviews were collected, distributed across each of the three groups.

The festival was subject to in-depth analysis guided by the research goal of mapping the role of the initial festival in Barcelona as a network 'hub', connecting different festival nodes around the world. Complete transcripts of the interviews were made, and these were first subject to open coding to identify concepts and categories in the data, which were then entered into a matrix for analysis (Miles *et al.*, 2013). The axial coding entered in to the data matrix facilitated the analysis by concepts and categories contained in the theoretical framework.

Because the festival has a substantial history, it was also important to extract a temporal dimension from both the interviews and the secondary documentation. The different festival events developed over time have therefore been selected as explanatory cases. The dimensions that were analysed for the events included the different programing and production models, the scale and dimensions of the event and their geographic location.

Barcelona as starting point

The Sónar Festival is an annual two-day music festival held in June in Barcelona. The event was founded in 1994, when the city was experiencing a lack of resources for culture and social investment, as a consequence of the high expenditure on the 1992 Barcelona Olympic Games. As Victor Nubla (personal interview, 2009) pointed out, the city faced a reduction in public sector funding following the Olympics. In the absence of public funding, civil society organisations and the commercial and voluntary sectors began to create new cultural initiatives, although not all managed to survive.

One of the few projects that thrived was the Sónar Festival, designed as a platform to promote and produce electronic culture. The edition of the festival was made possible thanks to the support of institutions such as the Sociedad General de Autores y Editores (SGAE), which is the Spanish national association with responsibility for copyright issues, and the CCCB. The CCCB is a multidisciplinary cultural institution in the centre of Barcelona, inaugurated in 1994, dedicated to the study of cities and urban culture. One of the CCCB's main goals is staging temporary exhibitions related to contemporary urban culture and other related events and festivals.

Thanks to such support, and healthy box office revenues, Sónar was successful from the very first edition. The local administration adopted the festival as a strategic initiative in 1996, when the Barcelona City Council became Sónar's main partner. Sónar fitted the strategy of festivalisation (Häußerman and Siebel, 1993; Karpińska-Krakowiak, 2009; Hitters, 2007; Jakob, 2013) of the Catalan capital, although some partners of the festival also had different aims and goals. For example, SGAE aimed to construct a platform in Barcelona dealing with electronic music and therefore helped Sónar to build a network of professionals and musicians involving highbrow, experimental and electronic musicians, which also included professional associations, such as the Asociación Española de Editores de Música (Spanish Association of Music Publishers) (Magaudda and Colombo, 2010). In 2005 Advanced Music SL, the promoter of the festival, assumed full control of the festival organisation, gradually becoming the main actor in Sónar's development after SGAE left the organisation in the same year.

Because the Sónar Festival appeared at a critical moment in Barcelona's development, several local stakeholders and administrations identified the event as a strategic tool for the city. Probably because the main costs of the event were covered by the box office revenues, most of the public partners saw the event as an opportunity to associate themselves with a popular cultural event that did not need much financial support. As a result, the festival was embraced by different local cultural institutions and administrations who have helped the organisation to develop a strong relationship with the city, embedding the festival firmly in the cultural scene of Barcelona, but also in the international networks provided by the stakeholders. This local embedding has arguably enabled the festival to develop a global network, which now delivers value both to the event itself and to the city.

Sónar as a model

In the early 1990s, the electronic music scene in Spain was divided between the wild nightclubs on the Valencian coast (Sáenz 2008) and a minimal scene interested in new rhythms generated by electronic trends going beyond the 'dance floor'. At that time, Spain had no clear offer of non-conventional music, such as alternative, experimental or electronic music. Therefore, in 1994 the Sónar Festival offered an innovative platform where different kinds of music could gain an audience.

During the early editions, the festival maintained its original focus on electronic music and became part of a global network of electronic music and culture. Two pieces of evidence highlight this situation: (1) from the beginning the festival programmed internationally well-known musicians and artists, such Laurent Garnier (programmed in the first edition, 1994), Richie Hawtin (set in 1996) and Jeff Mills (in 1997) among others; and (2) from the second and third edition, as Teglietti pointed out (personal interview, 2013), "the festival audience, as well as accredited professionals, changed from being local and national to being international". In this sense, from the beginning, Sónar started to be internationally well known as a festival with its specific aesthetics and iconography related to electronic music and electronic culture.

At the same time, from the early editions onwards, Sónar established a structure that made the festival unique. Sónar presented different platforms for different music streams, such as experimental and alternative music, as well as a platform focused on electronic and different dance music labels. This division led to the basic and most characteristic structure of the festival, the contrast between Sónar By Day, where experimental and advanced music from well-known and unknown artists is presented, and Sónar By Night, featuring big concerts with both well-established artists and newcomers.

During recent decades, Sónar has adapted its specific language and iconography to international trends in electronic culture, and to advanced and experimental music and culture. As Luis Hidalgo explained (personal interview, 2009), "the festival has focused its aesthetics on an ambiguous concept (advanced music), so that could easily be adapted to the trends of new times, globally".

With these features, the Sónar Festival was able to introduce itself to the global cultural scene with a clear and specific identity, as a summer festival in a sunny Mediterranean European city where the latest trends in music, culture and art can be discovered. At the same time, the festival presents itself to local audiences and to the local music scene, as a well-connected and internationally recognised music festival with a special focus on the latest international trends. These different positions give the event a dichotomous identity, which makes it locally, nationally and internationally different. "I love Sónar By Day, the better part of the festival, more than the big rave at night, because there is more space for experimental sounds. So By Night is like all the other festivals, but By Day is special," explained Olaf Bender, manager of Level Raster Norton in Germany (interviewed during the festival in 2009).

As Enrique Palau pointed out (personal interview, 2010), from the first edition: "the festival has been an international event and has had a clear international projection with artists, audience and professionals from all over the world".

In that sense the festival has been always linked with international and global networks, and therefore, through this aesthetic, the festival becomes internationally connected.

Taking into account both the festival structure and the context, Sónar has globally generated content and, at the same time, also has strong links to international stakeholders. Therefore the festival is embedded in the global 'space of flows' (Castells, 2009, 2010), transforming these flows through the concrete use of local places. Over the years the festival has expanded the number of networks links and places (nodes) established through network relationships; the event has built a global network based on a specific Sónar model, in which it has a central role.

Exporting the festival

The Sónar Festival has developed innovative strategies to transform its international relationships into an established network of collaborations. The most obvious example has been the desire to present the festival around the globe, developing diverse festival formats in several cities and countries around the world.

During the last few years, Advanced Music SL, the festival promoter (from now on AM), has exported the festival characteristics, the image, the structure and aesthetics, or 'brand', to different cities, countries and audiences. The festival has been adapted and cloned around the world as Ricard Robles explains: "the quality of art direction, event format, characteristics, sound level standards and technical equipment has branded itself" (Bernárdez, 2011); but, as Luis Hidalgo suggests, Sónar did "not introduce itself as a brand, rather the festival got the brand after several years demonstrating its viability" (interviewed in 2009). Therefore the Barcelona Sónar DNA is adapted or cloned in different ways, but always with the spirit and the supervision of the Barcelona event and team, ensuring the coherence of the brand.

In this sense the festival organisation has transformed the local event structure into an international one, exporting the event through different formats. This process has been long, spread over several years in which different formats, such as the *A Taste of Sónar* or *SónarSound*, have been developed.

For the festival organisers, *A Taste of Sónar* is basically an appetiser held early in the year, before the main Barcelona festival. If we take *A Taste of Sónar London* as an example, it can be seen that the event has been presented over several years in the period prior to the Barcelona event (in March 2012, 2011, 2010 or in May 2009) and also that most of the artists presented at *A Taste of Sónar London* also performed in Barcelona in the same year. Hence, it could be considered that this format represents a promotional strategy, aimed at energising "an audience that would be talking about the Sónar for a while, developing a promotion for the festival in Barcelona" as Ricard Robles argued (Bernárdez, 2011). Similar tasters have been presented during the last decade in several cities, including Cape Town and Osaka.

The *SónarSound* is a different large-scale presentation of the festival around the world. Normally longer than the *Taste*, this event has diverse formats, depending on the city where it is located. In Seoul (2006), for example, it consisted of a few selected performances, whereas in São Paulo (2004) it had practically the same format as the festival in Spain. Therefore, in this format some artists at the festival represent the global Sónar brand, while the rest of the programme is filled with local artists. Then it could be understood that this format reaches local audiences at the same time that it links the festival with the local music sector. *SónarSound* has been presented in many cities around the world, notably Tokyo and several cities in the United States and Latin America.

Besides these two general exporting models, other sporadic network-building initiatives have been taking place, such as *HyperSounds*, a series of concerts, DJ sessions, installations and screenings based around sound research; a parallel festival in A Coruña (2010); and *Sónar on Tour*, developed in 2012 as a one-off experimental tour around the United States.

Through all these different initiatives, AM has developed a network of professionals, artists and places around Sónar. Especially with the *Taste*, the festival reaches international audiences, who supposedly will also attend the event in Barcelona, while through the *Sound*, the festival links more closely with local audiences and the local music sector.

Although AM initially started to develop this network of events around Europe, in the last few years they have been more interested in initiating collaboration with countries in South America (starting in 2004), Asia (2006), North America (2009) and Africa (2012). As Taglietti (personal interview, 2013) pointed out "as the audiences in Europe are already the ones going to the main festival in Barcelona", AM wants to focus on new target markets.

This indicates that the creation of the network is based on AM's interest in generating attention for the main event in Barcelona. The Barcelona event could therefore be considered as the focal point for the original Sónar concept, where all actors and flows of the network converge. Therefore, after 20 years of network-building at an international level, the festival has come to be understood as a 'hub', linking different nodes around the world.

Strategies to increase network value

Sónar has transformed the original Barcelona festival into a global network of festivals, which may contribute to the music sector as a whole, creating relationships between professionals, markets and industries in what Castells (2010, 2012) terms the global 'space of flows'. The special kind of cultural aesthetics related to advance music and multimedia art is now well known around the world, at least partly thanks to the Sónar Festival and its networks. Therefore it seems that the festival organisers may generate network value through the festival, by using it to link different festival collaborators around the world, from promoters to artists to audiences.

For the well-known French musician and producer Laurent Garnier (Font and Salat, 2007),

> the professionals and artists need to be at the Sónar Festival to know what's happening in the music world, when the brand goes big and strong and crosses frontiers, the people talk about it, the organisers bring different things to different places.

With this comment, the artist suggests two general ideas: on the one hand, that the Barcelona event is a platform where the professionals need to be to know what's happening in the advanced music scene and, on the other hand, that the festival organisers move artists and performances around the world through the festival network.

Related to the first idea, the festival has been delivering surprises because the audience often do not know what they would like to see, until they have already seen it. As Ben Osborne (ibid.), a professional music journalist from the magazine *DJ* comments: "even if I'm working in the field and I usually receive new material from diverse artists, the Sónar people always get some performances and artists that are new for everyone". This gives the festival the possibility to present a programme with a high proportion of unknown artists to the international advanced music scene. This characteristic is interesting for professionals who want to know the new tendencies and performances in the field. Therefore the festival has become the 'place to be' for the international advanced music sector. This, in turn, increases the network value of the event because it has become a 'hub' through which all the key actors in the scene have to pass in order to ensure their own position in the scene.

In terms of using the festival network, well-known DJ and producer Jeff Mills comments that the "festival organisers travel all year round to find new artists and musicians to bring them to play at the (Barcelona) festival" (ibid.). This also suggests that the festival organisers take special care with the programme, researching new influences, performances and artists to present an interesting experience. The festival organisers therefore have the possibility to contact international artists, producers and agents to sound out the new trends around the globe, as well as to be able to present artists to different places. Effectively, the network delivers novelty in two ways: new acts can be introduced to the electronic music field through the Barcelona 'hub', and these acts can then be staged in different places around the globe to create new programmes in new locations.

We can therefore see the Barcelona event as a central place in a globalised network, as a 'hub' where professionals need to be present to be part of the new trends in the electronic music scene. At the same time, the network, built through the festival contacts and exporting model, generates valuable knowledge about global music trends. The larger the size of the network, the greater the value of the Sónar Festival as a 'hub', which can build relationships and knowledge and also generate interest for different locations (or nodes) in the network. In order to make this possible, AM has had to develop different strategies in forming relationships with partners and institutions. These might broadly be grouped into (1) organic relationships, (2) commercial relationships and (3) developmental relationships.

We see *organic relationships* as those developed in a 'natural' way with other professionals. Having attended the festival over ten years, Olaf Bender (manager Level Raster Norton Germany, interviewed during the festival in 2009) suggests,

> we are every time at Sónar, and we grew up with the festival. The Sónar Festival has developed as the music sector, like us; in the beginning the festival was more experimental and then it grew up to more popular sounds. I think that's the development of Sónar, I don't know if it's good or bad, but it has developed.

Seth Hodder, promoter of Novamute (Font and Salat, 2007) also commented "Sónar has been growing and changing as the sector has done, at the same rhythm, on the same direction, adapting themselves to new perspectives and tendencies." Sónar has long-established relationships with music professionals, which have also developed and changed in the same way as the festival has. Therefore we consider these relationships as 'organic'.

In contrast, *commercial relationships* are usually developed in collaboration with local partners. The local professionals know the audience, the market and the local industry, and generally suggest marketing strategies, logistics and production, as well as some ideas about local musicians and performances. In this sense, the content of the local festival, and also the 'hub' in Barcelona, thrives in the context where the festival takes place. For example, since the festival has been taking place in Tokyo there is a significant presence in the Barcelona programme of Japanese performers. The local professionals have commercial exchanges with AM to be able to present the festival in the new location, sometimes on a regular basis and sometimes just once. Georgia Taglietti explains (personal interview, 2013):

> our relationship with local partners is always different in each case; for example, we could sell the brand, parts of the programme, we could organise the event, but in any case we are always there, working with the local partner, controlling the quality and operative aspects.

In this sense the commercial relationships give AM the possibility to tour Sónar around the world and, at the same time, to gather information and knowledge about different local music scenes.

Finally, the *developmental relationships* are based on the growth of the local music scene in different places around the world. As festival director Enric Palau commented, "sometimes you feel that the festival also enriches the local scene, as you find artists from the same city at the festival that do not know each other". The festival therefore generates information exchanges for professionals, creating a platform for local music sector development. As Seoul-based artist Fortune

Cookie commented, "I think we need a festival like this to help us create a scene of electronic music" (Font and Salat, 2007). These developmental relationships are those the festival has with professionals, generating progression in their area of expertise or their career. These kinds of relationships are really strong, as some professionals have a sense of belonging to a global Sónar community.

These different types of relationships deliver various types of value to the festival and to its wider network. The organic relationships create embedded trust that helps to cement the position of Sónar as the 'hub' or the 'place to be' in the music scene. This, in turn, can be used to generate economic value by using the reputation of Sónar to develop commercial relationships with partners in other parts of the world, which, in turn, help to develop the local music scene. The spread of electronic music around the globe also helps to cement the position of Barcelona as the original Sónar city, and to increase its influence and value as a festival 'hub'.

Conclusions

Sónar illustrates the need for a network approach to the study of events. The festival is no longer just a single event, but a 'hub' in a broader network. The 'hub' function generates network value by creating different kinds of relationships locally and globally that create economic, social, cultural and symbolic capital. In many cases the symbolic capital created by achieving a certain position in the 'scene' delivers much more value than the purely economic spin-off that most events (including Sónar) usually underline as a major source of value creation.

The study of value creation also benefits from a longitudinal approach such as that adopted in this chapter. Seen over time, the festival can be viewed as a slowly extending network that links the local cultural space of Barcelona with an emerging global electronic music scene. Within this network some actors have achieved a more central position over time, and they have been able to consolidate themselves as fixed nodes in the Sónar value network – for example, those cities where the festival has taken place several times. The network has spread through the formation of different kinds of relationships that have allowed Sónar to experiment with different versions of the event in different locations. The growth of the network has not only strengthened the central position of Sónar as the 'hub' event in the network, but it has also increased the cultural and symbolic value of Barcelona as the home of Sónar.

Developing a network event such as Sónar (and there is a growing number of examples of similar 'exporting' festivals (Ferdinand and Williams, 2013) such as Rock in Rio and the Hay on Wye Literature Festival) requires not just an understanding of the basic content being circulated through the network, but also of the distribution of value. In contrast to traditional value chains, the power relationships between the different actors in a value network remain relatively fluid. At any point in time the power of different actors depends on their ability to link the local 'space of places' with the 'global space of flows', leveraging global and local network value. AM has understood this dynamic well, managing the globalisation of the Sónar concept without loss of originality by collecting and mixing content and ideas from a large range of different locations. Rather than diminishing the power of the original festival, therefore, AM has skilfully managed to generate value from multiple editions of the festival globally and to use this value to strengthen the local 'hub'. These kinds of dynamics call for a network approach to events that considers the distribution of value among all network actors, rather than simply an event and/or its host city.

This Sónar study illustrates the capacity of a music event to generate a value based on a network, transforming the original event as a 'hub', to be linked to several local nodes. This capacity underlines the value that the festival has for the global music industry, as well as for the development of the local music scene. Therefore there is an interdependence between the city where the festival takes place and the festival itself as a 'hub'.

This chapter illustrates several important points about the generation of network value through events such as Sónar. As predicted by the theoretical principles of network value, the total value of the Sónar network has increased as the number of actors associated with it has grown. The addition of new nodes to the network has not only increased the total network value, but it has also strengthened the position of Barcelona as the network 'hub', and as the location of the 'original' festival. Sónar has also stimulated competition between cities around the globe to become nodes in the network and to establish their own position as regular venues for different editions of the event. It therefore also seems that some local actors are better able than others to extract value from the linkages provided by the network.

These findings suggest a number of fruitful avenues for future research on network value and on the role of events in generating network value. In particular, the types and qualities of relationships developed between network hubs and nodes seem to be of importance in value creation. It would be interesting to examine in more detail the volume and types of value created by the different types of relationships between the 'hub' and the network nodes. Does an organic relationship, for example, offer a richer diversity of types of value than a commercial relationship, which seems to be based mainly on economic value? How do power relationships – for example, between global and local actors – affect the value generated for the different partners and for the network as a whole? Is it important for a 'hub' to secure its centrality in the network in order to minimise competition with emerging nodes and to prevent a potential loss of power and symbolic value?

References

Bærenholdt, J.O. (2012). Enacting destinations: the politics of absence and presence. In R. Van der Duim, C. Ren and G.T. Jóhannesson (eds), *Actor–Network Theory and Tourism: Ordering, Materiality and Multiplicity*. Abingdon: Routledge, pp. 111–27. ISBN: 0415620724

Bernárdez, J. (2011). *Caso: Sónar, el Festival Internacional de Música Avanzada y Arte Multimedia de Barcelona*. Online publication: http://www.slideshare.net/JorgeBernardez/caso-sonar-el-festival-internacional-de-msica-avanzada-y-de-arte-multimedia-de-barcelona-v-espaol-dic-2012

Castells, M. (2009). *Communication Power*. Oxford: Blackwell. ISBN: 0199595690

Castells, M. (2010). *The Rise of the Network Society. The Information Age: Economy, Society and Culture* (Vol. I). Malden, MA: Wiley-Blackwell, 2nd edition. ISBN: 1405196866

Castells, M. (2012). *Networks of Outrage and Hope: Social Movements in the Internet Age*. Cambridge: Polity Press. ISBN: 0745662854

Colombo, A. (2009). Expansive waves of festivals: approaches in economic impact studies of arts festivals. *La revista d'economia della cultura*, 3, 351–9. ISBN: 9788815129116

Colombo, A. (2015). How to evaluate cultural impacts of events? A model and methodology proposal. *Scandinavian Journal of Tourism Research*. doi:10.1080/15022250. 2015.1114900

Crowther, P. and Orefice, C. (2014). Co-creative events: analysis and illustrations. In G. Richards, L. Marques and K. Mein (eds), *Event Design: Social Perspectives and Practices*. London: Routledge, pp. 122–36. ISBN: 0415704642

Ferdinand, N. and Williams, N.L. (2013). International festivals as experience production systems. *Tourism Management*, 34, pp. 202–10. doi:10.1016/j.tourman.2012.05.001

Font, J. and Salat, J.M. (2007). *Sónar Around the World*. Documentary produced by TV3 – Televisió de Catalunya. 55 minutes.

Fredline, E., Jago, L. and Deery, M. (2003). The development of generic scale to measure the social impacts of events. *Event Management*, 8(1), 23–37. doi:10.3727/152599503108751676

Giorgi, L. (ed.) (2010). *European Arts Festivals: Cultural Pragmatics and Discursive Identity Frames*. Eurofestival Project. European Arts Festivals and Public Culture. Project. 215747. SSH-2007-5.2.2 'Creativity, Culture and Democracy'. EU: Seventh Framework Programme.

Häußerman H. and Siebel W. (1993). *Festivalisierung der Stadtpolitik: Stadtentwicklung durch grosse Projekte*. Opladen: Westdeutscher Verlag. ISBN: 3531125079

Hitters, E. (2007). Porto and Rotterdam as European capitals of culture: towards the festivalization of urban cultural policy. In G. Richards (ed.), *Cultural Tourism: Global and Local Perspectives*. New York: Haworth Press, pp. 281–301. ISBN: 0789031175

Jakob, D. (2013). The eventification of place: urban development and experience consumption in Berlin and New York City. *European Urban and Regional Studies*, published online, 3 October, 20, 447–59, doi:10.1177/0969776412459860

Karpińska-Krakowiak, M. (2009). Festivalisation of the city: contemporary examples. *Urban People*, 11(2), 338–50.

Magaudda, P. and Colombo, A. (2010). The Sónar festival. In L. Giorgi (ed.), *European Arts Festivals: Cultural Pragmatics and Discursive Identity Frames*. Eurofestival Project. European Arts Festivals and Public Culture. Project. 215747. SSH-2007-5.2.2 'Creativity, Culture and Democracy'. EU: Seventh Framework Programme, pp. 130–50.

Miles, M., Huberman, M. and Saldaña, J. (2013). *Qualitative Data Analysis: A Methods Sourcebook*. Thousand Oaks, CA: Sage. ISBN: 1452257876

Oestreicher-Singer, G., Libai, B., Sivan, L., Carmi, E. and Yassin, O. (2013). The network value of products. *Journal of Marketing*, 77(3), 1–14 doi: http://dx.doi.org/10.1509/jm.11.0400

Richards, G. (2013). Events and the means of attention. *Journal of Tourism Research and Hospitality*, 2, 2. doi:10.4172/2324-8807.1000118

Richards G. and Palmer, R. (2010). *Eventful Cities: Cultural Management and Urban Revitalisation*. London: Butterworth-Heinemann. ISBN: 075066987X

Richards, G. and Wilson, J. (2004). The impact of cultural events on city image: Rotterdam. Cultural capital of Europe 2001. *Urban Studies*, 4(10), 1931–5. doi:10.1080/0042098042000256323

Richards G., Marques, L. and Mein K. (eds) (2014). *Event Design: Social Perspectives and Practices*. London: Routledge. ISBN: 0415704642

Sacco, P.L. (2017). Events as creative districts generators? Beyond the conventional wisdom. In J. Hannigan and G. Richards (eds), *The SAGE Handbook of New Urban Studies*. Thousand Oaks, CA: Sage.

Sáenz, D. (2008). *La ruta. Ministerio de cultura*. Madrid: Ministerio de cultura. ISBN: 9788461249930

Seaman, B. (2003). Economic impact of the arts. In R. Towse (ed.), *A Handbook of Cultural Economics*. Gloucester: Edward Elgar, pp. 224–31. ISBN: 0857931032

Smith, A. (2012). *Events and Urban Regeneration: The Strategic Use of Events to Revitalise Cities*. New York: Routledge. ISBN: 0415581486

Stabell, C.B. and Fjeldstad, Ø.D. (1998). Configuring value for competitive advantage: on chains, shops, and networks. *Strategic Management Journal*, 19, 413–37. doi:10.1002/(SICI)1097-0266(199805)19:53.0.CO;2-C

Yin, R.K. (2009). *Case Study Research: Design and Methods*. Thousand Oaks, CA: Sage, p. 312. ISBN: 1452242569

Part II

Assessing the value of events

6 The use and non-use values of events

A conceptual framework

*Tommy D. Andersson, John Armbrecht
and Erik Lundberg*

Introduction

The fundamental economic principle of comparing output to input, or value produced compared to cost of utilised resources, presents challenges for many activities financed by public authorities. Normally, the problem is not to assess the cost of resources but to assess the value produced. That is probably the reason why much of the political debate is cost-centred, with a focus on how much public money should be spent on, for example, schools, hospitals or cultural activities. To an economic mind it is incomprehensible how reasonable costs of utilised resources could be determined without an understanding of the value produced by the same resources. The major thrust of this chapter is, therefore, that methods to assess value produced are badly needed to improve decision-making regarding public funding, not least of the cultural sector, but also for the events and festivals sector. There is a burgeoning literature about the value of cultural activities, but so far only a scarce amount of research on how to measure the value produced has been published. This is even more true for research on events.

The objective of this chapter is to review major constructs used to put a value on cultural activities in terms of use value and non-use value and discuss how these concepts, models and methods can be used in an event context.

The remaining parts of this chapter are structured as follows. First, the concept of value, including use value, option value and non-use value, is introduced. Then, methods to measure these values are described. A literature review of studies that have applied these concepts on events is presented. The chapter ends with a conceptualisation of relevant concepts for event research, as well as suggested methods for their measurement and recommendations for future research.

Value

From an economic perspective, value is related to the concept of utility. Bentham (1789/2000) describes the meaning of utility as the "property in any object, whereby it tends to produce benefit, advantage, pleasure, good, or happiness" (p. 14). This description of utility is also referred to as 'experienced utility' (Kahneman, 2000). Bentham's (1789/2000) conception shifted towards a consumer-oriented perspective – that is, utility represented the benefits and pleasure that individuals derive from consuming services and products. Utility is thus used to explain choices and may be labelled decision utility (Kahneman, 2000). Decision utility represents aspects that influence individuals' satisfaction and can explain choices individuals make. According to Hanley and Barbier (2009), positive and negative changes in utility are referred to as benefits and costs that lead to the formation of value. Usually benefits and costs reveal something about changes in a society's state of welfare (Garrod and Willis, 2001).

Value will henceforth refer to utility and include positive as well as negative perceptions – and can be understood as a function of both positive and negative perceptions. One established categorisation of value in environmental and cultural economics is 'use values' versus 'non-use values' (Frey, 2003; Throsby, 2010; Garrod and Willis, 2001), which is presented in the following sections and applied to the event context. These categorisations are also discussed as the concept of total economic value (TEV) by Dwyer and Forsyth in Chapter 7 of this book.

Use values

In general terms, services provide a range of different values to individuals and society. These values may arise through experiences as a combination of different sensory, spiritual, religious and other impressions. From an economics perspective, these types of individual experiences are conceptualised as *use values* and arise in one way or another for any good or service that is consumed. Having a restaurant meal, admiring a painting or listening to a rock concert may generate spiritual and sensory impressions. Garrod and Willis (2001) use the term "*current use* value" to refer to such experiences in order to separate them from future use values and non-use values. Current use values may either be consumptive (enjoying a meal) or non-consumptive (looking at a painting) (Hanley and Barbier, 2009). The former are values associated with an activity that consumes the resource in question. The latter refers to the value associated with an activity that does not consume the resource.

Consumptive and non-consumptive values that are *directly* connected to a resource, such as an event, are labelled *direct use values* because they presuppose active use. Boyle and Bishop (1987) argue for the inclusion of *indirect use value*, described as valuable activities indirectly associated with the resource. People who, for example, have visited a major sport event and thus experienced a *direct use value* may also derive satisfaction, and *indirect use value*, from reading about the event in newspapers. Another value referred to as indirect use value by Boyle and Bishop (1987) arises from research related to a particular event (i.e. reducing the ecological footprint of events as a result of event research). In an event context, Andersson *et al.* (2016) and Andersson and Armbrecht (2014a) define the direct use value as the experiential value inside the event area, whereas the indirect use value is defined as the value that event visitors experience before and after the event at the event destination but incurred by the event (use value = indirect use value + direct use value).

Non-use values

While use values relate to experiences, non-use values may be perceived disregarding any use of resources. An early study on the Nidaros Cathedral in Trondheim (Norway) revealed that a large proportion of the value destroyed through weathering and/or corrosion by air pollution impacted on preservation motives (Navrud and Ready, 2002). Use value accounted for only 14 per cent of the total value. Non-use values, as measured by Navrud and Ready (2002), are also referred to as passive use or existence values (Hanley and Barbier, 2009; Garrod and Willis, 2001). Sometimes these values are referred to as intrinsic values because they are embedded in the resource itself (Pearce and Turner, 1990). Boyle and Bishop (1987), as well as Desvousges *et al.* (1983), describe non-use values as intrinsic values, which may arise unrelated to any human perceptions, or as a value that resides within resources but is dependent on individuals' perceptions.

There is no straightforward consensus as to which categories of non-use values should be included in an economic assessment. The lack of agreement may arise through differing theoretical perspectives and conceptualisations and/or through studies of differing study objects.

Existence value

From a motivational point of view, non-use values may arise either due to selfish or altruistic motives (Hanley and Barbier, 2009). Altruistic motives are relevant in terms of the current generation, future generations or simply one's own heirs (sometimes referred to as paternalistic altruism (Lazo *et al.*, 1997)). Motives such as *sympathy, gift, or bequest* or *rights* (of animals…) or *stewardship* (earth is more important than people inhabiting it) are discussed. These values are, however, not related to vicarious benefits – that is, securing pleasure because others derive a (use) value.

Frey (2003) describes existence value as the pleasure people derive from knowing that a cultural good exists. Particular examples are historic buildings and heritage, which, once destroyed, could never be built again. Greenley *et al.* (1981) describe the same value category from an environmental economics perspective as the willingness to pay "for the knowledge that a natural environment is preserved" (p. 657).

Throsby (2003) uses the term 'collective benefits' to describe the benefits that arise because a museum: (1) makes a contribution to the public debate, (2) plays a role in the cultural identity, (3) influences the creative industries, (4) provides the option of visiting the museum, (5) offers bequests for future generations, (6) offers educational benefits, (7) helps us learn more about cultures and (8) exists.

Option value

Event visitors derive value from an event through actual use – that is, experiences. Some individuals will, however, derive satisfaction through having the option to visit and experience events. This potential value (as opposed to realised use value) is referred to as option value by economists. Pearce and Turner (1990) describe option value as an expression of preference which may be measured in terms of willingness to pay. Inhabitants in a community may, for example, preserve the option to take part in the annual half marathon event though they have never done so before. The preservation of the possibility to experience the half marathon refers to the use of the event and may, therefore, be included as a use value. The negative consequences if events vanish, both in theory and in practice, tell us that option values on an aggregated level tend to be positive.

While some researchers argue that there is no such thing as option value (Mitchell and Carson, 1989), others consider option value to be a non-use value. Cicchetti and Freeman, (1971), Arrow and Fisher (1974) and Krutilla (1967) conclude, for example, that the 'option demand' or 'option value' for goods with public characteristics needs to be considered as part of non-use values. Still other researchers may describe option value as a separate value category as compared to use and non-use values. Krutilla (ibid.) defines option value as individuals':

> willingness to pay for retaining an option to use… [a resource]… that would be difficult or impossible to replace and for which no close substitute is available. Moreover, such a demand may exist even though there is no current intention to use the area or facility in question and the option may never be exercised.
>
> Ibid., p. 780

While Hanley and Barbier (2009) define option value as use-related value, they describe it as something akin to an insurance premium which should be considered as something separate from the TEV. Pearce and Turner (1990) describe option value as arising as a consequence of uncertainties in supply or demand or both. Given the presence of uncertainty, (risk-averse) individuals will be willing to pay more than solely the expected consumer surplus in order to preserve a resource. The total value in terms of willingness to pay is referred to as option price and is the sum of expected consumer surplus plus option value, where option value relates to the willingness to pay to ensure the future availability of a resource (ibid.). 'Vicarious' should rather be ascribed to the benefits belonging to the class of option values. Frey (2003), in a cultural setting, recognises that individuals may draw considerable benefit from the existence and knowledge about a cultural supply even though he or she does not make use of it at that moment.

Quasi option price represents another concept related to the option of using a resource. In an environmental context, quasi option value may represent the potential value of, at some point, extracting pharmaceuticals from a specific forest. While it may not be known how to extract or make use of particular substances, these uncertainties may be overcome in future. In view of the risk that a particular forest may be destroyed in future, the quasi option value is represented by the worth of preserving the forest, considering a potential increase in knowledge of how to extract and use specific substances for pharmaceutical use (Pearce and Turner, 1990).

Bequest value

Individuals may value cultural assets not for themselves but for future generations (Frey, 2003). This type of non-use value is referred to as *bequest value* and is important because future generations are not in a position to express their prefer-ences via today's markets.

Examples of use and non-use values: results from qualitative interviews

Armbrecht (2012) undertook a limited number of qualitative interviews to under-stand the concepts proposed above. Table 6.1 illustrates a tentative synthesis, which shows that individuals were able to describe use value in a cultural setting relatively well. Several of these values also relate to public values. Direct use value is found to be a relatively broad concept, capturing, for example, health and pleasure benefits. This, however, also makes the concept somewhat vague.

Option value – that is, the potential future value – seems to be related strongly to the use value that individuals perceive. Option and bequest values also show conceptual overlap. Both value concepts are future oriented, but bequest values are further away in terms of time and may refer to individual benefits to a lesser extent than option value does. Assuming that uncertainty increases in the future, it is reasonable that respondents have less knowledge about benefits that may accrue to future generations. This uncertainty may be reflected in Table 6.1, where the bequest value is not described as distinctly as use values are.

Table 6.1 How use and non-use values of cultural institutions are described by respondents

Direct use value	Indirect use value	Option value	Bequest value	Existence value
improved test scores		improved test scores		
improved self-efficacy				
learning skills	learning skills	learning skills	learning skills	
health	health		health	health
social bonds/ capital	social bonds		social capital	social bonds/ capital
economic effects		economic effects		
pleasure	pleasure	pleasure	pleasure	
captivation		captivation	captivation	
cognitive growth		cognitive growth		
expanded capacity for empathy		expanded capacity for empathy		
identity		identity	identity	identity
communal meaning			communal meaning	communal meaning
			economic impacts	economic impacts

Source: Armbrecht (2012)

Methods used to assess the value

The concepts use value and non-use value are part of a cost–benefit framework which must be viewed as a holistic perspective. Cost–benefit analysis (CBA) aims to assess all major impacts for all members of a society (Hanley *et al.*, 1993). In a CBA, both tangible and intangible costs and benefits should be assigned a value. Examples of intangible benefits can be a cleaner environment or better working conditions. Intangible costs may be lost access to public areas or the degradation of working conditions due to the festival (Andersson *et al.*, 2004; Mules and Dwyer, 2005). The primary interest is economic efficiency – that is, the welfare contribution (Hicks, 1939). To measure the welfare contribution of actions, Hicks (ibid.) and Kaldor (1939) suggested assessments of whether the benefits, preferably measured in monetary terms, are large enough to hypothetically compensate for the costs measured in monetary terms. Thereby a net benefit is estimated.

The major challenge with a CBA is to assign monetary values to intangible costs and benefits (Getz, 2005). Not all benefits and costs have market prices and therefore it is necessary to evaluate these using other methods. There is a gamut of methods used to assess the values of costs as well as benefits. These methods are often categorised into revealed preference methods or stated preference methods.

Revealed preference methods

Revealed preference methods are characterised by being based on actual behaviour, which is assumed to reveal the value consumers place on an activity. Revealed preference methods have been used extensively in environmental economics (Poor and Smith, 2004). Lately, the techniques have also gained popularity in other areas such as cultural heritage sites (Alberini and Longo, 2006; Bedate *et al.*, 2004; Mayor *et al.*, 2007; Ruijgrok, 2006). An example may be the travel cost event visitors are prepared to undertake to attend an event. The travel cost method assumes that, apart from the price paid for entrance, the travel costs incurred represent the price that visitors are willing to pay to access a site (Fleming and Cook, 2008). The method uses the cost of travelling as a proxy for the value of benefits provided (Driml, 2002) and assumes that costs increase with increasing distance (Hotelling, 1947). An increase in distance (and travel costs) is expected to result in a falling visitation rate. This represents an indirect, so-called Clawson–Knetsch method (Cesario, 1976), and can be used to estimate individuals' consumer surplus (Garrod and Willis, 2001; Hanley and Barbier, 2009; Tietenberg and Lewis, 2008). While useful, the relevance of revealed preference methods has been limited in public goods settings and event settings since they measure behaviour and therefore fail to cover non-use values.

Stated preference methods

The contingent valuation method (CVM) is a stated preference method and assesses individuals' willingness to pay for a specific scenario (Mitchell and

Carson, 1989) by creating a hypothetical market (Mmopelwa *et al.*, 2007). Measuring willingness to pay is achieved through value statements from respondents. Throsby and Withers (1983) were early to use willingness to pay in cultural settings and the method has been used since to measure the value of historic sites (Rolfe and Windle, 2003), theatres (Bille Hansen, 1997), monuments and landmarks (Kling *et al.*, 2004; Powe and Willis, 1996), broadcasting (Schwer and Daneshvary, 1995), world heritage sites (Del Saz Salazar and Montagud Marques, 2005; Kim *et al.*, 2007; Maddison and Mourato, 2001; Tuan and Navrud, 2008), museums (Bedate *et al.*, 2009) and festivals (Snowball, 2005; Andersson *et al.*, 2012; Andersson and Lundberg, 2013).

While popular, the method is contested for its hypothetical character leading to negative effects on its reliability and validity (Bedate *et al.*, 2009; Arrow *et al.*, 1993). The endorsement and guidelines proposed by the National Oceanic and Atmospheric Administration have contributed to methodological refinements in support of the method (Mmopelwa *et al.*, 2007).

Studies of the value of culture, festivals and events

Cultural institutions produce experiences that create values for consumers. The value to the consumer can be defined as an "interactive relativistic preference experience" (Holbrook, 1999, p.5). 'Interactive' implies that consumer value is created through an interaction between a subject (consumer) and an object (e.g. art). 'Relativistic' refers to the comparison of value statements originating from one person – I like opera more than theatre – but also the illegitimate comparison of value statement between subjects – I like opera more than you do. Furthermore, relativistic implies that value statements are individualistic and situational. The term 'preferential' suggests that value statements rely on preferences. Finally, 'experience' states that value does not reside in the possession of an object but rather in the experience of it (ibid.).

Two types of use values can be distinguished, as discussed above: (1) direct use value and (2) indirect use value (Mitchell and Carson, 1989). The former refers to experiential values during a play or an exhibition. It reflects the value created through the core cultural experience. Indirect use value concerns experiences that arise before or after the main event. An opera creates direct use values during the performance (e.g. pleasure, well-being and captivation), but also indirect use values when visitors socialise, interact, have a cup of tea etc.

Non-use value in a cultural context

Research on the value of culture from an economic perspective accelerated in the late 1980s as William Baumol (1986) described the un-normal and random return rates of paintings since the sixteenth century. The unexpected low return rates paved the way for speculation and research on explanations for this situation. Among others, social, psychic and prestige-related returns have been identified as external effects that deserve consideration when discussing the value of cultural goods and services.

Recognising the distinction between values that arise in terms of experiences, as well as values that arise in terms of non-use values, has fed a vital area of research within cultural economics. Frey and Pommerehne (1989) were early to list and describe the public, non-use values of cultural goods and services, and performing arts in particular. They are existence value, options value, education value, prestige value and bequest value.

Since then, the evaluation of cultural resources has grown considerably and studies on non-use values in cultural settings have emerged continuously (Ruijgrok, 2006; Bille Hansen, 1997; Dutta *et al.*, 2007; Tohmo, 2004; Aabø and Audunson, 2002).

In relation to existence value, Throsby (2001) gives the example of the pyramids, which are valuable to the public since they constitute part of humanity and human identity. Once destroyed, they may never be rebuilt. Furthermore, they would not be authentic to individuals even if rebuilt. Existence values refer to the satisfactory feeling of knowing that a resource is preserved. The attractiveness and pride derived from living in an area with cultural assets is therefore valuable (ibid.). Boyle and Bishop (1987) argue that existence values reflect the value a cultural institution has within society.

The option value of cultural institutions constitutes another non-use value (Throsby, 2001; Frey, 2003) and reflects the worth individuals perceive when knowing they have the possibility to access a resource, even though they do not exercise this option (Weisbrod, 1964). If plans exist to close down a theatre, the option value may well not be observable in the market, but should play a role in the decision-making process. Throsby (1999) describes option value as a desire to preserve the option to use the resource at some point in the future.

The number of studies focusing on describing, measuring and analysing the use and non-use value of cultural institutions increases steadily and a complete literature review of the field is outside the scope of this chapter. But Aabø and Strand (2004) provide a somewhat dated but useful overview of studies.

Use and non-use values in an event context

Mules and Dwyer (2005) argue for the use of CBA in event evaluation since a mere economic impact evaluation does not take all benefits and costs into account. Instead of relying solely on visitor expenditure, the economic impact analysis should be a part of a CBA. One obstacle is the time consuming and costly effort required to collect all data needed for a CBA. This problem has also been highlighted by other researchers (Getz, 2005; Jackson *et al.*, 2005).

CBA has been applied in festival and event contexts. One of the first examples is found in the study of the Adelaide Grand Prix by Burns *et al.* (1986). Several CBA studies have followed, looking at such phenomena as televised events

(Fleischer and Felsenstein, 2002), sport events (Noll and Zimbalist, 1997), and festivals, events and conventions in general (Andersson *et al.*, 2004; Armbrecht and Lundberg, 2006; Dwyer *et al.*, 2000; Andersson *et al.*, 2012). Table 6.2 includes an overview of recent event studies undertaking value assessments based on the categorisation of use and non-use values and applying CVM methodology.

There have also been several ex ante studies on the 2012 London Olympics (Atkinson *et al.*, 2008; Walton *et al.*, 2007). In particular Atkinson *et al.* (2008) and Walton *et al.* (2007) use a refined CBA to measure intangible costs and benefits.

Table 6.2 Event studies describing use and/or non-use values

Type of event	Study	Country	Values involving direct use	Values not involving direct use
Sports event				
The Davis Cup (Tennis)	Barget and Gouguet (2007)	France		Option value, legacy value, existence value
European Athletics Indoor Championships 2013	Andersson *et al.* (2016)	Sweden	Direct use value, indirect use value	Bequest value, existence value, option value
Music event				
Way Out West Festival	Andersson *et al.* (2012)	Sweden	Direct use value, indirect use value	Bequest value, existence value, option value
Iberian Organ Festival (one of four case studies)	Bedate *et al.* (2004)	Spain	Direct use value	
Peace and Love music festival in Borlänge, Sweden, in 2012	Heldt and Mortazavi (2015)	Sweden	Use value	
Visual arts event				
Singapore Biennale 2008 and Singapore Arts Festival 2009	Chang and Mahadevan (2013)	Singapore	Use value	Legacy value, non-use value

Conclusions

Use values and non-use values represent a development rooted in the very origins of economic thinking. Utility was a central concept in the eighteenth century and in many ways more central to economics than money was. Contributions from Pareto, Kaldor and Hicks paved the way for CBA, which was developed in the middle of the last century and made comparisons of value and cost of social projects much more holistic than traditional project assessments. With a focus on the value (income) side of CBA, use and non-use values were suggested as a way to include not only benefits for citizens from direct use of resources, but also benefits accruing to other citizens. This perspective is suitable for assessments of the value of natural resources such as untamed rivers and wild forests and it was also mainly developed within environmental economics. The perspective is, however, also suitable to assessments of culture as well as festivals and events.

The direct use value of an event can be defined by the value experienced by event participants during the event. An event with entrance fees provides a straightforward example of the direct use value. We know that the entrance fee represents what participants regard as the minimum expected value, otherwise they would hardly have paid the ticket price. Depending on the quality of the event, the experienced value may differ from the expected value. Assessments of experienced direct use value draw upon CBA methodologies. An event provides ideal circumstances for such studies since we know the number of attendants and the ticket price represents a natural anchoring point for assessments as well as a very good vehicle for estimates of willingness to pay. Straightforward questions such as: "What is the maximum amount you would pay for the entrance ticket and still think that it was worth the price for the event you just have experienced?" can be used to assess the direct use value of an event.

The indirect use value is less well defined in space and time than the direct use value. Indirect use value is defined by the joy and expectations that visitors experience before the event as well as the pride, joy and social and cultural value experienced after the event. This is a challenging definition for empirical research. For several reasons a more limited definition has been suggested, where the value of indirect use value is limited in space and time to the days of the visit at the event destination and related to the event. There are two major reasons for this limitation. First, it makes the concept operational and easier to handle in empirical studies. Second, it makes indirect use value relevant for tourism studies and provides possibilities to separate event experiences from other destination experiences since it is possible to evaluate and estimate consumer surplus generated at the destination but outside the event premises. The indirect use value thus describes the value generated by the tourism industry at the destination, which was an objective for Andersson *et al.* (2012) who proposed this operational definition of indirect use value.

Non-use value of an event is normally assessed by asking citizens whether they are in favour of public financial support to a specific event or festival.

Those in favour of public support are asked for the maximum amount of tax increase they are willing to pay to keep the event or festival alive. Those against public support are asked whether they need a compensation to be willing to accept (WTA) having the event or festival at the destination. Taxes are therefore the vehicle of payment and there may, in some societies, be issues with strong antipathy against taxes generally that may make this vehicle of payment less suitable.

Non-use values have, in several studies, turned out to be of a magnitude comparable to economic impacts (Andersson *et al.*, 2012, 2016), which indicate that the social impact for local residents may be as important as the economic impact for the local industry.

Challenges

If it can be said that events with entrance fees provide an ideal setting for an empirical study; the same cannot be said for free festivals without entrance fees, where sampling techniques and other reliability issues are more challenging. This is the case not only for assessments of use value, but equally for other assessments of, for example, economic impact, satisfaction and experienced quality.

Another methodological challenge is related to valid measures of the sub-categories of non-use value: existence value, option value and bequest value. It is a problem of concept overlap and therefore not easy to define and measure. A qualitative study by Armbrecht (2012) described how various concepts cover different types of value in terms of intrinsic/extrinsic and individual/society respectively (cf. Figure 1.2).

The separation of non-use value into sub-categories can be achieved by asking respondents to, first, estimate the willingness to pay for the non-use value and, thereafter, to distribute that value (e.g. in terms of percentages) among a selected number (e.g. three to five) sub-categories, such as option value and bequest value. The problem is that the descriptions of these sub-categories tend to be abstract and difficult for the respondents to make sense of, which is clearly demonstrated by Figure 6.1. Surveys tend to give a fairly equal distribution of the values, which is probably a result of the problematic discriminant validity for these concepts. Respondents are not clear about the differences.

Figure 6.2 summarises our present knowledge and experiences from assessing values of events, in monetary terms, including not only extrinsic, but also intrinsic values. CVM is the most frequently used measurement technique, although other stated, as well as revealed preference methods are possible to use.

Environmental values present another challenge for a valid estimate of non-use values. There are some events that impact on nature and citizens' evaluations of these impacts may be included both in existence value and bequest value. But should only values experienced by humans be part of a holistic evaluation? Impacts on nature or the ecological system in addition to human beings may be considered part of the total impact.

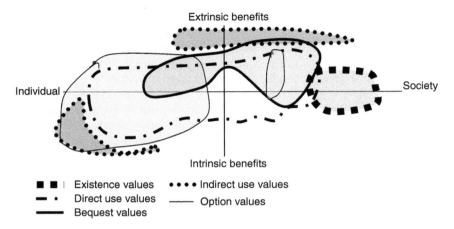

Figure 6.1 A description of sub-categories of use and non-use values for cultural events
Source: Armbrecht (2012)

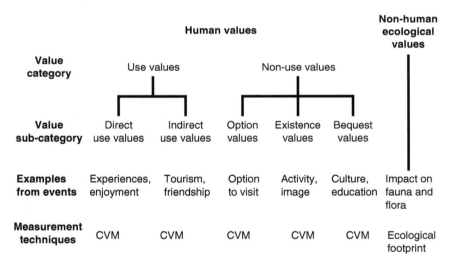

Figure 6.2 A summary chart of relevant measures of use and non-use values of events

References

Aabø, S. and Audunson, R. (2002). Rational choice and valuation of public libraries: can economic models for evaluating non-market goods be applied to public libraries? *Journal of Librarianship and Information Science*, 34(1), 5–15. doi:10.1177/096100060203400102

Aabø, S. and Strand, J. (2004). Public library valuation, nonuse values, and altruistic motivations. *Library and Information Science Research*, 26(3), 351–72.

Alberini, A. and Longo, A. (2006). Combining the travel cost and contingent behavior methods to value cultural heritage sites: evidence from Armenia. *Journal of Cultural Economics*, 30(4), 287–304.

Andersson, T.D. and Armbrecht, J. (2014a). Factors explaining the use-value of sport event experiences. *International Journal of Event and Festival Management*, 5(3), 235–46. doi:10.1108/ijefm-12-2013-0042

Andersson, T.D. and Armbrecht, J. (2014b). Use-value of music event experiences: a "triple ex" model explaining direct and indirect use-value of events. *Scandinavian Journal of Hospitality and Tourism*, 14(3), 255–74. doi:10.1080/15022250.2014.947084

Andersson, T.D. and Lundberg, E. (2013). Commensurability and sustainability: triple impact assessments of a tourism event. *Tourism Management*, 37(August), 99–109. doi: http://dx.doi.org/10.1016/j.tourman.2012.12.015

Andersson, T.D., Rustad, A. and Solberg, H.A. (2004). Local residents' monetary evaluation of sport events. *Managing Leisure*, 9(3), 157–70.

Andersson, T.D., Armbrecht, J. and Lundberg, E. (2012). Estimating use and non-use values of a music festival. *Scandinavian Journal of Hospitality and Tourism*, 12(3), 215–31. doi:10.1080/15022250.2012.725276

Andersson, T.D., Armbrecht, J. and Lundberg, E. (2016). Triple impact assessments of the 2013 European athletics indoor championship in Gothenburg. *Scandinavian Journal of Hospitality and Tourism*, 16(2), 158–79. doi:10.1080/15022250.2015.1108863

Armbrecht, J. (2012). *The Value of Cultural Institutions: Measurement and Description*. Kållered, Göteborg: BAS förlag.

Armbrecht, J. and Lundberg, E. (2006). From quality to expenditures: a case study of Storsjöyran Music Festival, Sweden. Master's degree thesis, Göteborg University.

Arrow, K. and Fisher, A. (1974). Environmental preservation, uncertainty, and irreversibility. *The Quarterly Journal of Economics*, 88(2), 312–19.

Arrow, K., Solow, R., Portney, P.R., Leamer, E.E., Radner, R. and Schuman, H. (1993). Report of the NOAA Panel on Contingent Valuation.

Atkinson, G., Mourato, S., Szymanski, S. and Ozdemiroglu, E. (2008). Are we willing to pay enough to "back the bid"?: Valuing the intangible impacts of London's bid to host the 2012 Summer Olympic Games. *Urban Studies*, 45(2), 419–44. doi:10.1177/0042098007085971

Barget, E. and Gouguet, J.J. (2007). The total economic value of sporting events theory and practice. *Journal of Sports Economics*, 8(2), 165–85.

Baumol, W.J. (1986). Unnatural value: or art investment as floating crap game. *The American Economic Review*, 76(2), 10–14.

Bedate, A., Herrero, L.C. and Sanz, J.Á. (2004). Economic valuation of the cultural heritage: application to four case studies in Spain. *Journal of Cultural Heritage*, 5(1), 101–11.

Bedate, A., Herrero, L. and Sanz, J. (2009). Economic valuation of a contemporary art museum: correction of hypothetical bias using a certainty question. *Journal of Cultural Economics*, 33(3), 185–99.

Bentham, J. (1789/2000). *An Introduction to the Principles of Morals and Legislation*. Kitchener, ON: Batoche.

Bille Hansen, T. (1997). The willingness-to-pay for the Royal Theatre in Copenhagen as a public good. *Journal of Cultural Economics*, 21(1), 1–28.

Boyle, K. and Bishop, R. (1987). Valuing wildlife in benefit–cost analyses: a case study involving endangered species. *Water Resources Research*, 23(943).

Burns, J., Hatch, J. and Mules, T. J. (1986). *The Adelaide Grand Prix: The Impact of a Special Event*. Adelaide: Centre for South Australian Economic Studies.

Cesario, F.J. (1976). Value of time in recreation benefit studies. *Land Economics*, 52(1), 32–41.

Chang, S. and Mahadevan, R. (2013). Fad, fetish or fixture: contingent valuation of performing and visual arts festivals in Singapore. *International Journal of Cultural Policy*, 20(3), 318–40. doi:10.1080/10286632.2013.817396

Cicchetti, C.J. and Freeman III, M.A. (1971). Option demand and consumer surplus: further comment. *The Quarterly Journal of Economics*, 85(3), 528–39. doi:10.2307/1885940

Del Saz Salazar, S. and Montagud Marques, J. (2005). Valuing cultural heritage: the social benefits of restoring and old Arab tower. *Journal of Cultural Heritage*, 6(1), 69–77.

Desvousges, W.H., Smith, V.K. and McGivney, M.P. (1983). *A Comparison of Alternative Approaches for Estimating Recreation and Related Benefits of Water Quality Improvements*. Washington, DC: Report to the US Environmental Protection Agency.

Driml, S. (2002). Travel cost analysis of recreation value in the Wet Tropics World Heritage Area. *Economic Analysis and Policy*, 32(2), 11–26.

Dutta, M., Banerjee, S. and Husain, Z. (2007). Untapped demand for heritage: a contingent valuation study of Prinsep Ghat, Calcutta. *Tourism Management*, 28(1), 83–95.

Dwyer, L., Mellor, R., Mistilis, N. and Mules, T. (2000). A framework for assessing "tangible" and "intangible" impacts of events and conventions. *Event Management*, 6(3), 175–89. doi:10.0000/096020197390257

Fleischer, A. and Felsenstein, D. (2002). Cost–benefit analysis using economic surpluses: a case study of a televised event. *Journal of Cultural Economics*, 26(2), 139–56.

Fleming, C.M. and Cook, A. (2008). The recreational value of Lake McKenzie, Fraser Island: an application of the travel cost method. *Tourism Management*, 29(6), 1197–205.

Frey, B.S. (2003). *Arts and Economics: Analysis and Cultural Policy* (2nd edn). Berlin: Springer Verlag.

Frey, B.S. and Pommerehne, W.W. (1989). *Muses and Markets: Explorations in the Economics of the Arts*. Oxford: Basil Blackwell.

Garrod, G. and Willis, K.G. (2001). *Economic Valuation of the Environment: Methods and Case Studies*. Cheltenham: Edward Elgar.

Getz, D. (2005). *Event Management and Event Tourism*. New York: Cognizant.

Greenley, D.A., Walsh, R.G. and Young, R.A. (1981). Option value: empirical evidence from a case study of recreation and water quality. *The Quarterly Journal of Economics*, 96(4), 657–73.

Hanley, N. and Barbier, E. (2009). *Pricing Nature: Cost–Benefit Analysis and Environmental Policy*. Cheltenham: Edward Elgar.

Hanley, N., Spash, C.L. and Cullen, R. (1993). *Cost–Benefit Analysis and the Environment*. Cheltenham: Edward Elgar.

Heldt, T. and Mortazavi, R. (2015). Estimating and comparing demand for a music event using stated choice and actual visitor behaviour data. *Scandinavian Journal of Hospitality and Tourism*, December, 130–42. doi:10.1080/15022250.2015.1117986

Hicks, J.R. (1939). The foundations of welfare economics. *The Economic Journal*, 49(196), 696–712.

Holbrook, M.B. (1999). *Consumer Value: A Framework for Analysis and Research*. London: Routledge.

Hotelling, H. (1947). Letter of June 18, 1947, to Newton B. Durry. Included in the report *The Economics of Public Recreation: An Economic Study of the Monetary Evaluation of Recreation in the National Parks, 1949*. Mimeographed. Washington, DC, Land and Recreational Planning Division, National Park Service.

Jackson, J., Houghton, M., Russell, R. and Triandos, P. (2005). Innovations in measuring economic impacts of regional festivals: a do-it-yourself kit. *Journal of Travel Research*, 43(4), 360–7. doi:10.1177/0047287505274649

Kahneman, D. (2000). Experienced utility and objective happiness: a moment-based approach. In D. Kahneman and A. Tversky (eds), *Choices, Values and Frames*. Cambridge: Cambridge University Press, pp. 673–92.

Kaldor, N. (1939). Welfare propositions of economics and interpersonal comparisons of utility. *The Economic Journal*, 49(195), 549–52.

Kim, S.S., Wong, K.K.F. and Cho, M. (2007). Assessing the economic value of a world heritage site and willingness-to-pay determinants: a case of Changdeok Palace. *Tourism Management*, 28(1), 317–22.

Kling, R.W., Revier, C.F. and Sable, K. (2004). Estimating the public good value of preserving a local historic landmark: the role of non-substitutability and citizen information. *Urban Studies*, 41(10), 2025-2041. doi:10.1080/0042098042000256369

Krutilla, J.V. (1967). Conservation reconsidered. *The American Economic Review*, 57(4), 777–86.

Lazo, J.K., McClelland, G.H. and Schulze, W.D. (1997). Economic theory and psychology of non-use values. *Land Economics*, 73(3), 358–71. doi:10.2307/3147173

Maddison, D. and Mourato, S. (2001). Valuing different road options for Stonehenge. *Conservation and Management of Archaeological Sites*, 4(4), 203–12.

Mayor, K., Scott, S. and Tol, R. (2007). Comparing the travel cost method and the contingent valuation method: an application of convergent validity theory to the recreational value of Irish forests. *Papers*. Dublin: Economic and Social Research Institute.

Mitchell, R.C. and Carson, R.T. (1989). *Using surveys to value public goods: the contingent valuation method*. Washington, DC: Resources for the Future.

Mmopelwa, G., Kgathi, D.L. and Molefhe, L. (2007). Tourists' perceptions and their willingness to pay for park fees: a case study of self-drive tourists and clients for mobile tour operators in Moremi Game Reserve, Botswana. *Tourism Management*, 28(4), 1044–56. doi:10.1016/j.tourman.2006.08.014

Mules, T. and Dwyer, L. (2005). Public sector support for sport tourism events: the role of cost–benefit analysis. *Sport in Society*, 8(2), 338–55.

Navrud, S. and Ready, R.C. (2002). *Valuing Cultural Heritage: Applying Environmental Valuation Techniques to Historic Buildings, Monuments and Artifacts*. Cheltenham: Edward Elgar.

Noll, R.G. and Zimbalist, A.S. (1997). *Sports, Jobs, and Taxes: The Economic Impact of Sports Teams and Stadiums*. Washington, DC: Brookings Institution Press.

Pearce, D.W. and Turner, R.K. (1990). *Economics of Natural Resources and the Environment*. Hemel Hempstead: Harvester Wheatsheaf.

Poor, P.J. and Smith, J.M. (2004). Travel cost analysis of a cultural heritage site: the case of historic St Mary's City of Maryland. *Journal of Cultural Economics*, 28(3), 217–29.

Powe, N.A. and Willis, K.G. (1996). Benefits received by visitors to heritage sites: a case study of Warkworth Castle. *Leisure Studies*, 15(4), 259–75.

Rolfe, J. and Windle, J. (2003). Valuing the protection of aboriginal cultural heritage sites. *Economic Record*, 79(Special Issue), 85–95.

Ruijgrok, E.C.M. (2006). The three economic values of cultural heritage: a case study in the Netherlands. *Journal of Cultural Heritage*, 7(3), 206–13.

Schwer, R.K. and Daneshvary, R. (1995). Willingness to pay for public television and the advent of "look-alike" cable television channels: a case study. *Journal of Media Economics*, 8(3), 95–109.

Snowball, J. (2005). *The Economic Valuation of Cultural Events in Developing Countries: Combining Market and Non-Market Valuation Techniques at the South African National Arts Festival*. Grahamstown, S. Africa: Rhodes University.

Throsby, C.D. (1999). Cultural capital. *Journal of Cultural Economics*, 23(1–2), 3–12.

Throsby, C.D. (2001). *Economics and Culture*. Cambridge: Cambridge University Press.

Throsby, C.D. (2003). Determining the value of cultural goods: how much (or how little) does contingent valuation tell us? *Journal of Cultural Economics*, 27(3–4), 275–85. doi:10.1023/A:1026353905772

Throsby, C.D. (2010). *The Economics of Cultural Policy*. Cambridge: Cambridge University Press.

Throsby, C.D. and Withers, G.A. (1983). Measuring the demand for the arts as a public good: Theory and empirical results. In W.S. Hendon and J.L. Shanahan (eds), *Economics of Cultural Decisions*. Cambridge, MA: Abt Books.

Tietenberg, T.H. and Lewis, L. (2008). *Environmental and Natural Resource Economics*. Boston, MA: Pearson Addison Wesley.

Tohmo, T. (2004). Economic value of a local museum: factors of willingness-to-pay. *Journal of Socio-Economics*, 33(2), 229–40.

Tuan, T. and Navrud, S. (2008). Capturing the benefits of preserving cultural heritage. *Journal of Cultural Heritage*, 9(3), 326–37.

Walton, H., Longo, A. and Dawson, P. (2007). A contingent valuation of the 2012 London Olympic Games: a regional perspective. *Journal of Sports Economics*. doi:10.1177/1527002507308769

Weisbrod, B.A. (1964). Collective-consumption services of individual-consumption goods. *The Quarterly Journal of Economics*, 78(3), 471–7.

7   Event evaluation

Approaches and new challenges

Larry Dwyer and Peter Forsyth

Introduction

Special events provide important social and recreational opportunities for local communities. They are associated with additional demand for destination goods and services generating increased sales, jobs, income and investment and export opportunities. Given their relevance to national identity and pride, destination image and branding (Marzano and Scott, 2006), they form a fundamental component of the tourism development strategy in many destinations (Jago and Dwyer, 2006).

Increasingly, event assessment is used by event convenors to support public funding of special events. Governments are often asked to provide financial support for special events, including the allocation of substantial funds to provide or upgrade the facilities required to stage the event. As a consequence, governments will generally require credible forecasts of the event impacts and comprehensive evaluations of the economic effects. At the same time, public sector agencies demand greater rigour in evaluation techniques (VAG (Victorian Auditor General), 2007). The problem faced by researchers is to provide techniques which give accurate results while at the same time providing practical use for policy-makers, who must make decisions on whether allocating resources in support of some event or festival is appropriate; and if so, to what extent.

This chapter will provide an overview of the main approaches to economic evaluation of special events. These are: economic impact analysis (EIA) and cost–benefit analysis (CBA). Two main types of modelling techniques are used for EIA: input–output (I–O) and computable general equilibrium (CGE) modelling. A variant of CBA analysis, based on the concept of total economic value (TEV), has received some support recently. In addition, there have been some recent attempts to develop mixed or hybrid approaches which combine elements of EIA and CBA. The details of these approaches are discussed, as well as their advantages and limitations. An approach is recommended that bridges the gap between welfare measuring CGE and CBA, in a way that has policy relevance for destination managers.

Economic impact analysis

Economic impact analysis involves estimating the additional expenditure generated by the event, and then using some form of economic model to estimate how this expenditure affects the destination economy. The economic model identifies and quantifies the linkages between different sectors of the local economy and linkages with other regions (Crompton, 2010). The injected expenditure of visitors and organisers/sponsors stimulates economic activity and creates additional business turnover, employment, value added, household income and government revenue in the host community. The relationship between expenditure and output, income, value added and employment (direct, indirect or induced) can be described by multipliers. The size of the multipliers will depend upon the type of model used to estimate the impacts (Dwyer *et al.*, 2005).

Before distinguishing the two major types of models used in EIA, we pose three general criticisms of this approach.

One criticism is that EIA alone usually cannot decide which is the best allocation of public resources in support of events since society has goals other than efficiency. The economic impacts of an event are not the same thing as the economic benefits that arise. Economic impact studies can only estimate the effect on economic variables such as output, gross domestic product (GDP), employment and the like. The impact on GDP, for example, is a gross measure of the change in value of output as a result of an event. This addition to output normally requires additional inputs, of land, labour and capital, to enable it to be produced. These inputs have a cost, and this cost must be deducted from the change in value of gross output if a measure of the net economic gain is to be made. Another way of putting this is to say that EIA has little or no policy relevance unless the requisite modelling outcomes include welfare measures (Dwyer *et al.*, 2015). While an increase in GDP (or gross regional product, GRP) may or may not be welfare enhancing, as a measure of welfare it has several limitations (ibid.). Importantly, since prices seldom reflect full benefits from consumption or full costs of production, the economic impacts of an event do not equate to its economic benefits. To enable the addition to GDP/GRP generated by a special event, inputs are needed: additional labour must be hired, additional capital must be made available, more land will be alienated and more natural resources will be used up, with attendant social and environmental costs.

A second criticism is that EIA provides only a partial perspective to decision-makers facing the problem of funding or subsidising an event. Event researchers typically have taken a piecemeal approach to evaluation – much of the impact assessment literature ignores any serious effort to value the social, cultural, environmental and other impacts of events, even though techniques are available to do so. In order for the government to be more comprehensively apprised, the evaluation exercise must transcend a narrow concern with economic issues and embrace the wider range of effects associated with events (Hede, 2007). The challenge then is how to compare values (economic, social and environmental) that seem to be 'incommensurable'.

A third criticism is that some types of EIA exclude resident values of events from the assessment process, treating resident event-related expenditure merely as 'transferred expenditure' playing no role in determining economic impacts (Dwyer *et al.*, 2015). How this exclusion of resident willingness to pay (WTP) for event attendance harmonises with views of the importance of resident perceptions of events is generally ignored by theorists and practitioners alike.

In much of the economic modelling of special events undertaken by tourism researchers, the models do not contain a welfare measure. We refer to this approach as 'standard' EIA. Standard EIA models comprise all input–output models and CGE models without a welfare function. In contrast, CGE models are perfectly capable of being formulated to contain a welfare measure, as demonstrated in Blake's study of the London Olympics (Blake, 2005). In the discussion below we refer to such models as 'welfare measuring' CGE.

Input–output modelling

The standard model used for economic impact estimation of special events has been the input–output (I–O) model (Crompton, 2006, 2010). I–O tables show the various industries that comprise the economy and indicate how these industries interlink through their purchase and sales relationships. In an I–O model, an exogenous injection of expenditure, such as an increase in visitor expenditure associated with the holding of a special event, generates an increase in output in supplier industries. This requires, in turn, an increase in inputs supplied to those industries, which again requires an increase in outputs by industries supplying these inputs. An I–O model traces and estimates these input requirements among industries. This forms the basis of the measures known as 'multipliers' that provide estimates of the effects on important economic variables such as GDP or value added. I–O modelling has been used, for example, to estimate the economic impacts of events such as the Euro 1996 Football Championship (Gratton *et al.*, 2000), the football World Cup in Germany (Ahlert, 2001) and the economic impacts of government financing of the 2010 FIFA World Cup held in South Africa (Mabugu and Mohamed, 2008)

In recent years, a growing number of researchers have argued that, based on its restrictive assumptions, I–O modelling generates exaggerated estimates of the economic impacts of events, particularly large events (Matheson, 2002; Dwyer *et al.*, 2004; Jago *et al.*, 2010), and is thus incapable of accurately informing event funding agencies or governments of the 'return on investment' estimated from event funding. The restrictive assumptions of I–O modelling (no capacity constraints and consequently no impact of the event on wages or prices) means that I–O modelling fails to capture the industry interactive effects that would be revealed in the use of a more sophisticated model for economic impact assessment (Blake, 2005; Madden, 2006). Compounding this problem is the propensity of consultants to deliver the biggest possible impact estimates for clients eager to develop events, by applying inappropriate multipliers (Crompton, 2006). It is well established, now, that the economic assessment models used for estimating the economic impacts of major events must reflect contemporary developments in economic analysis. In recent years, the literature on event assessment has moved away from the use of I–O models to provide the multiplier effects of the new expenditure, and towards the use of CGE models.

Computable equilibrium modelling

CGE models are designed to capture the complex pattern of price changes, feedback effects and resource constraints that exist in all economies following a demand side shock such as that occasioned by the holding of a special event (Blake, 2005; Bohlmann, 2006; Dwyer *et al.*, 2005; Madden, 2006; VAG, 2007; Giesecke and Madden, 2011). They include more specifications of the behaviour of consumers, producers and investors, thus permitting specific models to be calibrated to actual conditions for a particular event in a particular economy (Dwyer, 2015). In contrast to I–O analysis, which always produces a positive gain to the economy, however disastrous the event, CGE modelling recognises that price rises due to resource constraints may limit the increase in economic activity occasioned by a special event, and may even lead to contractions in economic activity in some sectors or the whole economy.

To make informed decisions about events policy, governments need to know the answers to questions such as: how much will the event add to economic activity and jobs after accounting for inter-industry effects? To what extent do the benefits of the event in the host region come at a cost to other regions? CGE modelling can address such questions. The advantages of CGE models for event economic impact assessment may be summarised as follows (Dwyer *et al.*, 2006):

- CGE models recognise that relative prices of land, labour and capital may change when an event causes businesses to change the composition of their inputs.
- Capacity constraints imply that the prices of inputs and wages will increase in the face of an increase in demand associated with an event. These price rises, including (for some destinations) any upward pressure on the exchange rate due to increased foreign expenditure associated with an event, will limit the extent of economic expansion associated with the event, and may even lead to contractions in economic activity in some sectors.
- CGE models recognise the behaviour of the government budget sector as relevant to the estimated economic impacts of a special event. For example, government support for additional infrastructure spending required by special events (e.g. expenditure on stadia, roads and transport facilities) will have a positive effect on spending, but it must be financed, through taxation or borrowing. This may moderate the growth in private consumption associated with the event, leading to downward pressure on the output of consumption-oriented industries.

- The distributional impact of a special event is often ignored. CGE models can provide information as to who gains and who loses, both within and outside the event location.
- CGE models can provide a net benefit or welfare measure. Unfortunately, tourism researchers continue to confuse the 'impacts' and the 'benefits' of tourism growth, ignoring the fact that tourism growth has an economic cost, since it requires the use of scarce resources. Welfare measures indicate how much better or worse off an economy is as a result of a tourism demand shock such as associated with a special event. To measure welfare, the analyst can adjust GDP simulations to include the cost of capital (Dwyer and Forsyth, 2009). Alternatively, Blake (2005), in his study of the London Olympics, employed the change in welfare by equivalent variation (EV), as a measure of economic welfare, which indicates how much the change in welfare is worth to the economy at the pre-simulation set of prices.
- The assumptions of a CGE model can be varied and the sensitivity to them tested to assess the economic impacts of an event. These include assumptions about factor constraints, workings of the labour market, changes in real wage rates and prices, and government taxing and spending policies. The fact that CGE simulations can be undertaken using different assumptions, the realism of which can be discussed and debated, provides a transparency to the event assessment process that rarely exists in I–O modelling. This can provide very useful information in predicting the economic impacts of particular types of events in different macroeconomic contexts.

CGE modelling is particularly relevant for estimating the economic impacts of large and mega events. Of course, estimating the economic impacts of tourism demand shocks in certain event contexts (local festivals and events) may not justify the expense of constructing a new CGE model if no suitable model already exists. The practical advantage of using an alternative technique in certain tourism contexts is, however, a separate issue from its theoretical status (Dwyer, 2015).

Using a welfare measuring CGE model, with information about the net economic benefits of the event, the government or funding agency is in a better position to make an informed decision about the extent to which it is prepared to support any event. Even so, the analysis omits wider costs and benefits that can be crucial inputs to policy. Event assessment that focuses only on economic impacts is too narrow in scope to provide sufficient information to policy-makers and government funding agencies and, where practical, a more comprehensive approach should be employed to embrace the importance of social and environmental impacts in addition to economic impacts.

Cost–benefit analysis

The success or contribution of a particular event should not be measured only by its economic impact. It is recognised that there may be other benefits from events, such as enhancing the image of a city or region, facilitating business networking and civic pride. Event organisers may emphasise the developmental benefits of targeted infrastructural investments in deprived areas and the long-term 'legacy' benefits that the increased exposure to the international media brings through increased tourist arrivals and tourism receipts in the years after (and before) a special event (Preuss, 2007). The Olympic Games and World Cup football are probably the best current examples of events with expected large flow-on benefits. Ethnic festivals or events for disadvantaged groups may help to address social/cultural issues in the community (Pillay and Bass, 2008). Events can also result in associated social and cultural benefits to a destination, providing for continuing education and training, facilitating technology transfer and the like. However, events are recognised to generate adverse social impacts such as disruption to local business and community backlash and adverse environmental impacts such as various forms of pollution (Baade and Matheson, 2002).

CBA can be used to capture, measure, weigh and compare all expected present and future benefits of a policy, programme or investment (such as a special event), with all its expected present and future costs. As a result of the holding of an event, individual firms, consumers, and/or workers may be better or worse off, through changes in their own consumption, income and level of effort, as well as the way they are affected by associated government expenditure. Firms can gain (or lose) if there is a change in the level of profits. Consumers gain (or lose) from the holding of the event and workers can gain from additional wages, less any costs of additional effort. Governments may gain through increased tax receipts at existing tax rates, and they will pass these gains on to the community in a number of ways – through tax cuts, or additional expenditures which benefit the community; or they may save their gains and pass them on to future generations.

CBA is an ideal approach to event assessment as it is holistic, including, in principle, all costs and benefits (welfare effects) associated with an event (Fleischer and Felsenstein, 2002; Shaffer *et al.*, 2003; VAG, 2007; Dwyer *et al.*, 2015). A measure of the net benefit of a special event to the community as a whole can be obtained by adding up the monetary evaluation of the gains and losses experienced by all in the community. For a special event to be socially acceptable, the sum of the benefits to society (including private and social benefits) must exceed the sum of the costs to society (including private and social costs). 'Value' or 'benefit' is measured by willingness to pay – what people are willing to pay (or give up) to get what an event provides – estimated by measuring the additional consumer surplus and producer surplus of a given option over the 'do nothing' or 'no event' case (Boardman *et al.*, 2011). Economic costs are measured by 'opportunity cost' – what people or a society give up by investing capital and employing workers in event-related activities as opposed to the best alternative. By quantifying the net benefits of projects, programmes and policies in a standard manner, CBA improves the information base for public sector decision-making, thereby assisting in the assessment of relative priorities (Dwyer, 2012). It is designed specifically to answer public policy questions.

While economic impact assessments of events emphasise the injected expenditure associated with events as the basis for estimating its significance, a CBA recognises that various 'surpluses', including the consumer surpluses of residents, are essential to event evaluation. Thus CBA estimates the sum of the surpluses of an event for a particular community. These welfare effects include:

- household consumer surpluses from direct enjoyment of the event (attendees)
- household consumer surpluses of attendees of offsite events/activities
- household benefits from indirect enjoyment of the event (non-attendees)
- surpluses to destination businesses (returns to destination-owned capital above opportunity costs)
- benefits to destination labour (above opportunity costs)
- follow-on benefits of future visitors to the tourism industry (brand benefit)
- ongoing (legacy) benefits from construction of assets for the event.

VAG, 2007; Dwyer *et al.*, 2015

Event-related costs can include:

- capital expenditures on event-related infrastructure
- operating expenditures such as event management and staging, marketing/promotion, catering and administration
- costs incurred by state government agencies such as road and traffic authority, police, ambulance, fire brigade and destination emergency services
- social and environmental costs such as disruption to business and resident lifestyles, traffic congestion, road accidents, crime, litter, noise, crowds, property damage, environmental degradation, vandalism, congestion, noise, air and water pollution and carbon footprint.

A major difficulty with a CBA is that it is primarily a partial equilibrium approach. This means that it is unable to go beyond the markets directly affected by the event. Thus an event may use labour, but often this labour is drawn from regions away from the event. There may be benefits or costs associated with this, but CBA cannot pick them up. CBA is unable to take account of externalities which are economy-wide or world-wide, such as the impact of an event on greenhouse gas emissions (the net effect on these emissions can be very different from the emissions directly attributable to the event). By contrast, CGE models are general equilibrium models, and they can measure and evaluate these externalities.

For special events, judgement can be made as to whether the economic benefits are greater than the costs, and also as to whether the event would represent the best use of the funds, when funds are limited and alternative calls on funds exist. The aggregate result of a CBA indicates whether the estimated gains exceed the costs to the community as a whole. If the estimated net social benefit of an event is positive (the total benefit exceeds the total cost), then the event is said to be an efficient use of society's economic resources. Standard EIA approaches cannot provide this information, though, of course, CGE models with welfare measures can.

A variant approach: TEV

The concept of total economic value (TEV) is used successfully to value environmental resources, distinguishing between user and non-user values (Smith, 1999; Richardson and Loomis, 2009). The TEV is the sum of the amenity's total use and total non-use values, such that: total economic value = total use value + total non-use value.

The TEV of environmental amenities comprises explicit use benefits as well as implicit non-use benefits. As used in resource evaluation, the concept refers to the value derived by people from a natural resource, a human-made heritage resource or an infrastructure system, compared to not having it.

Use values

Use values are conceived in terms of *direct* and *indirect* use value, which can be linked to different aspects of the event experience by participants, visitors and destination residents.

Direct use value is defined as the experiential value of persons inside the event area. This corresponds with the utility actually felt by the consumer at the event. Willingness to pay is partly shown by the expenditure needed to access the event (tickets) or for various purchases. In the study of the Way Out West (WOW) festival, direct use value was elicited using ticket price as payment vehicle in the question: "What is the maximum amount you would pay for your festival ticket and still think it was worth the money spent?" (Andersson and Lundberg, 2013).

In contrast, the indirect use value is defined as the value that event visitors experience before and after the event at the event destination but associated with the event. For example, people who have visited a major football event and thus experienced a direct use value, may also derive satisfaction and *indirect use value*

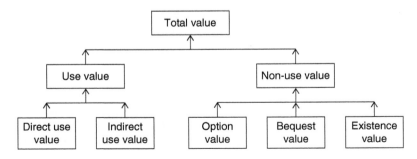

Figure 7.1 Total economic value

from reading about the event in newspapers or watching repeat games on TV. For the indirect use value associated with the WOW festival (Andersson *et al.*, 2012), total expenditure of all attendees (visitors plus residents) was used as payment vehicle in the question: "What is the maximum amount you would pay for all the experiences that you have had in Gothenburg and still think it was worth the money spent?" (Andersson and Armbrecht, 2014). Given information regarding the total WTP for their stay in Gothenburg, the direct use value was subtracted in order to estimate the indirect use value – that is, a monetary value for the experience outside the festival gates.

Based on some perceived similarities between resource evaluation and event evaluation, researchers have begun to explore the relevance of the TEV concept to assessment of special events and festivals. Figure 7.2 displays the framework adopted in a recent assessment of the European athletics indoor championship held in Gothenburg (Andersson *et al.*, 2015).

In the assessment framework of Figure 7.2, the net economic impact of a festival comprises direct expenditure and opportunity cost.

Direct expenditure

In Figure 7.2, direct expenditure includes both money spent on the event itself and related expenditure on items such as transport, accommodation, food and beverage, shopping etc. Multipliers can be applied to the direct economic impact to determine the total economic impact on the local economy. The authors argue that using a simple direct economic impact estimate will avoid debates on complex methodologies and debates on the inclusion or exclusion of multipliers and that direct economic impact ("in-scope expenditure") works well as a basis for straightforward comparisons to other events. This comparison would be meaningful only for small events. However, it is still possible to use the direct economic impact estimate for further analysis of the multiplier effects using economic models if required (Andersson *et al.*, 2012).

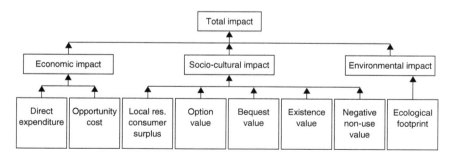

Figure 7.2 A measurement model describing the total festival impact from a sustainability perspective

Source: Andersson *et al.* (2015)

Opportunity costs

Visitor expenditure always has an alternative use that can be identified by collecting information, albeit highly hypothetical, about what visitors would have done if there had not been a festival. Noting that assessment of opportunity cost is imperative for complete estimations of economic impact, analysts exclude the expenditures of event attendees who are 'casuals', 'time switchers' and 'displaced' visitors (Andersson and Lundberg, 2013). However, contrary to standard practice of eliminating 'transferred expenditure' from consideration, included in economic evaluation of the WOW event is the expenditure of residents who attend the event but who, in the case of no event, would have travelled elsewhere. One justification for this is that, to some extent, it counterbalances the (unestimated) potential loss of expenditure from residents who would otherwise have left Gothenburg during the time of the event.

The estimate of opportunity cost in the WOW study conforms to standard practice in estimating 'in-scope', 'net injected' or 'new' expenditure associated with an event (Jago and Dwyer, 2006). This process is essential prior to an EIA. It does not, however, address the real cost of allocating funds to developing an event in terms of other investment opportunities foregone. An advantage of CGE and CBA is they treat seriously the issue of opportunity costs of event-related expenditure – that is, what a society gives up by investing capital and employing workers in event-related activities as opposed to the best alternative use of funds.

Non-use values

In the environmental evaluation process these relate to a wider group of stakeholders than resource users. They are usually categorised in terms of option and quasi-option value, existence value, bequest value and altruistic value.

1   *Option and quasi-option value*: Option values reflect the willingness to preserve an option for potential future use. In the environmental resources literature it relates to individuals' willingness to pay for retaining an option to use a resource that would be difficult or impossible to replace and for which no close substitute is available (Fisher, 2000). In the presence of uncertainty, (risk-averse) individuals will be willing to pay more than solely the expected consumer surplus in order to preserve a resource. Thus persons may wish to preserve the option to take part in an annual triathlon or music festival, now or in the future, even though they may never attend. Quasi-option value reflects the willingness to avoid irreversible commitment to development now, on the expectation that future information will give a clearer view of what its uses are. It reflects the extra value of choosing not to take irreversible steps associated with tourism development now if new information about the outcomes of alternative decisions might become available in the future. In an event context, quasi-option value would seem to work against developing large event facilities such as football stadia, velodromes or aquatic

complexes, which might be perceived to 'lock in' the community to particular types of events in the future, limiting the options to develop events of other types.

2   *Existence value*: Existence value reflects benefits from simply knowing that a certain good or service exists. It captures the intrinsic value of an environmental aspect in its own right, independent of human use. In the resource environmental literature it is an expression of willingness to forego current use to retain the amenity, irrespective of any future use. The concept may also include the benefits obtained from knowing that culturally important resources are protected and this could be important for some types of events. For event assessment, existence value equates to the utility a person derives from knowing that the event exists, with all that represents from the economic, social, symbolic and cultural points of view and positive effects on destination image (Richardson and Loomis, 2009).

3   *Altruism or vicarious value*: In environmental resource evaluation this concept reflects the value that people attach to knowing that other people enjoy features of natural environments – that is, the value that people attach to the knowledge that others are enjoying the natural environment passively or actively (Aldred, 1994). This concept certainly seems important for event evaluation – individuals may attach a value to the positive experiences that an event brings to others, whether users or non-users. The values that others are perceived to attach to an event can, in principle, cover a substantial range, including symbolic, educational, aesthetic, political, spiritual, lifestyle, prestige, community pride, social cohesion etc.

4   *Bequest (legacy) value*: In environmental resource evaluation this concept reflects the value attached to the benefits of preservation for the enjoyment of future generations (Richardson and Loomis, 2009). In the event context, bequest value is the value that the community attaches to the continuation of an event for future enjoyment by people. Closely linked to altruistic motives it relates to the satisfaction felt by members of the community as a result of handing down an event for future generations to experience. As such, the concept is most likely linked to events that carry on a 'tradition' or reflect particular cultural or heritage values.

In Figure 7.2, the researchers include local resident consumer surplus as a non-use value. Since consumer surplus is the difference between what one is willing to pay for a product or service and what is actually paid, we feel that this estimate is better included among use value as an additional economic benefit of an event.

The method most often employed to estimate non-use values is contingent valuation (CV), whereby value is determined through a survey of peoples' preferences in hypothetical market situations in which people state what they would do in a given situation(s) (Walton *et al.*, 2008). Residents are asked to state their maximum WTP for or, alternatively, their willingness to accept (WTA), specific intangible benefits and costs associated with an event. The aggregated WTP and

WTA provide an estimate of residents' perceived value of the intangible benefit and cost. Taken together, these (positive and negative) values will represent the net non-use value created by an event.

The cost of environmental impacts

Interestingly, Figure 7.2 attaches the above non-user values to the socio-cultural effects of a special event and not to the environmental effects, despite the historical relationship between the quest for environmental preservation and the TEV concept. In the evaluation of the WOW festival, the environmental impacts are estimated to be negative as they range only over carbon emissions and ecological footprint. While this may be appropriate for most events, there are some that involve preservation of valued environmental resources (e.g. a wilderness area for cross-country skiing). The value attached to preservation of such areas will include the types of non-user values identified above.

For many environmental effects, imputed valuation methods can be used (Smith, 1999). These assume that the value of an environmental amenity can be determined through the actual costs that people pay either to avoid degradation of the amenity or to repair or replace that amenity if it becomes degraded. In the WOW study, the ecological footprint was converted into a monetary measure by estimates of land lease cost per hectare in the area where the event takes place, while tons of CO_2 equivalents associated with the event were estimated with regard to the market price for emission rights. To estimate the impact more accurately, a 'green' CGE model would need to be employed, capturing the net changes brought about by an event consequent upon a change in industry composition (UNEP, 2014).

Given that CV enables estimates of non-use values, these can be added to use values to estimate the TEV of an event. As always, the jurisdiction selected for event evaluation will determine whose values are accounted for.

Is a tool from the environmental arena appropriate for conceptualising use and non-use values in the event context? The conceptual framework provides a view on value creation of events, including both visitors (users) and local residents (non-users). While the concept of TEV is useful in distinguishing user and non-user values and some sub-categories of these, it is really a 'partial' CBA, omitting many types of costs and benefits that are included in a detailed CBA. For the proposed framework, displayed as Figure 7.2, there are several issues that need to be addressed.

1   Strictly interpreted, in the TEV framework the user values relate only to expenditures through market transactions, excluding the consumer surplus of event attendees. Omission of consumer surpluses of event attendees, however, would omit an important benefit category associated with events. This issue is recognised by Andersson *et al.* (2012), who state that it could be included as an additional positive socio-cultural impact of an event. In this respect, however, the standard CBA framework seems better suited

to include this type of event benefit, making clear distinctions between the consumer surpluses of both attendees and non-attendees. Destinations that neglect the importance of special events to their own residents cannot be expected to make informed decisions regarding either an appropriate 'events budget' or appropriate levels of funding for particular events that may be proposed.

2 In the TEV framework, the non-user values of option, existence, altruistic and bequest value underpin the various surpluses experienced by non-users of an event. With the CBA approach, the primary type of non-user value, which presumably would be the aggregate of different non-user values, has been labelled 'psychic income' (Mules and Faulkner, 1996). While CBA generally lumps together the different values associated with non-user WTP for an event to take place, the TEV framework provides a useful way to classify the main types of underlying motives. This is recognised by Andersson and Armbrecht (2014), who have recently argued that more detailed analyses of the dynamics of experiences during an event would also further our understanding of the event experience.

3 In a CBA, the estimate of consumer surplus is typically an important part of the benefits of an event. A CBA of an event would typically divide consumer surpluses into three categories: household consumer surpluses from direct enjoyment of the event (attendees), household consumer surpluses of attendees of offsite events/activities; and household benefits from indirect enjoyment of the event to non-attendees (Abelson, 2011). The first category is generally quite substantial as it captures the enjoyment of locals in attending an event. In the TEV framework, however, this consumer surplus is not captured in the direct expenditure less opportunity cost estimate, thus requiring additional estimation, as acknowledged by Andersson *et al.* (2012). The second category would fall under indirect user values, while the third would be included within the various types of non-user values.

4 If an EIA is undertaken using the TEV direct expenditure estimate, this would exaggerate the economic impacts (and particularly so if an I–O model is employed). Only 'injected' or 'new' money is relevant to the EIA – the expenditure of residents equates to 'transfers' only. Analysts using the TEV framework must ensure that resident expenditure is eliminated from direct user expenditure for the purposes of an EIA, as well as make adjustments to non-resident expenditure to take account of 'casuals', 'time switchers' and 'displaced' visitors (Jago and Dwyer, 2006). While researchers employing the TEV framework address the latter under 'opportunity costs' (see Figure 7.2), a further adjustment needs to be made to direct expenditure to eliminate that of residents in order to estimate the event's economic impacts. This does not apply to EIAs of the CGE variety.

5 The TEV framework omits *business surpluses*. Business surpluses associated with a special event are the additions to operating profits (after tax) accruing to local owners of businesses. These gains are associated with additional expenditure by visitors less the cost of resources to service this

expenditure (Abelson, 2011). Major events can drive higher than average net profits for the accommodation and hospitality sectors. This is partly due to government policy, which favours events that occur in the shoulder or off-peak tourism seasons when businesses are unlikely to be operating at full capacity and the marginal cost of supplying goods and services would be lower than average. In principle, this can be addressed by use of CV applied to the business sector. A more objective approach, and one which is much less labour intensive, may be to follow VAG (2007) and estimate the event-related change in business surpluses using the net injected expenditure generated by the event, and published data on the level of indirect taxes as a percentage of business turnover, the cost of inputs as a function of revenue less indirect tax and the direct company income tax rate (Dwyer *et al.*, 2016). Where such values appear in a revised TEV framework is uncertain. If the TEV framework is used for event evaluation, it would seem that business surpluses would most appropriately be included among the user values, both direct and indirect.

6   The TEV framework omits *labour surpluses* – the net benefits to local labour associated with event-related work, after compensation for working and tax paid. Additional employment can be an extra source of net benefit associated with a special event. When a worker would be otherwise unemployed or under-employed, the opportunity cost is the value of leisure foregone. A labour surplus occurs when event-related jobs go to unemployed or under-employed resident workers to meet visitors' extra demands for goods and services, and these workers are employed at a wage higher than that which they would be prepared to accept to enter into employment. The difference between the cost of labour, evaluated at the market wage rate, and evaluated at the shadow or reservation wage, is an additional benefit from the increased economic activity associated with an event. An objective measure of labour surplus has been proposed by VAG (2007), based on the net injected expenditure generated by the event, the proportion of expenditure spent on labour (wages bill), adjusted for the percentage of that done by extra local labour to meet the extra demand flowing from the event (that is not diverted from other employment in the destination) and the percentage of wage that represents a surplus to the additional labour employed (Dwyer *et al.*, 2016). Within the TEV framework, labour values would seem most appropriately included among the direct and indirect use values.

7   While CBA treats costs seriously alongside benefits, the TEV framework neglects the cost side of developing and operating special events. In particular many special events require the construction of stadia and other infrastructure that must be set against the benefits to estimate net benefits (positive or negative). In principle, the various event-associated costs (capital expenditures, operating costs, event-related costs incurred by government agencies, social and environmental costs) can be subsumed into the opportunity cost box of Figure 7.2. That said, the TEV framework seems geared to highlight the benefits side of events, downplaying the costs.

The application of the TEV framework to event assessment is in its early stages. Refinements will undoubtedly be made to this approach to take account of issues just raised and other problems that arise. Since it is a subset of CBA, its usefulness will be judged in terms of its ability to simplify event assessment or enhance its accuracy. The TEV framework certainly has some strengths in identifying the different bases of non-user values (option, existence, bequest and altruism) and pointing to useful research directions in this respect. Its conceptual basis for event assessment and its relevance for policy formulation is less clear at this time.

A hybrid approach

The standard approach to event evaluation has been for researchers and consultants to estimate the economic impacts of an event and then, alongside these, consider some of the possible wider effects of events that are not captured in the economic modelling, but which can be estimated using a formal CBA or welfare measuring CGE model. This has resulted in a less than satisfactory approach to event evaluation since the EIA and the CBA can give conflicting results.

Since CBA and standard EIA are quite different in their purpose, method and application, in the area of event assessment, taken in isolation, confusions may occur as to the policy implications of holding (or funding) a particular event. For example, a pre-event estimate of the economic impact of the Vancouver Winter Olympics 2010 concluded that the event would generate over $10 billion in provincial GDP and more than 200,000 jobs (Shaffer *et al.* 2003), while a CBA projected that the same event would generate net costs to the Province of British Colombia of $1.2 billion. In Australia, CGE simulations of a Formula One Grand Prix event projected that event-related expenditure of $58.4 million injected into the state of Victoria from interstate and overseas generated positive macroeconomic consequences, with real gross state product (GSP) up by $62.4 million, increased state taxes up $3.5 million and 400 new jobs in the state (full-time equivalents). In contrast to the CGE, with its positive economic impacts on the state of Victoria, a CBA of the same event showed a net loss (costs exceed benefits) of $6.7 million (VAG, 2007, p. 83).

Standard EIA and CBA focus on different aspects of the evaluation problem. CBA is the established technique for assessing the wider benefits and costs of a project and, as such, it is an appropriate framework for classification and measurement of the projected outcomes of an event. In contrast to standard EIA, which ignores non-market consumption benefits and third-party effects, CBA measures the event-related changes in all sources of economic welfare, whether occurring in markets or as implicit values.

In contrast to I–O modelling, which treats resident expenditure on an event simply as 'transferred' expenditure which is then ignored, CBA emphasises that the residents of a destination may benefit from an event. In making residents' values central to the assessment, CBA improves the information base for public sector decision-making, thereby assisting in the assessment of relative funding priorities. The projected net benefits of a special event represent the 'bottom line' for determining the extent, if any, of support from public funds.

While a CBA addresses the extent of net social benefit to the host destination from the event itself, it cannot measure the level of economic activity generated from the event or the wider flow-on effects. It is, essentially, a partial equilibrium solution to a general equilibrium problem, neglecting the general equilibrium, economy-wide effects of the injected expenditure from special events. In the case of many special events, particularly large or mega events, their outcomes are not aimed specifically at providing benefits to local consumers, but rather at attracting tourists and their expenditure from outside the region. This requires EIA to identify and measure the level of economic activity associated with the event such as increased income to households, GDP/GRP and taxation revenues, which a CBA cannot do. For mega events, in particular, CGE modelling would pick up general equilibrium impacts which the partial equilibrium CBA is not capable of detecting. However, the estimated economic impacts of a special event address narrower public policy objectives, providing an inadequate basis on which to decide the level of public funding support (if any) that should be given to a special event.

Given these mixed messages, it is little wonder that the policy implications of standard EIA and CBA approaches in event evaluation have become confused. Since neither technique is completely comprehensive, there is a need for an integrated approach to event evaluation that includes the advantages of each separate approach. Three types of integrative approaches may be identified. One approach is to estimate producer and labour surpluses, essential for CBA, directly from the simulated outcomes of a CGE modelling of an event's economic impacts (Dwyer et al., 2006; Dwyer et al., 2016). The advantage of this approach is that the CGE modelling informs the destination manager about the direct and indirect economic impact effects of the event, as well as inter-industry and taxation effects, while at the same time providing a basis for the estimation of the business and labour surpluses essential to a CBA. The approach has its limitations – there are various other event-associated costs and benefits (social and environmental effects) that are not included in these measures.

A second approach involves the development of measures of economic welfare by adding additional assumptions to the standard CGE model. This procedure measures the economic impacts (e.g. on GDP), but also includes a measure of welfare, based on various assumptions about labour supply and external inputs (Blake, 2005; Dixon, 2009; Dwyer et al., 2015). However, the welfare measures used in CGE modelling to date do not capture the full range of welfare effects associated with special events, though they are capable of so doing. This approach can also measure, and potentially value, wide-spread externalities, such as greenhouse gas emissions (Dwyer, 2015).

A third approach is also promising. On this approach, the primary technique, either CBA or CGE, is 'backed up' by the other. Proposing three criteria by which an integrative model may be assessed – existence of a net benefit/welfare measure, accuracy in estimating event impacts and completeness of the approach in capturing important benefits and costs – (Forsyth and Dwyer, 2017) have identified two alternatives which rate highly on each criterion. These are a welfare measuring CGE with CBA back-up, and a CBA with back-up from a welfare measuring CGE.

Many issues relevant to the development of an integrative approach to event assessment demand further exploration. In particular, estimation tools required to measure welfare effects associated with special events need more detailed attention from researchers. An important outcome of the dual approach is that the advantages and limitations of each approach are exposed and the methods refined for future research.

Conclusions

There is growing recognition that no single approach is adequate to event assessment. Of the three major types of economic evaluation techniques, each has limitations. I–O modelling is both inaccurate given its unrealistic assumptions and overly narrow in scope. CGE provides more accurate assessments of event impacts, but, in the absence of a welfare measure, the estimates have limited policy significance. CBA can, in principle, measure all direct costs and benefits to residents and visitors associated with a special event, but cannot handle general equilibrium effects. A variant of CBA, using the TEV framework for event assessment, has yet to demonstrate its superiority over the CBA approach, which it falls under.

There is a growing recognition that the different approaches need to be integrated in some way. We have argued that some initial steps have been taken in this, but no accepted framework for evaluating the various types of event impact has been developed as yet. An approach is recommended that bridges the gap between welfare measuring CGE and CBA, in a way that has policy relevance for destination managers. The challenges arising from the task of estimating the net benefits of special events as part of a more analytical and evidence-based justification for the level of government funding support should dominate the economic research agenda regarding special events in the future.

References

Abelson, P. (2011). Evaluating major events and avoiding the mercantilist fallacy. *Economic Papers*, 30(1), 48–59.

Ahlert, G. (2001). The economic effects of the Soccer World Cup 2006 in Germany with regard to different financing. *Economic Systems Research*, 13(1), 109–27.

Aldred, J. (1994). Existence value, welfare and altruism. *Environmental Values*, 3(4), 381–402.

Andersson T.D. and Armbrecht, J. (2014). Factors explaining the use-value of sport event experiences. *International Journal of Event and Festival Management*, 5(3), 235–46.

Andersson, T.D. and Lundberg, E. (2013). Commensurability and sustainability: triple impact assessments of a tourism event. *Tourism Management*, 37, 99–109.

Andersson T.D., Armbrecht, J. and Lundberg, E. (2012). Estimating use and non-use values of a music festival. *Scandinavian Journal of Hospitality and Tourism*, 12(3), 215–31.

Andersson T.D., Armbrecht, J. and Lundberg, E. (2015). Triple impact assessments of the 2013 European athletics indoor championship in Gothenburg. *Scandinavian Journal of Hospitality and Tourism*, November, 1–22.

Baade, R. and Matheson, V. (2002). Bidding for the Olympics: fool's gold? In C.P. Barros, M. Ibrahimo and S. Szymanski (eds), *Transatlantic Sport: The Comparative Economics of North American and 20 European Sports*. London: Edward Elgar, pp. 127–51.

Blake, A. (2005) *The Economic Impact of the London 2012 Olympics*. Research report 2005/5. Nottingham: Christel DeHaan Tourism and Travel Research Institute, Nottingham University.

Boardman, A., Greenberg, D., Vining, A. and Weimer, D. (2011). *Cost–Benefit Analysis: Concepts and Practice* (4th edn). Chicago: Prentice Hall.

Bohlmann, H.R. (2006). Predicting the economic impact of the 2010 FIFA World Cup on South Africa. Working Paper Series: 2006–11. Department of Economics, University of Pretoria. Retrieved from https://www.researchgate.net/publication/24116729_Predicting_the_Economic_Impact_of_the_2010_FIFA_World_Cup_on_South_Africa, accessed 20 August 2016.

Crompton, J.L. (2006). Economic impact studies: instruments for political shenanigans? *Journal of Travel Research*, 45, 67–82.

Crompton, J.L. (2010). *Measuring the Economic Impact of Park and Recreation Services. Research Series*. Ashburn, VA: National Recreation and Park Association.

Dixon, P. (2009). Comments on the productivity commission's modelling of the economy: wide effects of future automotive assistance. *Economic Papers*, 28(1), 11–18.

Dwyer, L. (2012). Cost benefit analysis. In L. Dwyer, A. Gill and N. Seetaram (eds), *Research Methods in Tourism: Quantitative and Qualitative Approaches*. Cheltenham: Edward Elgar, pp. 227–41

Dwyer, L. (2015) Computable general equilibrium modelling for tourism policy: inputs and outputs. Statistics and TSA Issues Paper Series, UNWTO, Madrid.

Dwyer, L. and Forsyth, P. (2009). Public sector support for special events. *Eastern Economic Journal*, 35(4), 481–99.

Dwyer, L. and Jago, L. (2012). Economic contribution of special events. In S. Page and J. Connell (eds), *A Handbook of Events*. London: Routledge, pp. 162–77.

Dwyer, L., Forsyth, P. and Spurr, R. (2004). Evaluating tourism's economic effects: new and old approaches. *Tourism Management*, 25, 307–17.

Dwyer, L., Forsyth, P. and Spurr, R. (2005). Estimating the impacts of special events on the economy. *Journal of Travel Research*, 43(May), 351–9.

Dwyer, L., Forsyth, P. and Spurr, R. (2006). Assessing the economic impacts of events: a computable general equilibrium approach. *Journal of Travel Research*, 45, 59–66.

Dwyer, L., Jago, L. and Forsyth, P. (2015). Economic evaluation of special events: reconciling economic impact and cost–benefit analysis. *Scandinavian Journal of Hospitality and Tourism*, 1–15.

Fisher, A.C. (2000). Investment under uncertainty and option value in environmental economics. *Resource and Energy Economics*, 22(3), 197–204.

Fleischer, A. and Felsenstein, D. (2002). Cost–benefit analysis using economic surpluses: a case study of a televised event. *Journal of Cultural Economics*, 26(2), 139–56.

Forsyth, P. and Dwyer, L. (2017). *Evaluating events: comparison of alternative approaches*. Forthcoming.

Giesecke, J.A. and Madden, JR. (2011). Modelling the economic impact of the Sydney Olympics in retrospect: game over for the Bonanza story? *Economic Papers*, 30, 218–32.

Gratton, C., Dobson, N. and Shibli, S. (2000). The economic importance of major sports events: a case-study of six events. *Managing Leisure*, 5(1), 17–28.

Hede, A.M. (2007). Managing special events in the new era of the triple bottom line. *Event Management*, 11(1–2), 13–22.

Jago, L. and Dwyer, L. (2006). *Economic Evaluation of Special Events: A Practitioner's Guide*. Altona: Common Ground.

Jago, L., Dwyer, L., Lipman, G., van Lill, D. and Vorster, S. (2010). Optimising the potential of megaevents: an overview. *International Journal of Event and Festival Management*, 1(3), 220–37.

Mabugu, R. and Mohamed, A. (2008). The economic impacts of government financing of the 2010 FIFA World Cup. Stellenbosch Economic Working Papers: 08/08. Stellenbosch: University of Stellenbosch.

Madden, J.R. (2006). Economic and fiscal impacts of mega sporting events: a general equilibrium assessment. *Public Finance and Management*, 6(3), pp. 346–94.

Marzano, G. and Scott, N.R. (2006). Consistency in destination branding: the impact of events. In *Global Events Congress and Event Educators Forum*. Brisbane: University of Queensland Press, pp. 196–205.

Matheson, V. (2002). Upon further review: an examination of sporting event economic impact studies. *The Sport Journal*, 5(1), 1–7.

Mules, T. and Faulkner, B. (1996). An economic perspective on special events', *Tourism Economics*, 2, 2.

Pillay, U. and Bass, O. (2008). Mega-events as a response to poverty reduction: the 2010 FIFA World Cup and its urban development implications. *Urban Forum*, 19(3), 329–46.

Preuss, H. (2007). The conceptualisation and measurement of mega sport event legacies. *Journal of Sport and Tourism*, 12(3–4), 207–28.

Richardson, L. and Loomis, J. (2009). The total economic value of threatened, endangered and rare species: an updated meta-analysis. *Ecological Economics*, 68(5), 1535–48.

Shaffer, M., Greer, A. and Mauboules, C. (2003) *Olympic Costs and Benefits*. Vancouver: Canadian Centre for Policy Alternatives, February.

Smith, V.K. (1996). *Estimating Economic Values for nature: Methods for Non-Market Valuation*. Cheltenham: Edward Elgar.

UNEP (2014). *Using Models for Green Economy Policymaking*, Green Economy, United Nations Environmental Programme, www.unep.org

VAG (Victorian Auditor General) (2007). *State Investment in Major Events*. Victoria: Victorian Government, May.

Walton, H., Longo, A. and Dawson, P. (2008). A contingent valuation of the 2012 London Olympic Games: a regional perspective. *Journal of Sports Economics*, 9(3), 304–17.

8 Economic valuation of events

Combining methods based on revealed, stated and subjective preference data

Reza Mortazavi and Tobias Heldt

Introduction

Economic valuation of an event boils down to the evaluation of changes in the welfare of everyone who is directly or indirectly affected. The best way to make this evaluation is through a comprehensive cost–benefit analysis (CBA) (Mules and Dwyer, 2006). The basis of a CBA is to calculate benefits and costs and assert that activities that have a positive net present value are desirable from the society's point of view.

However, a comprehensive CBA is very demanding in terms of the information required. It must be determined whose benefits and costs should count and the effects must be quantified and valued in monetary terms (Boardman *et al.*, 2014). It may not always be straightforward to assess how the effects should be measured and quantified. Some of the effects may relate to goods and services that do not have an obvious market price. Nevertheless, since these goods and services are often publicly funded (for example, major sporting events), the benefits and costs should be valued in monetary terms.

A fundamental economic measure of the benefit a person receives from consuming a unit of a good or service is that person's willingness to pay (WTP) for that unit. Normally, the marginal benefit is assumed to be diminishing, which implies that WTP decreases for additional units. This gives rise to a downward sloping demand curve.[1] Total benefits to the consumers can then be calculated by integrating the aggregate demand curve. Consumer surplus (CS) is the net benefit when the expenditures (that is, price multiplied by quantity) have been deducted from the total benefits. Change in CS can be used to measure the impacts of a policy – for example, price change. The total benefits to the society are the sum of the CS and the producer surplus (PS). The latter is what producers receive in addition to the minimum amount they would be willing to accept for producing and selling one unit of a good or service. This element is less problematic with respect to valuation since sales, revenues and profits are already measured in monetary terms. Economic impact analysis – of events, for example – usually focuses on features that are mostly related to the PS – for example, the extra revenues received by local businesses.

Estimating CS is quite straightforward for goods and services that are traded in a market. In these cases, CS is the difference between what the consumers pay and the maximum they would be willing to pay (area under the demand curve above the price level). The same exercise is not as simple for goods and services that are not traded in a market – that is, those that have no clear market price, such as valuation of and estimation of demand for environmental goods (Kolstad, 2000). In such contexts, a fundamental concept is the distinction between price and value. When a consumer buys a market good with a price tag of $x, we could say that the consumer values that good as at least $x since he/she actually purchases the good at that price. However, 'things' that do not have a price tag do not necessarily lack value. Often, the impacts of a project (such as an infrastructure project or a special event) concern features that are not uncomplicatedly valued. For example, one of the most important benefit elements from an infrastructure project is travel time savings, the value of which is not always obvious. Economic valuation of some of the aspects of an event, say the sense of pride local people feel about hosting the event, is not obvious either. Also, even if some parts of an activity are priced, such as an entrance fee paid to enter a park or a festival, this fee may not include the additional costs to get to the park or the festival and, hence, the value of the activity.

Moreover, valuing something does not necessarily mean the direct consumption or use of that thing. Some things are valued for their mere existence. For example, some people may be willing to pay for a heritage site such as the Acropolis in Athens or the Peace and Love festival in Borlänge, Sweden, even if they actually never visit the place or event.

Various methods have been developed to estimate the value of non-market goods. The origins of these methods go back to the valuation issues concerning public goods such as air quality or a public park (Pearce, 2002). These methods can be divided into two categories: revealed and stated preference methods. Both methods concern various ways to infer monetary values for consumers' preferences. Revealed preference (RP) methods use information on actual behaviour in a related market (hedonic pricing) or in the consumption of the good or participation in an activity (travel cost method) to estimate the demand and, hence, the economic value of a good, resource, service, or activity. Stated preference (SP) methods use surveys in which people are asked about their WTP for a good or service. For example, a study may ask a sample of individuals the maximum amount they would be willing to pay to attend a festival under certain conditions.

A main difference between RP and SP methods is that, while RP methods may only capture the use-value[2] of something, SP methods may also capture the non-use values. Furthermore, while RP methods measure values based on observed behaviour, SP methods use hypothetical scenarios and may therefore suffer from hypothetical and response biases, especially when non-use values are concerned. These factors have led to criticism of SP methods (Kahneman and Knetsch, 1992; Hensher, 2010).

Shaw and Rogers's (2005) extensive literature review found very few articles in which the above-mentioned methods were used to estimate non-market values of events and festivals. Hence, the purpose of the present chapter is to introduce methods for estimating values of events and how these can be used for comparing the socio-economic values of events.

The above-mentioned measures of welfare and welfare changes, such as CS, are based on translation into monetary units. The focus is on the consumption of goods and services that bring the individual utility or satisfaction. Within this utility maximisation principle, income and prices determine the level of utility or satisfaction. Also, on a more aggregate level, the welfare level of nations has been measured by the level of income, such as gross domestic product (GDP) per capita. However, GDP fails to cover many aspects of social progress, such as income inequality, social cohesion and leisure and other non-market activities. Due to these shortcomings, other measures of a nation's well-being have been developed such as a human development index (HDI) (Fischer, 2009). This measure incorporates not only economic growth, but also other aspects such as life expectancy and educational level. Another indicator of the state of welfare within a society is perceived or subjective well-being (SWB). The concept of SWB and its average in the population is increasingly being seen as a relevant proxy for welfare and welfare change. SWB has been defined as "an individual's evaluation of the extent to which he or she experiences positive or negative affect, happiness, or satisfaction with life" (Frey, 2008, p. 3). It is often referred to as 'life satisfaction' or 'happiness' and is normally measured through surveys that ask people how satisfied they are in general with their lives (Kahneman and Krueger, 2006; Fischer, 2009).

The following section presents and discusses some recent attempts to economically value music events. The subsequent section shows how the method of stated choice can be applied to value welfare effects of events, including a short introduction to measuring SWB. To illustrate the method and how values can be estimated, a well-known Swedish music festival is used as a case of reference. The final section offers some conclusions.

Economic valuation of music festivals

How much a person is willing to pay[3] for leisure-related goods and services or to participate in leisure-related activities is the basic measure of that person's economic valuation of the service or the activity (see, for example, Peterson and Loomis, 2000). For example, the difference between the entrance fee and the maximum amount a person would be willing to pay to attend a music festival may be seen as that person's CS. Shaw and Rogers (2005) discussed use and non-use values of cultural events and festivals. Use values are attributed to the benefits that the attendees receive, while non-use values are attributed to factors such as some local residents being proud that their community offers a well-known event, even if those residents do not attend the event. Andersson *et al.* (2012) further divided the use values into two categories of direct and indirect use values. The former refer to the value of the core experience of attending a festival, while the latter refer to the experiences that arise outside a festival area, before, during and after the festival.

One non-market valuation method that is based on observed behaviour – that is, RPs – and is relevant for estimating use values is the so-called travel cost method (TCM). The basic idea that travel costs can be used as a proxy for price to value non-market goods was proposed by Harold Hotelling in 1947 as a response to a park service director on how to estimate the economic value of the park. Clawson and Knetsch (1966) applied and developed the idea further, which inspired many later studies on valuation of recreational sites.

TCM is based on the idea that the demand for a recreation site or an event, such as a music festival, can be derived based on the travel costs (time and money) incurred in getting to the event. A crucial assumption of the TCM is that people respond to a price change in the same way as they do to a change in travel cost. TCM should be applied to evaluate the economic benefits of a festival when travel, and hence a travel cost, is actually involved (many non-locals attend the festival and come from different geographical places, which means there is a variation in travel distance).

Applications of TCM to value the economic benefits of music events seem to be rare. One exception is Prayaga *et al.* (2006), who applied TCM to estimate the economic value of Gemfest in Australia. Another example is Heldt and Mortazavi's (2016) study, which provides detailed descriptions of how estimations of CSs are done in practice. That study found that the estimates of CS were sensitive to the functional form of the trip-generating function. Also, the estimates were very sensitive to whether time costs were included in travel costs; the estimates were almost twice as high if the time costs were included. The CS was in the range of 27–89 million SEK, depending on functional form.

Choice experiment applied to a music festival

An alternative approach to TCM to value benefits from a music festival is to use an SP method. Examples include contingent valuation, conjoint analysis and choice experiments (see Pearce *et al.* (2002) for a summary guide). In a contingent valuation survey, respondents are asked to state their WTP for something. In a conjoint analysis, different alternatives are defined by multiple attributes with varying levels and respondents are asked to rate or rank different combinations in descending order of preference. Choice experiment (CE) is basically the same, except that the different combinations are presented to the respondents as different choice options and the respondents are asked to make a choice from the choice set (Holmes and Adamowicz, 2003). The respondents are usually presented with a choice pair and asked to choose one of them. A general disadvantage of the SP methods is that they are based on hypothetical scenarios and valuations, which means the derived WTP values may suffer from this hypothetical bias compared to WTP values based on RPs (Hensher, 2010). The advantage is that many different situations can be simulated with a degree of variation in attributes and levels that is not always possible in actual markets. Furthermore, these methods can be used to estimate non-use values.

As was the case for TCM, it appears that few studies have used SP in general, and CE in particular, to value benefits from events in general or music festivals in particular. An exception is Andersson *et al.* (2012), who applied contingent valuation, which is a different type of SP method than CE, to estimate use and non-use values of a music festival (the Way Out West Festival in Gothenburg, Sweden). In the following, we illustrate the use of CE methodology to estimate economic values of different attributes of a music festival, such as the duration and number of attendees.

The Peace and Love music festival

Our case and data used in this study come from the 2012 Peace and Love festival, held in Borlänge, Sweden, from Tuesday, 25 June to Saturday, 29 June. The festival was established in 1999 as a movement to offset the increased violence that had escalated in the 1990s in the local area of Borlänge, a mid-sized town of approximately 50,000 people located some 180 kilometres north-west of Stockholm. Fewer than 1,000 people attended each of the first few years of the festival, but by 2006 the festival had approximately 30,000 visitors and has continued to grow. The number of visitors peaked in 2011, with 50,000 tickets sold. In the year of our analysis (2012), 48,621 tickets were sold.

Data were collected by a survey directed to 1,005 visitors to the 2012 Peace and Love music festival. Data collection followed a strategy to reduce selection bias. Visitors at the festival filled out a self-complete questionnaire on site within the festival area. The survey asked questions about the characteristics of the individual visitors, such as their gender, age, place of residence and their travel costs and chosen accommodation. The survey also contained a CE, as will be described in detail below. Further descriptions of data collection procedure and questionnaire can be found in Heldt and Olofsson (2011, 2012).

The choice experiment

The choice question for the CE was, "Which festival would you choose?" Before the respondents were asked to answer that question, they were presented with a description of the choice setting – that is, a scenario (see Figure 8.1). This description included the task of choosing between two options for the Peace and Love festival. The two options were described as being the same except for differences in three attributes: the price, the number of days the festival lasted for and the number of people attending the festival. The meaning of the three attributes had been described to the respondent prior to the choice question. Table 8.1 shows the attributes and the levels for each attribute in the CE.

The CE itself was conducted by providing the respondent with a scenario and the task of choosing among two alternatives according to Figure 8.1.

Figure 8.1 Example of choice set for the Peace and Love choice experiment

Choice set 1	Peace and Love A	Peace and Love B
Ticket price	1,345 SEK	1,745 SEK
Number of visitors	40,000	60,000
Number of days	4	5
I would choose:	Peace and Love A	Peace and Love B
I would refrain from visiting Peace and Love		

Table 8.1 Attributes and levels used for the choice experiment

Attribute	Description	Level
Price	Ticket price for the complete festival. It includes entrance fee for all days but not access to the camping area	1. 1,345 SEK 2. 1,645 SEK 3. 1,745 SEK 4. 1,945 SEK
Number of visitors	States the number of tickets that have been sold and is an estimate of the total number of visitors to the festival	1. 20,000 visitors 2. 40,000 visitors 3. 60,000 visitors
Number of days	States the number of days for the festival. It includes the Peace and Love forum that starts the festival	1. 4 days 2. 5 days 3. 6 days

Assume that you are confronted with the choice of buying tickets for the Peace and Love festival. There are two types of Peace and Love festival and you have to choose one of these. The only thing that differs between the two alternatives is the *price, number of visitors* and *number of days*. The festivals have the same bands as this year's festival, the same location and the same time of year. Which festival would you choose? You also have the option to refrain from visiting the festival.

The respondents made a choice between the Options A and B. There was also a third option to choose neither Option A or B. Only nine individuals in the sample chose this latter option – hence, these observations were disregarded in the final analysis.

Each respondent answered two choice sets; that is, each questionnaire included two choice sets. In total, the CE included 24 different choice sets constructed using a factorial design and distributed randomly to 12 different questionnaire versions (see Louviere *et al.* (2000) for details on the design of CE). Given the experimental design, CE can be used to estimate CS, but also visitors' preferences for attributes related to the choice scenario.

In a CE, the respondents must weigh the different attributes against each other. More formally, it is assumed that individuals compare the utility attached to each option and select the option with the highest utility. Since not every factor affecting choice is known with certainty, there is an element of unpredictability from the analyst's point of view. This so-called random utility framework is common when the purpose is to estimate WTP. The utility function can be written as: $U_{in} = V_{in} + \varepsilon_{in}$ where U_{in} is the total utility of alternative i for the individual n, V_{in} is the observable component or the indirect utility function, which is often assumed to be a linear function of the attributes of the alternatives, ε_{in} is the random unobserved component. The logit model, which assumes that the error part is independently and identically Gumbel-distributed, is commonly used to estimate the parameters of the indirect utility function. Based on this model, the probability of alternative i being chosen is calculated by: $P_{in} = \dfrac{\exp\left(V_{in}\right)}{\Sigma_{j \in J}\exp\left(V_{jn}\right)}$ where J is the total number of alternatives.

The logit model can be used to estimate the CS of the festival. The so-called log-sum (Small and Rosen (1981); Train (2003)) based on the binary logit is $\Delta E\left(CS\right) = \dfrac{1}{\beta}\left[\ln\left(\exp\left(V_i^1 + V_j^1\right)\right) - \ln\left(\exp\left(V_i^0 + V_j^0\right)\right)\right]$, which can be used to measure changes in the CS. The parameter β is the marginal utility of income, which is often replaced by a cost or a price variable. Applied to the Peace and Love festival, the data provides an average estimate of CS of 24.2 MSEK with a 95 per cent confidence interval of 17–31.4 MSEK.

The conditional logit model can also be used to estimate the effect of each attribute on the utility. However, in order to capture some observed individual heterogeneity, the attributes are also interacted with the age of each individual. The reason for just using one individual specific characteristic is to keep the model simple. The variable Age is used because it correlates with other variables such as income. The indirect utility function V_i (dropping the individual subscript) associated with option i is assumed to be $V_i = \beta_0 + \beta_1 x_{1i} + \beta_2 x_{2i} + \beta_3 x_{3i} + \beta_4 x_{2i} \times A + \beta_5 x_{3i} \times A$ where x_1 = Entrance price, x_2 = Number of attendees, x_3 = Number of days the festival lasts, $x_2 \times A$ is the interaction between attendees and age and $x_3 \times A$ is the interaction between number of days and age. The results are reported in Table 8.2.

According to the results in Table 8.2, ceteris paribus, the higher the entrance price the lower the utility, as expected. The effect of the two other attributes – number of attendees and days – now depends on the age of the individual. The primary interest here lies in WTP measures for the attributes. The marginal rate of substitution between two attributes, say x_1 and x_2, is defined as $MRS = -\dfrac{\partial V/\partial x_2}{\partial V/\partial x_1}$. The value of an additional day, for example, is the marginal rate of substitution between money and the festival lasting an extra day. Considering that the marginal utility of the attributes, number of attendees and days all vary with the age of the individual, we can estimate these for each individual in the sample. The average WTP for having the festival lasting one day longer is 60 SEK. The average WTP to avoid an additional

Table 8.2 Results from the conditional logit based on the choice experiment data

Attributes	Coefficient	Standard error	Z	P-value
Constant	−.2171754	.112941	−1.92	0.054
Entrance price	−.0021691	.0003155	−6.88	0.000
Attendees	.008692	.0096506	0.90	0.368
Attendees × Age	−.0009172	.0003808	−2.41	0.016
Days	.8600977	.229815	3.74	0.000
Days × Age	−.0301603	.0090907	−3.32	0.001
Number of observations	601			
LR chi2(6)	102.96			
(P-value)	(0.0000)			
Pseudo R²	0.1236			
Log likelihood	−365.01			

1,000 visitors attending the festival is 6.2 SEK. The WTP to avoid additional attendees may indicate over-crowding or that the price is too low in relation to demand, which also indicates that there is a considerable consumer's surplus related to the existing price.

Subjective well-being as a measure of welfare

Subjective well-being (SWB) can been defined as "an individual's evaluation of the extent to which he or she experiences positive or negative affect, happiness, or satisfaction with life" (Frey, 2008). The research literature uses SWB as a substitute for the term 'happiness'. Research in many different fields has shown a positive relationship between SWB and various individual expressions related to welfare. One example is volunteers, who regularly report being happier and claim to feel better than non-volunteers, on average (ibid.). Another example is Aknin *et al.*'s (2010) finding that SWB is positively affected by pro-social spending – for example, spending money to help others.

The most common SWB measurement is a direct question regarding current life satisfaction: "All things considered, how satisfied are you with life as a whole nowadays?" The scales have varied between different studies, but it is currently common to use an 11-step scale ranging from 0 (dissatisfied) to 10 (satisfied), as used, for example, by Michaelson *et al.* (2009) and the European Social Survey (2010).

Happiness and well-being are usually measured through surveys, though the method is not conclusive since well-being and happiness may be influenced by the cultural and social context at the time the aforementioned question is asked. Well-being fluctuates during the day, depending on performed activities. This has led some researchers to propose a method whereby well-being is measured at several points during the day, with a weighted average equalling the individual's happiness level (Kahneman *et al.*, 2004). Moreover, positive expectations affect well-being and happiness to the extent that many are happier in anticipation of a holiday than during the actual holiday (Nawijn *et al.*, 2010).

In relation to the welfare effects of events, we continue to use the case of Peace and Love to explore whether there is a correlation between individual WTP and individual subjective values of well-being. In the survey at the Peace and Love festival, the respondents were asked the following question: how satisfied are you with your life in general on a scale of 0–10? The average response was 7.9 with a standard deviation of 1.8.

Table 8.3 presents the estimates from a simple regression in which WTP to avoid more attendees at the festival is the dependent variable, while subjective value of well-being – which we will call 'happiness' – is one of the independent variables.[4]

The results indicate a statistically significant correlation between happiness and WTP to avoid more festival-goers, controlling for a few other variables. On average, people who are more satisfied with their lives have higher WTP to avoid an overly crowded festival. The same applies to visitors with a higher formal level of education. On average, the WTP decreases with the festival ticket price and travel cost, which could be due to the total budget considerations. We also see that, on average, females are less willing than males to pay to avoid too many attendees than males.

Concluding discussion

This chapter has introduced and discussed the economic valuation of events. We have explained that the measure of an individual's benefit from consuming a good or service is that person's WTP. In aggregate, the welfare benefits of visitors to an event are summed into the CS. The total benefits to the society are the sum of the CS and the PS.

To illustrate how benefits from a music festival can be valued in practice, we used the non-market valuation technique of CE to obtain an average estimate of CS for the Peace and Love music festival in Sweden. Moreover, we illustrated that the method could be used to estimate the effect of each

Table 8.3 Results from a regression of willingness to pay to avoid more attendees on subjective well-being and some other independent variables

Variables	Coefficient	Standard error	t-value	P-value
Constant	1.553036	.5503993	2.82	0.005
Happiness	.1772371	.0550328	3.22	0.001
Ticket price	−.0003172	.0001253	−2.53	0.012
Education	2.20013	.1106174	19.89	0.000
Travel cost	−.0005581	.0002135	−2.61	0.009
Female	−.6862846	.2033001	−3.38	0.001
Number of observations	526			
$F_{(5, 520)}$	44.34			
(P–value)	(0.0000)			
R^2	0.2989			
Adjusted R^2	0.2922			

attribute on the utility. For example, the average WTP for the festival to last one extra day was found to be 60 SEK. Finally, SWB or happiness is increasingly being seen as a relevant proxy in relation to discussions of welfare and welfare change. The concept of SWB was introduced and brought together with estimations of WTP for features of the event. The results indicated that there was a statistically significant correlation between happiness and WTP to avoid more attendees at the festival. The general policy implication of such a result would be that, with knowledge of what influence individual's happiness, event producers and other actors have the opportunity to increase the overall welfare of society.

However, it should be noted that we have discussed and demonstrated methods to evaluate events that are based on SP methods – that is, choices made in hypothetical settings. These methods may suffer from different sorts of biases. Also, even though we found a correlation between WTP for an attribute of an event and the respondents' stated level of life satisfaction, it is not clear how one can use this result as a monetary measure of welfare. In the case of observed or stated choices, one can estimate the value of an attribute as the marginal rate of substitution between money and that attribute, based on a utility maximisation principle. More research is needed about the proper way to translate measures of SWB into monetary valuation of welfare changes.

Notes

1 The so-called inverse demand curve, with price on the vertical axis and quantity on the horizontal axis, is meant in this text.
2 Pearce *et al.* (2006) defined use and non-use values as follows: use values concern the actual usage of the good or service (such as a visit to a national park), while non-use values are categorised into existence value, altruistic value and bequest value.
3 An alternative measure is willingness to accept (WTA), which measures the minimum amount of money a person is ready to accept to give up an object in his/her possession. WTA measures may be relevant when a policy implies that some people or a whole society have something taken away and must be compensated for it. Also a WTA measure might be preferable to WTP since the latter depends on income. Hanemann (1991) offers an in-depth analysis of the differences between WTP and WTA.
4 We also ran a regression of willingness to pay for the length of festival on the same independent variables as in Table 8.3, but did not report it, due to space constraints; this regression also indicated a significant correlation between 'happiness' and willingness to pay.

References

Aknin, L.B., Barrington-Leigh, C.P., Dunn, E.W., Helliwell, J.F., Biswas-Diener, R., Kemeza, I. and Norton, M.I. (2010). *Prosocial Spending and Well-Being: Cross-Cultural Evidence for a Psychological Universal* (NBER Working Paper 16415). Cambridge: National Bureau of Economic Research.
Andersson, T.D., Armbrecht, J. and Lundberg E. (2012). estimating use and non-use values of a music festival. *Scandinavian Journal of Hospitality and Tourism*, 12(3), 215–31. doi:10.1080/15022250.2012.725276

Boardman, W., Greenberg, D.H., Vining, A.R. and Weimer, D. (2014). *Cost-Benefit Analysis: Concepts and Practice* (4th edn). New Jersey: Pearson Education.

Clawson, M. and Knetsch, J.L. (1966). *Economics of Outdoor Recreation.* Baltimore: Johns Hopkins University Press.

European Social Survey (2010). Retrieved from: www.europeansocialsurvey.org, accessed December 2010.

Fischer, J.A.V. (2009). Subjective well-being as welfare measure: concepts and methodology. MPRA Paper 16619. University Library of Munich, Germany.

Frey, B.S. (2008). *Happiness: A Revolution in Economics.* Cambridge, MA and London: MIT Press.

Hanemann, W.M. (1991). Willingness to pay and willingness to accept: how much can they differ? *The American Economic Review*, 81(3), 635–47.

Heldt, T. and Mortazavi, R. (2016). Estimating and comparing demand for an event using stated choice and actual visitor behavior data. *Scandinavian Journal of Hospitality and Tourism*, 16(2), 130–42. doi:10.1080/15022250.2015.1117986

Heldt, T. and Olofsson, M. (2011). *Peace and Love 2011: Estimating The Festival's Economic Impact Using Segmentation* (In Swedish: *Uppskattning av festivalens ekonomiska betydelse via segmenteringsansatsen*). Högskolan Dalarna – Arbetsrapport, No. 6, Högskolan Dalarna, Borlänge. ISBN: 978-91-85941-39-1

Heldt, T. and Olofsson, M. (2012). *Peace and Love 2012.* Memo, Högskolan Dalarna, Borlänge.

Hensher, D.A. (2010). Hypothetical bias, choice experiments and willingness to pay. *Transportation Research Part B*, 44(6), 735–52. dx.doi.org/10.1016/j.trb.2009.12.012

Holmes, T.P. and Adamowicz, W.L. (2003). Attribute-based models. In P.A. Champ, K.J. Boyle and T.C. Brown (eds), *A Primer on Non-Market Valuation.* Dordrecht: Kluwer Academic.

Kahneman, D. and Knetsch, J. (1992). Valuing public goods: the purchase of moral satisfaction. *Journal of Environmental Economics and Management*, 22, 57–70.

Kahneman, D. and Krueger, A.B. (2006). Developments in the measurement of subjective well-being. *Journal of Economic Perspectives*, 20(1), 3–24.

Kahneman, D., Krueger, A.B., Schkade, D., Schwarz, N. and Stone, A. (2004). Toward national well-being accounts. *AEA Papers and Proceedings*, 94(2).

Kolstad, C.D. (2000). *Environmental Economics.* New York: Oxford University Press.

Louviere, J.J., Hensher, D.A. and Swait, J.D. (2000). *Stated Choice Methods: Analysis and Application.* Cambridge: Cambridge University Press.

Michaelson, J., Abdallah, S., Steuer, N., Thompson, S., Marks, N., Aked, J., Cordon, C. and Potts, R. (2009). *National Accounts of Well-being: Bringing Real Wealth onto the Balance Sheet.* London: New Economics Foundation.

Mules, T. and Dwyer, L. (2006). Public sector support for sport tourism events: the role of cost–benefit assessment. In H. Gibson (ed.), *Sport Tourism: Concepts and Theories.* London: Routledge, pp. 206–23.

Nawijn, J., Marchand, M.A., Veenhoven, R. and Vingerhoets, A.J. (2010). Vacationers happier, but most not happy after a holiday. *Applied Research Quality Life*, 5, 35–47.

Pearce, D. (2002). An intellectual history of environmental economics. *Annual Review of Energy and the Environment*, 27, 57–81.

Pearce, D., Özdemiroglu, E., Bateman, I., Carson, R.T., Day, B., Hanemann, M., Hanley, N., Hett, T., Jones-Lee, M., Loomes, G., Mourato, S., Sugden, R. and Swanson, J. (2002). *Economic Valuation with Stated Preference Techniques: Summary Guide.*

London: Department for Transport, Local Government and the Regions. Retrieved from: https://www.gov.uk/government/uploads/system/uploads/attachment_data/file/191522/Economic_valuation_with_stated_preference_techniques.pdf, accessed 15 October 2015.

Pearce, D., Atkinson, G. and Mourato, S. (2006). *Cost–Benefit Analysis and the Environment: Recent Developments*. Paris: OECD.

Peterson, G.L. and Loomis, J.B. (2000). Trends in leisure value and valuation. In W.C. and D.W. Lime (eds), *Trends in Outdoor Recreation, Leisure, and Tourism*. Cambridge, MA: CABI, pp. 215–24. doi:10.1079/9780851994031.0215

Prayaga, P., Rolfe, J. and Sinden, J. (2006). A travel cost analysis of the value of special events: Gemfest in Central Queensland. *Tourism Economics*, 12(3), 403–20.

Shaw, W.D. and Rogers, J. (2005). *Review of Non-market Value Estimation for Festivals and Events: A Discussion Paper*. Retrieved from: https://www.researchgate.net/profile/William_Shaw4/publication/237610666_Review_of_Non-market_Value_Estimation_for_Festivals_and_Events_A_Discussion_Paper/links/0f31752f3e5161c21d000000.pdf, accessed October 2015.

Small, K.A. and Rosen, H.S. (1981). Applied welfare economics with discrete choice models. *Econometrica*, 49, 105–30.

Train, K. (2003). *Discrete Choice Methods with Simulation*. Cambridge: Cambridge University Press.

9 Valuing the inspirational impacts of major sports events

Girish Ramchandani, Richard Coleman, Larissa Davies, Simon Shibli and Jerry Bingham

Introduction

In the UK, the potential benefits, and hence the value, of hosting major sporting events are well articulated in the event evaluation framework *eventIMPACTS*. This is an online resource which enables those who stage events to assess the impacts of their events on a number of different dimensions, notably: economic; environmental; media coverage; place marketing; and social impacts. An increasingly important social impact is evaluating the potential of events to inspire people to engage in increased levels of participation in sport and active recreation. Reducing physical inactivity is a desired outcome of investment that resonates with policy-makers world-wide, given its negative health effect on various diseases and life expectancy (Lee *et al.*, 2012). The value proposition is this: sporting events can provide the conditions whereby people are receptive to messages or influences that can lead to a change in attitude or indeed behaviour.

This notion that events can deliver positive externalities has been part of UK policy rhetoric for 30 years since the publication of the Coe Report (Coe, 1985). Even though the evidence, to date, of sport and physical activity legacies associated with major sports events is inconclusive, their use as a policy tool to foster participation has been documented in a number of countries. Hogan and Norton (2000) provide specific examples of strong political belief in favour of the inspirational value of elite performance underpinning sport development policy in Australia, New Zealand and the USA. Weed *et al.* (2009) liken such political and policy-making thinking in relation to the potential physical activity and sport benefits of major events to the 'Wimbledon effect', through which there is claimed to be an increase in the use of tennis courts in the UK in the two to three weeks around the All England Lawn Tennis Championships (Wimbledon) each year.

This chapter is concerned with research conducted in the run-up to the 2012 Olympic and Paralympic Games, which evaluated the potential of major sporting events to inspire people to increase their participation in sport and active recreation. In the first instance, we analyse the potential of events to stimulate attitudinal changes towards participation in sport and active recreation; we then report on a follow-up study investigating whether or not attitudinal change had converted into actual behaviour change some 12 months later.

Political context

There is a heightened political context that underpins this chapter surrounding the International Olympic Committee's decision in July 2005 to award the 2012 Olympic and Paralympic Games to London. Paris was widely perceived to be the city most likely to win the right to stage the Games and London was a distinct second favourite. What is thought to have been a deciding factor in London's favour was the pledge to deliver a lasting legacy, which was subsequently operationalised into four legacy outcomes. Of particular relevance to this chapter is the promise to harness the UK's passion for sport to increase grassroots participation, particularly by young people – and to encourage the whole population to be more physically active (DCMS, 2010).

In England (one of four nations that comprise the UK and home to 84 per cent of the UK's population), two targets were set for the planned increases in participation in sport and physical activity. The first target was to achieve 1 million people taking part in *more sport*. This target was designed to increase the proportion of the population taking part in three 30-minute bouts of moderate intensity sport per week (the 3 × 30 indicator). In essence, this target was about converting people who were already doing one or two 30-minute bouts of moderate intensity sport per week into people who achieved the 3 × 30 indicator. The second target was to achieve 1 million *more people* taking part in sport and physical activity more generally. In business strategy parlance, the intentions behind the sport and physical activity targets can be described as attempts to drive up the demand for these products on two broad market segments, namely the already active and the inactive. These are best articulated by using the Ansoff Matrix, as shown in Figure 9.1.

The first target, to encourage 1 million people to do more sport, is a market penetration strategy as it is predicated on the existing market for sport (participants) consuming a product (sport) that they already consume more intensively. In short, market penetration is concerned with persuading already active people to become even more active. By contrast, 1 million more people doing sport and physical activity is a market development strategy as it seeks to attract current non-consumers (i.e. sedentary people) to the existing products of sport and physical activity. Market development is concerned with converting inactive people into active people. In policy terms, while both market penetration and market development are laudable aims, the latter is perceived as being the 'Holy Grail' for governments because it is through a market development effect that the proportion of the population taking part in sport and active recreation increases.

Participation legacies of sports events

Evidence that mega events such as the Olympic Games create a 'demonstration effect' or 'trickle-down effect', whereby people are inspired by elite sporting events and as result increase their participation in physical and sporting activity, is both mixed and limited. Mahtani *et al.* (2013) carried out a review of systematic reviews to examine if there is an increase in participation in physical or sporting activities

		PRODUCTS	
		Existing	New
MARKETS	Existing	**Market penetration** *1 million people doing more sport* *e.g. 1 x 30 and 2 x 30 achieving 3 x 30*	**Product development**
	New	**Market development** *1 million more people doing sport and physical activity* *e.g. 0 x 30 achieving at least 1 x 30*	**Diversification**

Figure 9.1 Ansoff Matrix
Source: Adapted from Ansoff (1965)

following an Olympic or Paralympic Games and concluded that there was a paucity of evidence to support the notion that it leads to increased participation in the host country. A previous systematic review of the health and socio-economic impacts of major events by McCartney *et al.* (2010) was inconclusive. It cited evidence that found that there was an upward trend in sport participation from the early 1980s until 1994 in association with the 1992 Barcelona Olympic Games, but in other cases, such as the 2002 Manchester Commonwealth Games, overall participation decreased by 2 per cent. Weed *et al.*'s (2009) systematic review of the evidence for developing a physical activity and health legacy from the London 2012 Olympic and Paralympic Games similarly suggested mixed evidence for a demonstration effect on participation. In both systematic reviews the quality of evidence was considered to be poor. Other studies of specific mega events have drawn similar inconclusive findings (e.g. Veal, 2003). Even if there was evidence that participation in sport had increased after hosting a major sporting event, this does not mean that any such increase is necessarily attributable to hosting the event. It is concerning this issue of attribution that our study reveals some interesting issues and complexities.

There is some evidence that actually participating in non-mega events has a positive impact on engagement in sport, although the longitudinal effects of increased participation are unknown. For example, Bowles *et al.* (2006) concluded that novice cycle riders significantly increased their participation one month after a mass participation cycling event. Lane *et al.* (2008) showed that the

Dublin mini marathon engaged far more than just already active women within the Irish population and that training for the event was an important stimulus to action for most participants. Furthermore, Crofts *et al.* (2012) examined the physical activity patterns of participants in a women-only mass participation triathlon event and found that 50 per cent of women who were considered 'insufficiently' active before the event remained 'sufficiently' active three months later. However, there is little (if any) evidence on the link between attending a non-mega event in a non-participant capacity (i.e. as a spectator) and subsequent increases in sports participation.

Conceptual models of participation and engagement in sport

There are numerous theories that have been used to explain participation and engagement in sport and physical activity and several authors have identified these previously. Boardley (2013) and Foster *et al.* (2005) outlined some of the more popular theories applied in this context including Bandura's social cognitive theory and self-efficacy theory (Bandura, 1996, 1997), Deci and Ryan's self-determination theory (Deci and Ryan, 1985; Ryan and Deci, 2000), Ajzen and Madden's (1986) theory of planned behaviour, Fishbein and Ajzen's (1975) theory of reasoned action and Prochaska *et al.*'s (1992) transtheoretical model (TTM). Boardley (2013) suggested that these models reveal several themes that have relevance to the debate surrounding the potential for a demonstration effect resulting from major events, including confidence and competence; attitudes and norms; and stages of participation.

Weed *et al.*'s (2009) systematic review of literature for developing a physical activity and health legacy from the 2012 Olympic and Paralympic Games identified three models that have been widely used to examine engagement with sport and physical activity, although none of them were originally developed in this context. These are the TTM model (Prochaska *et al.*, 1992), the exercise adoption model (EAM) (Brooks *et al.*, 1996) and the psychological continuum model (PCM) (Funk and James, 2001). A common theme of these models is that each suggests a staged process of engagement in physical activity and sport and describes initial stages or processes that relate to changes in attitude, intention and awareness, rather than actual behavioural change with participation as a defined outcome (Boardley, 2013).

The TTM is the most widely adopted and researched in the literature relating to engagement with sport and physical activity (e.g. Marshall and Biddle, 2001; Foster *et al.*, 2005; Spencer *et al.*, 2006; Weed *et al.*, 2009). Originally developed within the psychology discipline to understand addictive behaviours, the TTM suggests that modification of behaviour involves progression through five stages: pre-contemplation (not ready, no intention of becoming active), contemplation (getting ready, thinking about becoming physically active), preparation (ready, making small changes in physical activity behaviour), action (meeting a criterion of activity, but only recently) and maintenance (meeting a criterion of activity for a sustained period of time). The TTM is a dynamic framework where people move forwards and backwards through stages in the process of change (Mair and Laing, 2013). An adaptation of the model to the notion of inspiration and participation is shown in Figure 9.2.

The TTM allows us to understand *when* change occurs (stages of change) and *how* change occurs (process of change). Prochaska *et al.* (1992, p. 1107) suggested that change processes are "covert and overt activities and experiences that individuals engage in when they attempt to modify problem behaviours". They go on to suggest ten change processes that have been identified across various health-related problems (see Figure 9.3). If physical inactivity or under-activity is considered to be the problem behaviour and, by attending an event, people become inspired to do more sport or physical activity, then inspiration is acting as a catalyst for, and predictor of, change.

Mair and Laing (2013) suggested that the first three stages and associated processes can be considered to have an attitudinal dimension, focusing on changing attitudes, with the fourth and fifth stages and associated processes having behavioural dimensions. It is therefore the early stages of the TTM that appear to be most susceptible to messages delivered through events and the points at which the inspiration effect, as an intermediary outcome, may later influence the process of behaviour change.

It is likely that, in the early stages, inspiration gained from attending an event increases people's awareness of sport (conscious raising) and gives them belief in their own ability to change (self-liberation). The latter processes of change (behavioural), such as helping relationships (finding people supportive of change) and stimulus control (using reminders and cues that encourage positive participation behaviour), are more likely to be linked to strategies, interventions and programmes seeking to help people increase exercise behaviour. It is unclear whether inspirational effects increase the likelihood of staged progression towards participation (market development and market penetration) or influence different 'early' stages for existing participants and non-participants.

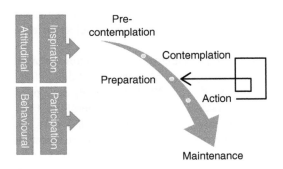

Figure 9.2 Stages of change (TTM)

Source: Adapted from Prochaska *et al.* (1992) and Mair and Laing (2013)

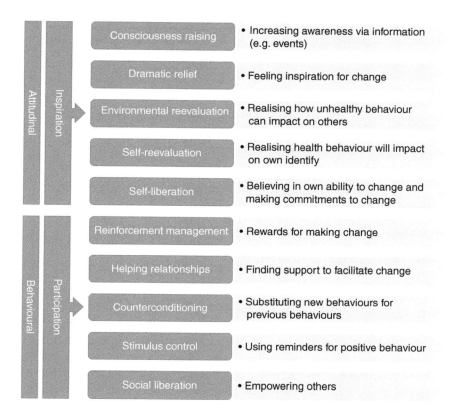

Figure 9.3 Processes of change (TTM)
Source: Adapted from Prochaska *et al.* (1992) and Mair and Laing (2013)

Methods

The research was conducted in two phases. The first phase (Phase I) was concerned with identifying whether there was an inspiration effect which could be measured at the attitudinal level among spectators at ten events held in England between 2010 and 2012. That is to say, as a result of attending a sporting event, did those who were interviewed say that the event motivated them to want to do more sport and active recreation? By contrast, the second phase (Phase II) followed up with a sub-sample of those who provided contact details for subsequent research and was concerned with measuring actual behaviour change among a cohort who had already reported an attitudinal change. The research was concerned solely with adults, who are defined as people aged 16 years or over.

In Phase I, a standard self-completion questionnaire was used at each of the ten events. The content of the questionnaire was essentially the same throughout,

Table 9.1 The events

Event	Location and dates	Unique specta-tors (estimated)	Phase I sample	Phase II sample
Women's Hockey Champions Trophy	Nottingham 10–18 Jul 2010	5,100	781	52
Triathlon World Championships Series	London 24–25 Jul 2010	14,300	781	31
Women's Rugby World Cup	Guildford/London 10 Aug–5 Sep 2010	8,800	750	50
World Junior Rowing Championships	Eton Dorney 4–7 Aug 2011	2,947	752	35
London Grand Prix Athletics	Crystal Palace 5–6 Aug 2011	Not known	793	32
World Badminton Championships	Wembley 8–14 Aug 2011	15,265	768	39
BMX Supercross World Cup Series	Stratford, London 19–20 Aug 2011	5,112	778	54
Trampoline and Tumbling World Championships	Birmingham 17–20 Nov 2011	5,719	741	53
European Figure Skating Championships	Sheffield 23–29 Jan 2012	5,786	465	NA
UCI Track Cycling World Cup	London 16–19 Feb 2012	16,210	849	88

albeit with some new response options being added to certain questions for the 2011 and 2012 events. Overall, nearly 7,500 responses were achieved across the ten events. Nine of the ten events (excluding the athletics event) were funded by UK Sport, the national agency responsible for elite sport and major events, who commissioned the programme of research. An overview of these events and the sample size achieved in each instance is presented in Table 9.1.

While it cannot be claimed that the samples were fully representative of the crowds who attended each event, on each occasion we sought to achieve what we considered to be a reasonably representative cross-section of spectators in terms of age, gender and ethnicity within the limited windows of opportunities available to interview. Steps to ensure that the survey samples collected during fieldwork were reasonably representative of their population included: professional research design; training interviewers to Market Research Society standards; overseeing fieldwork by using senior staff at the events; and interviewing as many spectators in as many different locations as possible to minimise bias.

In Phase II, respondents from Phase I who had provided their contact details were invited to complete an online survey approximately one year following the conclusion of each event in order to explore actual changes in their post-event participation behaviour and contributory factors. In the case of the track cycling event, the follow-up period was six months in order to minimise any contamination effects caused by the build-up to the London 2012 Olympic Games. No follow-up research was undertaken with the figure skating sample; therefore the Phase II research focused on nine events. The online questionnaire was emailed to 1,441 eligible respondents, of whom 434 (30 per cent) responded with fully completed surveys. While this is a good response rate for an online survey, the sub-samples across the events were too small for event by event analysis and thus our analysis focuses on the pooled headline data only.

A limitation of the research is that it relies on a self-report methodology, which could be affected by response bias and thereby undermine the validity of the findings. During both phases of data collection, the research attempted to mitigate this issue by ensuring confidentiality of responses.

Results: Phase I

Phase I: Sample profile

Across the ten events, 53 per cent of the spectators were female and 47 per cent were male. Nearly a quarter of the sample was under the age of 25 (16–24: 24 per cent); some 43 per cent were aged 25–44; and, the rest (33 per cent) were aged 45 plus. Less than one in ten respondents considered themselves to have a disability (7 per cent). Around 90 per cent of respondents were UK residents, of whom 92 per cent classed their ethnic origin as 'white'.

Compared with the population generally, spectators surveyed at the sporting events were extremely active. Some 47 per cent of the sample undertook sport or recreational physical activity on a regular basis (at least three times per week for 30 minutes) and a further 42 per cent were occasional sports participants (i.e. they had done at least 30 minutes sport or physical activity on between one and 11 days in the four weeks before interview). The vast majority considered doing sport or physical activity to be a ('very' or 'quite') important part of their lives (89 per cent) and 51 per cent were supporting a particular athlete or team at the event at which they were interviewed.[1] Moreover, all ten events attracted substantial numbers of participants of the sport featured,[2] with, in most cases, high proportions of those participants also being club members of that sport. Clearly, then, those people who chose to attend the events in question were very different to the population as a whole in terms of their interest in and engagement with sport.

The inspiration effect

Figure 9.4 shows the headline level of inspiration reported by spectators interviewed at the ten events. Overall, around 57 per cent of respondents either 'agreed' or 'strongly agreed' that their event attendance had inspired them to do sport or recreational physical activity more frequently than they did normally. This is an average score across the sample of events. The inspiration effect was highest at the World Series Triathlon (76 per cent). The European Figure Skating Championships and the BMX Supercross event at the Olympic Park feature at the

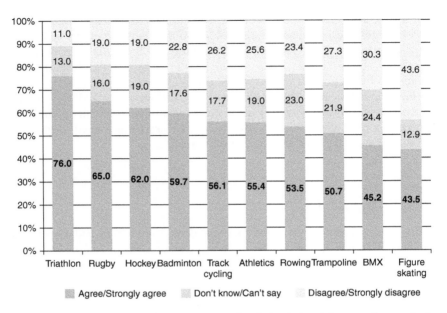

Figure 9.4 "I am inspired to do sport or recreational physical activity more frequently than I normally do": by event

lower end of the spectrum – less than half of the respondents at these events reported being inspired by them.

We speculate that the high inspiration effect at the World Series Triathlon event may be linked to the fact that running parallel to the elite event was a mass participation triathlon event at which many of the spectators were the friends and family of the amateur triathletes taking part. In this instance, it may have been the case that when spectators experience the considerable sporting endeavours of ordinary people like them, this may enhance the inspiration effect. By contrast, figure skating and BMX Supercross are highly technical and highly skilful sports that require specialist facilities. The levels of skill, equipment and facility required to take part in these sports are such that, while people enjoy watching the events, this may not translate so readily into an attitudinal change to do more sport.

Of those spectators who said they had been inspired, 57 per cent said their sense of inspiration was related to wanting to take part more often in the specific sport featured at the event.[3] This response was most common in the case of the World Badminton Championships, where 80 per cent of respondents said they would like to play badminton more often. On average, around 53 per cent said they felt inspired to do a sport other than the one featured at their event, or sport generally. This figure was considerably higher at the BMX World Cup (80 per cent) and the Grand Prix Athletics (76 per cent).

Who is inspired?

Among spectators at the ten events, the inspiration effect is above average in the 16–24 age group (70 per cent). This statistic falls to 58 per cent for 25–44 year olds and declines further to 47 per cent for those aged 45+, which implies a negative correlation between age and inspiration (see Figure 9.5). There is a gap of 23 percentage points between the most inspired age group (16–24: 70 per cent) and the least inspired age group (45+: 47 per cent). Differences in the inspiration effect are much more subtle when the data is broken down by gender, disability status and, for UK resident respondents, their ethnic origin. Even though black and minority ethnic (BME) groups reported, on average, a higher inspiration effect than the overall sample average for the ten events (62 per cent versus 57 per cent), BME groups also comprised a small proportion of respondents at each event.

As shown in Figure 9.5, inspiration is also positively associated with existing levels of participation in sport and physical activity. Of those spectators considered 'inactive' (zero days of activity in the past four weeks), around 40 per cent reported that they had been inspired to participate more frequently as a result of attending an event. This figure increased to 57 per cent for those who had undertaken occasional activity (one to 11 days of activity in the past four weeks), which in turn increased to 60 per cent for those considered to be regularly active (12+ days of activity).

As stated previously, taking part in sport and recreational physical activity was important to 89 per cent of the sample across the ten events. In addition, the more

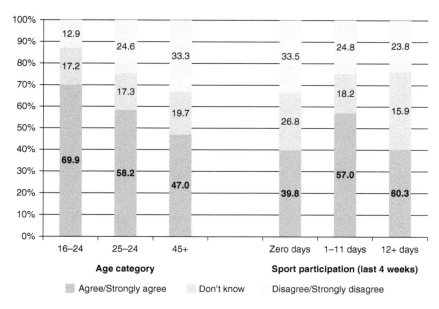

Figure 9.5 "I am inspired to do sport or recreational physical activity more frequently than I normally do": by respondents' age and participation levels

important sport was to respondents, the more likely they were to agree – and agree strongly – that they had been inspired by the event they had attended. The notion that the inspirational effect is felt more strongly by those already 'within' sport is further supported by results that consider respondents' participation in the sport featured at each event. Around 65 per cent of those spectators who took part in the sport featured at the event that they attended reported that they had been inspired by their experience, whereas this figure fell to under 50 per cent for those who were non-participants.

These findings indicate two distinct but related conclusions. First, the inspirational effect itself can be felt by both active and inactive people; however the effect is more pronounced on those who are already active. Second, major events tend to attract spectators who take part in sport or physical activity much more often than the general population. As a result, the inspirational effect is 'communicated' through events to a greater number of active people than inactive people. If this is correct, then any inspirational effect generated by a major sporting event on spectators will primarily be a 'market penetration' effect, rather than a 'market development' effect (see Ansoff Matrix in Figure 9.1).

The study suggests that while major events are less successful at supporting market development, they can still have some impact in inspiring currently inactive people. Across the ten events, around 40 per cent of the respondents who indicated that they were not active sports participants at the time of interview reported an inspirational effect. Scaling this finding to the estimated number of inactive spectators at nine of the ten events[4] (*c.* 8,000), it could be claimed that some 3,200 individuals who were completely inactive in the four weeks prior to being interviewed at least felt inspired to take up sport as a result of their event experience.

Given that two out of five inactive people reported an inspirational effect, the action most likely to increase overall market development could be the introduction of measures designed to attract more inactive people to major sporting events.

Attitudinal changes and the likely causes of the inspiration effect

When 'inspired' spectators were asked to evaluate in more detail how their attitude towards taking part in sport and physical activity had changed, their most common responses were:

- being reminded about the enjoyment of sport (89 per cent);
- being inspired to get fitter (85 per cent); and
- a desire to improve their own ability or to achieve personal sporting success (80 per cent).

When asked to rate the particular features of an event that had resulted in the inspiration to do more sport or physical activity, spectators tended to highlight those things connected to the inspirational standard of the competition and athletes, as opposed to the ancillary presentation and 'show' of the event (see Table 9.2). The primary drivers of inspiration were: the 'skill and ability of the athletes' (63 per cent of respondents said that this factor had had a 'high' impact on them); the 'quality of the competition' (51 per cent); and, the 'performance of any team or athlete being supported' (46 per cent). Together, these findings all provide useful pointers for event organisers who may have an interest in maximising the sport development impact of a major event they are staging.

These surveys have sought to measure feelings of inspiration rather than absolute commitments to action. Although the results are largely positive, particularly in relation to the frequency with which those who are currently active participate and, to a lesser extent, stimulating sedentary audiences to take up sport, there is no guarantee that the motivation generated by spectating experiences actually translates into increased participation, whether in the near future or in the longer term. On the basis that people may need active encouragement to convert intention or aspiration into action, survey respondents were asked to indicate the degree of importance they attached to nine different types of intervention which might harness their inspiration, as shown in Table 9.3.

The highest scoring interventions (in terms of their importance) were both concerned with the provision of information: either about sports that people can do at an appropriate level given their fitness and ability (68 per cent of respondents rated this as 'very important' or 'quite important') or about local sports clubs (67 per cent). Moreover, information about opportunities to try sport as a family was also regarded as an important factor by nearly half (49 per cent) of inspired respondents. Interestingly, only one in ten respondents across the aggregate spectator sample reported receiving any such information at the event that they attended. These findings highlight the value of using major sporting events as an effective platform for sport providers to 'signpost' potential participants when

Table 9.2 Drivers of inspiration as indicated by spectators (%)

Factor	High	Moderate	Low	NoneN /A
The whole atmosphere	35	47	9	9
The physical environment in which the event is taking place	32	45	13	11
The skill and ability of the athletes	63	25	4	8
The quality of the competition	51	34	7	9
The performance of the team/athlete I have been supporting	46	30	6	18
Activities that have been going on around the main event	11	32	29	28
Information I've received while I've been at the event	6	21	27	46
The sense of being part of a big event*	32	38	15	15

Note: * Option included for 2011 and 2012 events only

Table 9.3 Potential levers to participation (%)

Factor	Very important	Quite important	Not particularly important	Not at all important	Don't know
Taster sessions in [featured sport] (or other sports) here at the event	16	27	32	13	12
Taster sessions in [featured sport] (or other sports) where I live	21	33	24	10	11
Information about sports that I can do where I live at a level that is appropriate to my fitness and ability	25	43	15	6	11
Information about local clubs or centres where I could have a go	26	40	16	7	10
The chance to talk to sports people about the right types of sport for me to try	20	37	24	9	10
The chance to meet athletes and hear how they got started in their sport	23	33	26	8	10
The chance to try sport in a non-threatening environment (with other inexperienced people)	25	37	20	8	11
The chance to try a new sport where I could meet new friends*	20	41	21	6	12
Information about opportunities to try sport as a family*	17	32	26	13	13

Note: * Options included for 2011 and 2012 events only

seeking to capitalise on the excitement and enthusiasm generated among those who attend them.

There are, of course, many subsequent causal factors beyond the control of a major event that determine whether people translate any sense of inspiration into actual behavioural change. These may include, for example, health issues, monetary and lifestyle considerations and the availability of opportunities to participate. What this study does show, however, is that major events can play an important role at the start of what is a complex process, sparking people's desire to participate or to participate more frequently, and signposting them towards the next stage of that journey. After the encouraging results of Phase I in demonstrating that there was a positive inspiration effect for the majority of the sample at the attitudinal level, Phase II was conducted to measure the extent to which this translated into actual behaviour change.

Results: Phase II

The Phase II sample

This section evaluates the findings from Phase II based on the cohort of 434 respondents who engaged with both phases of the research. Before presenting the main findings, we present a brief summary of the characteristics of the Phase II sample. There was a fairly even split between male (54 per cent) and female (46 per cent) respondents. The age breakdown of respondents was as follows: 14 per cent were aged 16–24; 46 per cent were 25–44; and, 40 per cent were aged 45 and over. The majority did not have a disability that limited their daily activities (95 per cent). Prior to their attendance at the events at which they were surveyed in Phase I, just over half (51 per cent) had taken part in some sport on average three or more days per week in the previous four weeks (very active) and a further 39 per cent had participated on one to 11 occasions (occasionally active), whereas 10 per cent were inactive during that period. Furthermore, 63 per cent had said during Phase I that they felt either strongly inspired (17 per cent strongly agreed) or inspired (46 per cent agreed) by a specific event to take part in sport more frequently than they did normally.

The level of participation in sport by the sample as a whole is worth putting into context with the adult population of England. Within the sample, 51 per cent met the 3 × 30 criterion whereas among the adult population in England as a whole the corresponding statistic was 21 per cent. When we consider people who took part in some but less than 3 × 30-minute bouts of moderate intensity activity per week, the sample score was 39 per cent and for all adults in England the score was 28 per cent. This, in turn, means that 10 per cent of the sample respondents were classified as inactive compared with 51 per cent of the population as a whole. We therefore conclude that the sample is atypical of the population by virtue of its much higher levels of sport participation, and that therefore the results should not be generalised more widely.

Changes in participation behaviour

Analysis of post-event data revealed different types of changes in participation behaviour of respondents following their attendance at one of the events.

- Overall, 35 per cent of the sample had either taken up sport, or increased their frequency of participation in sport, in the three months following their attendance at one of the nine events (an 'initial' increase).
- Some 61 per cent of respondents were doing about the same amount of sport in this period compared with their pre-event activity levels whereas only 4.6 per cent reported an initial decline in sport participation.
- Over two-thirds of those who reported an initial increase were still participating more often at the time of the follow-up survey (i.e. 12 months later, apart from the track cycling event) than they were prior to their event attendance. Hence, 24 per cent of the overall sample demonstrated a 'sustained' improvement in sport participation post-event.
- In addition, there was also a 'lagged' increase reported by 11 per cent of respondents (i.e. not initially but at the time of the follow-up survey).

While these findings provide some evidence of positive changes in activity behaviour among the sample, they do not imply that this was necessarily caused by and attributable to any event as these changes may well have occurred regardless of attendance at an event. The initial, sustained and lagged effects could therefore be regarded as being 'gross' rather than 'net' changes in participation. In order to test the extent to which an event may, in fact, have stimulated such a change, we have converted the 'gross' figures into 'net' figures. The conversion process takes into account two down-weighting factors.

- First, we discount the proportion of respondents who did not report being inspired by an event during Phase I of the research.
- Second, we consider the perceived level of influence on participation that respondents attributed to a given event. The event influence was measured on a four-point scale ranging from 'very influential' to 'not at all influential'.

The calculation of the net effects of event attendance on participation is presented in Table 9.4 and explained below.

As stated previously, some 35 per cent of respondents reported an initial increase in participation following their event attendance. During Phase I, around three-quarters of this group had reported that they felt inspired (to some extent) as a result of attending an event to participate in sport more frequently than they did normally. Consequently, the gross initial change had been reduced from 35 per cent to 26 per cent. The latter figure was adjusted further to account for the proportion of those who had increased participation initially and reported an inspiration effect, and who also cited their attendance at an event as being at least 'slightly influential' in leading them to do more sport. This adjustment meant that the net initial increase in participation was 24 per cent. This figure corresponds to an index score of 69, meaning that 69 per cent of any change in behaviour can be attributed to the event. Repeating this exercise

Table 9.4 Derivation of net changes in post-event participation

Calculation components		Initial increase	Sustained increase	Lagged increase
Gross change %	*A*	34.8	24.2	11.3
Inspiration factor %	*B*	75.5	74.3	73.5
Adjusted change %	*C (= A × B)*	26.3	18.0	8.3
Event influence factor %	*D*	91.2	94.9	86.1
Net change %	*E (= C × D)*	24.0	17.1	7.1
Index score	*F (= E / A × 100)*	69	71	63

revealed a net sustained increase of 17 per cent (index = 71) and a net lagged increase of 7 per cent (index = 63). It is interesting to note that for those reporting a lagged increase in participation, the index score of 63 is the lowest across the three groups and is primarily driven by a lower 'event influence factor' relative to the other two categories. These findings point to the conclusion that other contaminating factors must have been present and contributed at least in in part to the behaviour changes reported.

Those who reported any positive effects were asked to identify the broad sport categories in which they had increased their participation levels – that is, the sport featured at the event they were interviewed at or other sports and activities. This analysis is shown in Table 9.5, which demonstrates the reported changes expressed in terms of the overall sample (as opposed to only those who indicated some type of an increase).

There are two key findings that emerge from Table 9.5. First, the highest gross and net changes are found in sports and activities other than the sport featured at the event at which respondents were interviewed. This is a surprising finding as the basic thinking behind the 'demonstration' effect is that, having seen a particular sport demonstrated at an event, those who are inspired to take up sport would gravitate towards the sport featured in the event. Second, the index scores for other sports and activities are all lower than the corresponding scores for the featured sports. This, in turn, means that the catalytic effect or extent of attribution is lower for other sports and activities than for the sport featured at the event. This interpretation, in turn, supports the notion that other contaminating factors must also be involved.

There is some crossover between the two broad categorisations, with some respondents undertaking more of a particular sport and also other sports. This phenomenon explains why the sum of the two categories exceeds the overall figures (for each type of increase) explained previously.

The analysis thus far has not differentiated between those who were already active in sport and those who were not. Consideration of people's predisposition to sport is important in order to make inferences about the market penetration (people doing more sport) and market development (more people doing sport) potential of events. This concept is examined in the next section.

Table 9.5 Gross and net changes in sport-specific and other participation

		Initial increase	Sustained increase	Lagged increase
	Gross change %	20.0	13.4	6.5
Featured sport(s)	Net change %	15.4	10.6	4.4
	Index	77.0	79.3	67.9
	Gross change %	25.3	18.4	9.7
Other sports	Net change %	16.8	12.4	6.0
	Index	66.4	67.5	61.9

Respondent clusters

In this section we examine the data for the following four respondent clusters, which have been developed, based on their sport participation profile prior to them attending one of the nine events in this research:

• respondents undertaking sport on a regular basis (3+ times per week for at least 30 minutes at moderate intensity) and a participant in the sport that was featured at the event that they attended (34 per cent of the sample);
• respondents undertaking sport on a regular basis but a non-participant in the sport that was featured at the event that they attended (17 per cent of the sample);
• respondents not undertaking sport regularly but a participant in the sport that was featured at the event that they attended (23 per cent of the sample); and,
• respondents not undertaking sport regularly or at all and a non-participant in the sport that was featured at the event that they attended (26 per cent of the sample).

In broad terms, any increase in participation for the first two clusters corresponds to a market penetration effect and for the last two clusters a market development effect. The analysis for these clusters focuses on the net (rather than gross) increases in post-event participation as these are attributed by respondents to event attendance. Consistent with the overall picture, event-related behaviour change across all clusters is most likely to occur in the initial post-event period, with the majority of this increase being sustained six months to one year following an event; the lagged increases are generally modest in comparison (see Table 9.6).

There is also indicative evidence, given the small sub-sample sizes associated with each cluster, that the largest increases in initial and sustained participation were among infrequent sport participants who also took part in the sport featured at an event. Around one third of this group (32 per cent) increased their participation initially, with more than one in five (22 per cent) sustaining this increase. Conversely, those who were not regularly or not at all active and did not participate in the sport featured at an event were least likely to demonstrate positive changes in initial and sustained participation levels. However, this cluster was most likely to demonstrate positive lagged changes. Comparisons

between the different clusters also indicate limited variations in lagged participation effects.

Figure 9.6 presents the net changes in sport-specific and other participation,
whether initial or lagged, by the four clusters. There are only marginal differences
between the proportionate increases in the two categories of participation for the
two clusters involving existing participants in the sport featured at an event. For
the two other clusters involving non-participants in a specific sport, however, the
likelihood of increased participation in other sport was around twice as much as
any increase in the sport featured at the event. Thus, even though respondents
may not necessarily participate in the sport they watched at an event, the data for
this sample suggests that there have been wider market penetration and market
development effects that would probably not have been expected and which are
without precedent in the literature.

Attribution and impact of other factors

Events do not take place in a vacuum. Despite the evidence presented in favour
of the net effects of event attendance on increasing participation, it would be
somewhat naive to infer that by simply attending a one-off sporting event people
will be driven to be more active in sport, not least because of the sheer volume of
such events that audiences may experience on a regular basis. For example, UK
Sport helped to stage in excess of 100 major sporting events in the UK in preparation for the London 2012 Olympic and Paralympic Games. In recognising that
there may have been other influences on post-event changes in participation, we
present in Figure 9.7 the factors reported by respondents (over and above their
event attendance) that had some impact on their participation.

The two most influential factors were linked to watching other major sports
events (apart from those included in this research), either on television or live
at the event. The relative impact of other factors listed in Figure 9.7 (e.g. taster
sessions, meeting athletes etc.) might be limited by the extent to which

Table 9.6 Net changes by respondent clusters

Cluster	Increase type (%)		
	Initial	*Sustained*	*Lagged*
Regular sport participant and participant in featured sport	27.2	18.4	8.8
Regular sport participant and non-participant in featured sport	18.3	14.1	5.6
Infrequent sport participant and participant in featured sport	32.0	22.0	4.0v
Infrequent/non-sport participant and non-participant in featured sport	14.5	10.9	9.1
Overall	24.0	17.1	7.1

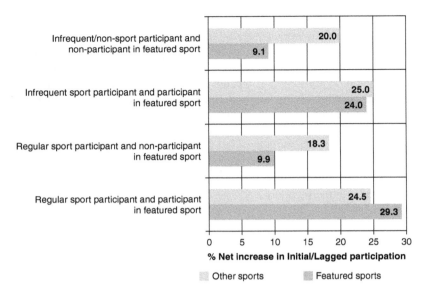

Figure 9.6 Net changes in sport-specific and other participation by respondent clusters

respondents had the opportunity to experience them between Phase I and Phase II. Moderate to strong correlations were found between the overall impact ratings of the factors and the impact ratings according to the different respondent clusters examined ($0.5 < r < 0.9$). Therefore, a broadly consistent pattern emerged in the importance of factors for each cluster, regardless of respondents' sport participation profile. The main implication of these findings is that the attribution of post-event net increases in participation by previously active and sedentary audiences to a specific event is not necessarily clear cut. In practice, various factors are likely to have an influence on behaviour change that compromises our ability to attribute any such change to attendance at a specific sporting event. At best events can be said to be contributory factors to attitudinal and behaviour change, but there is no evidence yet to isolate events *per se* and to claim that they have causal powers.

Conclusion

Historically, the 'value' of sporting events has been judged based on their ability to deliver direct economic/tourism benefits for the communities in which they are held. However, there is a growing acceptance that not all events that are 'major' in sporting terms are also 'major' in economic terms. Hence it is important to consider different types of value for which events can serve as a catalyst, including but not limited to social and environmental outcomes. The findings from this study have provided organisers and funders (primarily UK Sport in this instance)

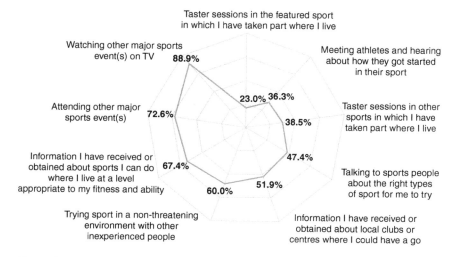

Figure 9.7 Influence of other factors on participation increases

Note: The data presented in this figure relates to respondents for whom there was a net change in initial or lagged participation

of ten events in England with an independent appraisal of the inspirational value created by their events in terms of promoting sport participation among those who attended them. The wider societal value of promoting sport participation is clear. Undertaking regular physical activity, including sport, is known to reduce the risk of many chronic health conditions and consequently helps to reduce healthcare costs. Taking part in sport also has a positive impact on the well-being and happiness of individuals.

If events are attended primarily by those who are already engaged in sport, then the scope for achieving market development effects would appear to be limited. While market penetration effects have their merits, in this context they do not lead to more people taking part in sport. Further thought is required about how those seeking market development effects can attract inactive individuals to sports events and have an inspirational impact on them that leads to positive behaviour change. In the context of the TTM, the research presented in this chapter has investigated the process of 'counterconditioning' (see Figure 9.3), namely the substitution of new behaviours for previous behaviours. The findings indicate that the counterconditioning process is more evident in the case of existing participants, which is in line with the evidence from previous systematic reviews (Weed *et al.*, 2009; McCartney *et al.*, 2010; Mahtani *et al.*, 2013). However, it is difficult to pigeonhole the changes in respondents' attitudes and behaviours to the specific stages of the TTM (see Figure 9.2) because the research was not set up to achieve this. This represents both a limitation of the current research and an area for consideration in the design of future research.

The results demonstrate that attendance at non-mega sports events can, to some extent, stimulate increases in participation at grassroots level. While these findings imply that there appears to be an inspiration effect, it is too simplistic to expose people to an event in the hope of changing their activity behaviour as they are inspired in different ways. In addition, despite the apparent positive changes, it can be problematic to attribute causality for improvements in activity behaviour to a single event, particularly in relation to any longer-term participation legacy. This is due to the range of factors that audiences may experience with the passage of time which may include contaminants such as other events and the simple act of watching other sports events on television. In terms of a value proposition, our evidence indicates that the inspirational effect of sports events and its subsequent potential to bring about measurable behaviour change is far more complex and nuanced than previously thought.

In order for events to drive the maximum possible sport participation benefits, certain mechanisms need to be in place. For example, watching a sports event might inspire someone to take up sport or increase their frequency of participation at a given point in time. However, how that feeling of inspiration (attitudinal change) is subsequently harnessed (e.g. through signposting and the provision of appropriate exit routes) will determine whether or not it eventually converts into sustainable behaviour change. There is, therefore, a need for greater cohesive working between the various event stakeholders (e.g. organisers, funders, sport development agencies and national governing bodies) and to build sport participation strategies well in advance of hosting an event. This view is also supported by Taks *et al.* (2014), who argue the case for formulating and implementing strategies and tactics in order to leverage sport participation outcomes. It is only then that any health and well-being benefits associated with increases in participation will be realised.

Notes

1   These two figures are based on nine events, excluding the European Figure Skating Championships, where this question was not asked.
2   In the case of the BMX and Track Cycling events, interviewees were asked whether they took part in those particular disciplines and/or other forms of cycling. At the Trampoline and Tumbling World Championships, interviewees were asked whether they took part in trampolining and/or other forms of gymnastics. A similar distinction was made at the European Figure Skating event between figure skating and other forms of ice skating.
3   For the Track Cycling, Trampoline and Figure Skating, this figure is based on the extent to which respondents at these events felt inspired to take part more often in those particular disciplines of the sports concerned, as well as other generic forms of the sport (i.e. cycling, gymnastics and ice skating).
4   Excluding the Aviva London Athletics Grand Prix, for which spectator numbers are not available.

References

Ajzen, I. and Madden, T.J. (1986). Prediction of goal-directed behavior: attitudes, intentions, and perceived behavioral control. *Journal of Experimental Social Psychology*, 22(5), 453–74. doi: 10.1016/0022-1031(86)90045-4

Ansoff, H.I. (1965). *Corporate Strategy*. New York: McGraw-Hill.

Bandura, A. (1996). *Social Foundations of Thought and Action: A Social Cognitive Theory*. Englewood Cliffs, NJ: Prentice-Hall.

Bandura, A. (1997). *Self-efficacy: The Exercise of Control*. New York: W.H. Freeman.

Boardley, I.D. (2013). Can viewing London 2012 influence sport participation? – a viewpoint based on relevant theory. *International Journal of Sport Policy and Politics*, 5(2), 245–56. doi: 10.1080/19406940.2012.671185

Bowles, H., Rissel, C. and Bauman, A. (2006). Mass community cycling events: who participates and is their behaviour influenced by participation? *International Journal of Behavioral Nutrition and Physical Activity*, 3(1), 39. doi: 10.1186/1479-5868-3-39

Brooks, C.M., Lindenfeld, C.M. and Chovanec, S.A. (1996). *Understanding Exercise Adoption Behaviour*. Boston, MA: International Health and Racket Sports Association.

Coe, S. (1985). *Olympic Review: Preparing for '88*, London: GB Sports Council.

Crofts, C., Schofield, G. and Dickson, G. (2012). Women-only mass participation sporting events: does participation facilitate changes in physical activity? *Annals of Leisure Research*, 15(2), 148–59. doi: 10.1080/11745398.2012.685297

Deci, E.L. and Ryan, R.M. (1985). *Intrinsic Motivation and Self-determination in Human Behavior* (3rd edn). New York: Plenum.

DCMS (Department for Culture Media and Sport) (2010). *Plans for the Legacy from the 2012 Olympic and Paralympic Games*. London: DCMS.

Fishbein, M. and Ajzen, I. (1975). *Belief, Attitude, Intention, and Behavior: An Introduction to Theory and Research*, Reading, MA: Addison-Wesley.

Foster, C., Hillsdon, M., Cavill, N., Allender, S. and Cowburn, G. (2005). *Understanding Participation in Sport: A Systematic Review*. London: Sport England.

Funk, D.C. and James, J. (2001). The psychological continuum model: a conceptual framework for understanding an individual's psychological connection to sport. *Sport Management Review*, 4(2), 119–50. doi: 10.1016/s1441-3523(01)70072-1

Hogan, K. and Norton, K. (2000). The "price" of olympic gold. *Journal of Science and Medicine in Sport*, 3(2), 203–18. doi: 10.1016/s1440-2440(00)80082-1

Lane, A., Murphy, N.M. and Bauman, A. (2008). *The Impact of Participation in the Flora Women's Mini-Marathon on Physical Activity Behaviour in Women*, Research Report 1. Ireland: Waterford Institute of Technology and Irish Sports Council.

Lee, I.M., Shiroma, E.J., Lobelo, F., Puska, P. Blair, S.N. and Katzmarzyk, T. (2012). Effect of physical inactivity on major non-communicable diseases worldwide: an analysis of burden of disease and life expectancy. *The Lancet*, 380(9838), 219–29. doi: http://dx.doi.org/10.1016/S0140-6736(12)61031-9

Mahtani, K.R., Protheroe, J., Slight, S.P., Demarzo, M.M.P., Blakeman T., Barton, C.A., Brijnath B. and Roberts, N. (2013). Can the London 2012 Olympics inspire a generation to do more physical or sporting activities? An overview of systematic reviews. *BMJ Open*, 3(1), e002058–e002058. doi: 10.1136/bmjopen-2012-002058

Mair, J. and Laing, J.H. (2013). Encouraging pro-environmental behaviour: the role of sustainability-focused events. *Journal of Sustainable Tourism*, 21(8), 1113–28. doi: 10.1080/09669582.2012.756494

Marshall, S.J. and Biddle, S.J.H. (2001). The transtheoretical model of behavior change: A meta-analysis of applications to physical activity and exercise. *Annals of Behavioral Medicine*, 23(4), 229–46. doi: 10.1207/s15324796abm2304_2

McCartney, G., Thomas, S., Scott, J., Hamilton, V., Hanlon, P., Morrison, D. and Bond, L. (2010). The health and socioeconomic impacts of major multi-sport events: systematic review 1978–2008. *BMJ*, 340(May), c2369–c2369.

Prochaska, J.O., DiClemente, C.C. and Norcross, J.C. (1992). In search of how people change: applications to addictive behaviors. *American Psychologist*, 47(9), 1102–14. doi: 10.1037/0003-066x.47.9.1102

Ryan, R.M. and Deci, E.L. (2000). Self-determination theory and the facilitation of intrinsic motivation, social development and well-being. *American Psychologist*, 55, 68–78. doi: 10.1037/0003-066X.55.1.68

Spencer, L., Adams, T.B., Malone, S., Roy, L. and Yost, E. (2006). Applying the transtheoretical model to exercise: a systematic and comprehensive review of the literature. *Health Promotion Practice*, 7(4), 428–43. doi: 10.1177/1524839905278900

Taks, M., Green, B.C., Misener, L and Chalip, L. (2014). Evaluating sport development outcomes: the case of a medium sized international sport event. *European Sport Management Quarterly*, 14(3), 213–37. doi: 10.1080/16184742.2014.882370

Veal, A.J. (2003). Tracking change: leisure participation and policy in Australia, 1985–2002. *Annals of Leisure Research*, 6(3), 245–77. doi: 10.1080/11745398.2003.10600924

Weed, M., Coren, E., Flore, J., Mansfield, L., Wellard, I., Chatziefstathiou, D. and Dowse, S. (2009). *A Systematic Review of the Evidence Base for Developing a Physical Activity and Health Legacy from the London 2012 Olympic and Paralympic Games.* London: Department of Health.

10 Understanding the value of events for families, and the impact upon their quality of life

Raphaela Stadler and Allan Jepson

Introduction

Drawing on previous conceptual and empirical research (Jepson and Stadler, 2017), this chapter explores the contemporary issue of quality of life (QOL) and opens critical discourse to ascertain how festival and event attendance could potentially improve QOL for families, individuals and communities. The research presented here clearly has overlap with many other areas of investigation such as: leisure provision, constraints and participation levels (see Hinch *et al.*, 2005), or designing events to enhance social interaction (see Nordvall *et al.*, 2014). Our focus here, though, is upon family orientated festivals and events. Our discussions of value are set in the context of what events mean to families and the potential family socialisation value they could gain from attending them, which in turn has the potential to enhance a family's overall QOL.

Our chapter begins with a review of literature which investigates and defines festival studies, the role of children within families, QOL research and individual and family QOL, in order to provide empirical and conceptual context to understanding the relationship between QOL, festivals and events. Following this discussion, our chapter explores current methods being used to capture and analyse empirical data in respect of QOL. We use our research methods (Jepson and Stadler, 2017) to demonstrate how QOL research is carried out in distinct stages. The subsequent section then presents analysis under the frame conditions of *time and space, money/wealth* and *rest, health and happiness*, which impact upon QOL and event attendance. The final section of our chapter draws conclusions from our current research in the area of QOL, it examines the gap between event research and praxis, and discusses the key conditions needed when families visit events – such as the potential for social bonding, belonging and attachment to place.

Festival studies

As a field of academic enquiry festival studies are deeply rooted and established within cultural anthropology and sociological fields of study, connected by a number of seminal works. Van Gennep (1909) discovered that the nature of ritual ceremonies accompanying the landmarks of human life was universal, apart from the detail – which varied from one culture to another. Turner (1969, 1974, 1982) documented the ritualistic liminal psychology associated with cultural festivals, events and rites of passage. Geertz (1973) theorised the role of rituals in social change and made us aware of the potential for conflicting views in society to be played out in the dramas created for ritualistic events and festivals. Abrahams (1982, 1987), in his research, discussed the symbolic meaning and importance of events and their multi-faceted components in a consumer-driven society. Falassi's (1987) book *Time Out of Time: Essays on the Festival* is thought to be the most cited literature in festival studies, either to set context and define or to seek to understand a festival's unique phases, patterns of behaviour, morphology, or its various rites of valorisation, conspicuous display, exchange, consumption and rites of competition. Manning's (1983) research was the first to explore the construction of festivals and the connections between festival development and its authenticity or perceived authenticity. The following discussions are used to contextualise individual and family QOL in the extant festival studies literature. Currently, there is a lack of understanding on the impact and value festivals can have on upon family QOL. The vast majority of research has focused primarily upon an individual's QOL. Our research demonstrates that there is a need for a stronger focus on families, friends, or groups of people within communities to better understand value creation and QOL. Therefore, our research aims to investigate and analyse the impact of festival and event attendance upon family QOL by highlighting the social values created through family event attendance.

The role of children within families

The role of children within the family has increased in importance over recent decades; this has been recognised since the mid- to late 1980s, with a steady increase in family-centred service delivery. This delivery is characterised by family choices, a family strengths perspective and further recognition of the family as a support unit to all members (Poston *et al.*, 2003). Research now shows that a family day out is more than just about satisfying adults, and that children's satisfaction comes above the needs of parents. For example, a Mintel Marketing Intelligence report (2004) revealed that from the top five enjoyment factors associated with going on a family holiday over 70 per cent of respondents wanted to engage in activities that their children would enjoy as opposed to more traditional antecedents such as weather and relaxation. Robinson (2008) adds to this debate by summarising that happy and satisfied children should result in happy and satisfied parents, guardians or carers. Further research, also by Mintel (2005), reveals that children like spending time with their families (85 per cent of seven year olds), although, as one might expect, this figure falls as children mature and seek to become more independent (71 per cent of 14 year olds). Robinson (2008) further adds to this debate by stating that parents, guardians or carers gain happiness and satisfaction from watching their children have fun and learn new things, especially if this aids their intellectual, physical or emotional development. Poria *et al.*'s (2003) research has similar findings and suggests that the increase in visits to stately homes and museums has a lot to do with the types of experience and educational re-enactments and activities which they promote. Light's (1996) research also noted that historical and cultural heritage sites lose out on attracting visitors due in part to a lack of practical experiences and facilities offered to children. They concluded that, although many sites appeared to be family friendly, there are issues surrounding what exactly this means and what is or should be included on site. Successful family attractions create memorable experiences and appeal to all age ranges; Robinson (2008) cites Thomas Land (within Drayton Manor Park and Zoo, Staffordshire) as a prime example which is based around the characters from the successful television series (and book) *Thomas the Tank Engine*. Its success is a model combining nostalgic memories for parents and present-day memories and association for children. This suggests that if the right environment is created for families then rewarding and enriching educational and cultural experiences are realised through parents and children. It can be concluded that family bonding and social cohesion are powerful leisure motivators, and that festivals and events can provide a platform for this to happen. Earlier research by Uysal *et al.* (1993) began to show that events can encourage family togetherness. This was reinforced by Crompton and McKay (1997), who found that the need for interaction and socialisation within the family is often inhibited by the independent actions of individuals in the home environment, which may be accompanied by a desire for culture enrichment outside the normal environment. Family togetherness, socialisation and resultant bonding can therefore be seen as the most important motivational influence for families attending festivals and events.

An introduction to quality of life research

The search for QOL has gained momentum and become a growing concern for individuals, families, communities and governments as a result of a rapidly changing world and a desire to find and sustain satisfaction, happiness and belief in the future (Eckersley, 1999; Mercer, 1994; Lloyd and Auld, 2002). Defining QOL is a hugely complicated task as it relates directly to a personal state of mind and all those factors which shape individual and group well-being (Rapley, 2003). The term well-being or 'bien-être', of French origin, can be traced back to the sixteenth century: "agréable procurée par la satisfaction des besoins du corps et ceux de l'esprit" ("an agreeable sensation procured from satisfying the needs of the body and those of the mind") (Pasquier, 1555, p. 301). QOL research has been approached from various academic fields: economics (Fox, 1974); marketing (Sirgy *et al.*, 1982; Sirgy *et al.*, 1985; Sirgy, 1986); population ecology and environment (Bubloz *et al.*, 1980; Murrell and Norris, 1983); public health (Murrell, 1973; Kimmel, 1977; Siegel *et al.*, 1978; Murrell *et al.*, 1982; Bell *et al.*, 1983; Nguyen *et al.*, 1983) and community psychology (Murrell, 1973; Hirsch, 1980; Mitchell *et al.*, 1981; Riger and Lavrakas, 1981). Rapley (2003, p. 27) summarises how the term QOL has been used in the literature in many different ways:

> Happiness; life satisfaction; well-being; self-actualization; freedom from want; objective functioning; "a state of complete physical, mental and social well-being not merely the absence of disease" (WHO, 1997: 1); balance, equilibrium or "true bliss" (Kant, 1978: 185); prosperity; fulfilment; low unemployment; psychological well-being; high GDP; the good life; enjoyment; democratic liberalism; the examined life (*pace* Socrates); a full and meaningful existence (cf. Sheldon, 2000).

A QOL theory was first developed by Sirgy (1986) from Abraham Maslow's (1954) human developmental perspective model. Maslow (ibid.) concluded that developed societies involve members who are mostly preoccupied in satisfying higher-order needs (social, esteem and self-actualisation needs), whereas less-developed societies involve members who are mostly preoccupied in satisfying lower-order needs (biological and safety-related needs). Sirgy (1986) recognised that QOL could also be defined in terms of the hierarchical need satisfaction level of most of the members within a society. Sirgy (ibid.) concluded that the higher the needs satisfaction of the majority in a given society, the greater the QOL of that society. From a festival studies perspective this is an important relationship as QOL goals could then be defined as: "the satisfaction of human and developmental needs in a community or society" (Sirgy, 1986, p. 331).

The discussion of hierarchical dimensions in both Maslow's (1954) and Sirgy's (1986) models, however, has its limitations. A major discussion point in relation to defining QOL is that it is inherently subjective as individuals assess themselves psychologically against multiple life domains and, in doing so, identify and prioritise the aspects of their life they feel are important for social and cultural well-being. Life domains are also value laden and do not necessarily fit into a hierarchical structure, such as education, family, health, job, friends and relationships, which relate to an individual's psychological space, where memories related to specific kinds of experiences and feelings are stored (Andrews and Withey, 1976; Campbell *et al.*, 1976; Day, 1978, 1987; Diener, 1984; Rapley, 2003). More recent studies in QOL, particularly within QOL marketing (Lee *et al.*, 2004), have relied on the development of satisfaction hierarchy models to explain the relationship between consumer well-being and life satisfaction. Life satisfaction is defined as a reflection of a person's considered evaluations of life or stages within it (Campbell *et al.*, 1976; Michalos, 1980; Diener *et al.*, 1985).

Defining individual and family quality of life

One of the first studies on family QOL by Kuyken (1995) was undertaken on behalf of The World Health Organization (WHO). The project set out to develop an international QOL assessment and, in doing so, produced multi-dimensional profiles of families across six main and 24 sub-domains of QOL. Kuyken (1995, p. 1405) defined QOL as an: "individual's perception of their position in life in the context of culture and value systems in which they live and in relation to their goals, expectations, standards and concerns". The identified six domains of QOL include: physical domain, psychological domain, level of independence, social relationships, environment and spirituality/religion/personal beliefs (Kuyken, 1995). Rapley (2003) highlights that the WHOQOL definition benefits from comprehensiveness and efforts to relate the idea to cultural, social and environmental contexts and to local value systems. While these QOL domains and the original definition are still used, a variety of theoretical and conceptual approaches have since been applied to the concept of QOL. Most of them, however, emphasise the importance of social relationships (and personal relationships in particular) and social values, as well as opportunities to participate in recreation/leisure in one way or another (ibid.). In relation to festival and event studies, researchers have thus far mainly focused on the individual's experience of QOL (see, for example, Small *et al.*, 2005; Liburd and Hergesell, 2009; Packer and Ballantyne, 2010; O'Shea and Leime, 2012). Family QOL considers all family members in terms of what it takes for them to have a good life and their "aggregated" perspective (Poston *et al.*, 2003, p. 139). Agate *et al.* (2009) found that it is not necessarily the amount of time that families spend together engaging in leisure activities, but how meaningful they are to individual family members and the family as a whole. Special events, for example, can provide such out-of-the-ordinary experiences, which bring the family together in different and new ways. In their study of 50 parents/guardians with children in Birmingham, Yorkshire and London, Foster and Robinson (2010) identified that children are crucial in the event decision-making process of families and parents are willing to compromise if the event is satisfying for the child(ren). 'Family togetherness' was thereby found to be the most important motivational factor, as well as having an impact on family QOL. Their study is, however, limited to motivational factors for attending events as a family and does not apply the broader concept of family QOL.

More recent studies in this area such as Tayler *et al.* (2006) looked at how a festival could help build relationships between parents and children to enrich a child's creativity. Packer and Ballantyne's (2010) research employed positive psychology theories to explore the impact of music festival attendance on young people's psychological and social well-being. Positive psychology, according to Seligman and Csikszentmihalyi (2000), seeks to understand and build upon those factors that can improve the QOL and enable individuals, communities and societies to thrive rather than just survive. Packer and Ballantyne's (2010) study offers a good insight into building theoretical frameworks to understand how festivals can impact on an individual's well-being. Their adapted framework utilised Laiho's (2004) psychological functions of music in adolescence, namely interpersonal relationships, identity, agency and emotional field. Packer and Ballantyne's (2010) framework also included psychological well-being (Ryff and Keyes, 1995), subjective well-being (Keyes *et al.*, 2002) and social well-being (Keyes, 1998). They found that the festival experience tended to begin months before people attended, and that the experience of attendance enabled a transitory state of subjective well-being which became a part of and strengthened a person's identity through strong emotional connections with music, people and place. Packer and Ballantyne's (2010) study found that feeling part of the festival performances was essential as this created a sense of belonging and enabled social integration during and beyond the event. Another interesting aspect of their research was the discovery that those who attended a festival every couple of years (rather than annually) reported a greater level of well-being outcomes than those who attended less or more frequently. Liburd and Hergesell (2008) conducted a preliminary study on the Wadden Sea Festival in Denmark to try to ascertain how a cultural event might influence individual participant's QOL. This study gave preliminary findings in regard to economic growth and tourism, but also went on to suggest that differentiation needs to take place between subjective definitions of QOL (Andereck *et al.*, 2007) and those concerned with life satisfaction (i.e. feelings of contentment or fulfilment with one's experiences in the world). This should be taken forward in future studies and psychological definitions which refer to the actualisation of one's self-potential (Liburd and Hergesell, 2008).

Foster and Robinson's (2010) paper was the first to explore families in the context of events; they did so by providing analysis of motivational factors that influence attendance. Their study provides useful context as it explored the role and importance of children as a key determinant in decision-making regarding the type of events which were attended. The study (ibid.) also identifies the key motivations for festival and event attendance as socialisation and family togetherness, which were previously identified in numerous other studies (Uysal *et al.*, 1993; Mohr *et al.*, 1993; Backman *et al.*, 1995; Scott, 1996; Schneider and Backman, 1996; Formica and Uysal, 1996, 1998; Crompton and McKay, 1997; Faulkner *et al.*, 1999; Lee, 2000; Tomljenovic *et al.*, 2001; Nicholson and Pearce, 2001; Lee *et al.*, 2004; Bowen and Daniels, 2005). Foster and Robinson (2010) identified children as the prime factors in deciding which type of festivals and events to visit and that their satisfaction comes ahead of that of parents', guardians' or carers'. It could be argued that studies by Usyal *et al.* (1993), Crompton and McKay (1997), Packer and Ballantyne (2010), Tayler *et al.* (2006) and Foster and Robinson (2010) give the closest connection to research on the value of festival and event attendance upon family QOL. However, no research within event or festival studies has investigated how family togetherness, socialisation and bonding could create social values and impact upon a family's QOL. Therefore, one could suggest that another research domain is emerging on 'family values and impact discourse'.

Appropriate methods to investigate the impact of events upon family quality of life

Based on the review of existing literature, significant gaps and a lack of understanding in regard to the impact of festivals and events on QOL have been identified. The first phase of our research adapts theoretical perspectives (Ragheb and

Tate, 1993; Lloyd and Auld, 2002; Poston *et al.*, 2003; Packer and Ballantyne, 2010), which are used to form discussion themes and questions within family focus groups (please refer to Appendix for further details). Critical realism (Collier, 1994) has been identified as the most appropriate research philosophy for this study as it will test theories of QOL, but assumes that relationships are present between variables and facts. Fairclough (2003) gives further justification for this approach when he concludes that social events contain social practices that exist within social structures, which are all part of reality.

The research project is the first of its kind and hence a mixed methodological approach is employed. Due to the complexities and diversities of local communities, a singular research methodology would not fully explain or provide accurate conclusions on how community festivals and events impact upon an individual's or family's QOL. The research project therefore consists of three stages (see Figure 10.1): Phase 1 includes an initial qualitative exploration of individual and family QOL domains through focus group discussions with families in Hertfordshire, UK. Findings from this research phase are presented below and will also feed into Phase 2: semi-structured interviews with families pre- and post-event attendance. The third and final stage will bring together findings from focus groups and semi-structured interviews in order to develop a QOL measurement scale for events and festivals which will test findings on a broader scale. It is important to note that this research project is iterative and ongoing; this chapter presents only the first phase of our research.

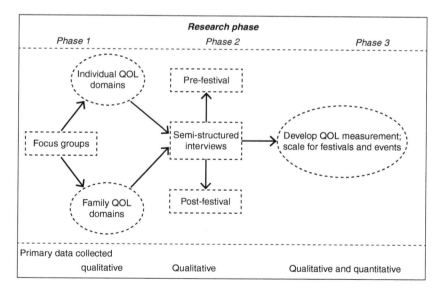

Figure 10.1 QOL research methods diagram
Source: Authors, 2016

Focus groups

Focus groups can provide a responsive context for people who have not traditionally been encouraged to voice their perspectives on sensitive topics
(Krueger, 1994; Rubin and Rubin, 1995). Our focus groups gathered subjective
accounts of personal QOL around the three variables of life satisfaction, happiness and morale, as identified by Lloyd and Auld (2002). The focus groups also
tested Ragheb and Tate's (1993) theory of frequency of engagement against
levels of satisfaction in festivals and events. It is suggested that the outcome of
the focus groups is the emergence of major QOL themes and sub-themes,
which, after comprehensive analysis, will be adapted into semi-structured interviews or questionnaires in future studies. This study, though, is only concerned
with the data derived from family focus groups which were conducted in St
Albans and Welwyn Garden City, in Hertfordshire, where festivals are an established part of community life. We employed a mixture of snowball sampling,
contacting local communities through cultural groups, toddler groups and
social media sites, and by visiting local events in Hertfordshire to recruit families. Our focus groups consisted of four families (with small children aged
between new born and four years). At the time of writing, three focus groups
had taken place between June and October 2015. We used the term 'family'
loosely when constructing our focus groups, but employed the definition put
forward by Poston *et al.* (2003, p. 319). All focus groups were held in a neutral
and close-by environment (local church halls or community centres), where
participants could leave and get home quickly if they needed to. They lasted for
60 minutes in duration. Open-ended questions were used to encourage discussion without intentionally introducing the chosen theoretical constructs (please
refer to Appendix).

All participants were made aware of the purpose of the research and
completed consent forms before the focus groups took place. Participants
were also advised that they could withdraw from the focus group discussions
at any time should they feel uncomfortable (nobody withdrew from the
groups). Focus groups were audio-recorded (iPad and iPhone) digitally, but
not videoed; they were then later transcribed for thematic analysis. More
specifically, they were coded and sorted using NVivo after transcription, in
order to identify major and minor QOL themes emerging from the discussions. We then employed the constant comparative method of analysing data
to generate categories, sub-categories and codes to interpret patterns and
themes, and ensure rigour (Glaser and Strauss, 1967; Lincoln and Guba,
1985; Lincoln, 1995). Trustworthiness in this study was achieved through
incorporating the concepts of credibility, transferability and dependability
(Lincoln and Guba, 1985; Lincoln, 1995; Rapley, 2003). Finally, we employed
a second phase of 'thematic data analysis' (Rubin and Rubin, 1995) to further
understand the importance of the relationship between festivals, families and
social values which reaffirmed our key themes and frame conditions to
achieve QOL.

Findings and discussion

Our findings, presented here, suggest three interconnected themes as important conditions for family QOL: time and space, money/wealth and rest, health and happiness (see Figure 10.2). We suggest that, in order to achieve family QOL through festival attendance, these three conditions need to be positive, and also need to be taken into consideration by event organisers and stakeholders. The following sections explore and discuss our qualitative data, framed by the thematic conditions mentioned above. Findings are presented here through anonymised and encoded responses from family members across two focus groups (Focus Group 1/FG1, Respondents A–D, and Focus Group 2/FG2, Respondents E–F).

Time and space

Participants in our focus group discussions highlighted time as a key element of QOL and linked this clearly to personal and family health and well-being. More specifically, there was a perception of rushed behavioural practices; parents identified that there was little down time and that events and activities were difficult to attend due to the extended preparation to get from home to the event location. According to our participants, in order to achieve socialisation and family bonding, time often needs to be strategised to long-term dates rather than being able to react quickly, unless events are local and happened upon within the normal day. Respondents also identified that there is a clear trade-off between domestic responsibilities and attending events together to create opportunities for socialisation. Usyal *et al.* (1993) and Crompton and McKay (1997) emphasised the need for interaction and socialisation within the family, which can be achieved through event participation; however, our focus group participants found this to be difficult to achieve when time is limited or needs to be spent on other domestic responsibilities.

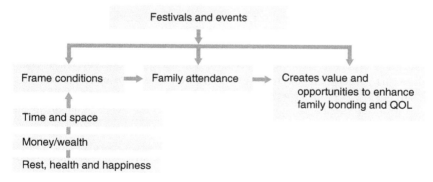

Figure 10.2 Festival and event value creation and the impact upon family QOL
Source: Authors, 2016

Similarly, Harrington (2015) discussed the need for parents to bond with their children during family leisure experiences, yet she doesn't make reference to the amount of time needed to ensure this is successful. Participants within our focus groups all agreed that time is a crucial element, but in order for children and parents to bond with each other and create social value and family happiness, time and space need to be brought together effectively. Semi-permanent event spaces can be created in order for socialising activities and family bonding to be achieved. However, finding activities that all the children can take part in sometimes divide the family rather than bring them together, which presents a clear challenge to event producers constructing and utilising temporary space.

F: Sometimes on the weekend we're finding now that me and my husband, we'll split up. Like my husband will take him out, while I stay at home and take care of the baby. That works, but then you're not actually spending any family time together. And also you're missing out. Because he'll take them to football lessons, and I don't really know what's happening at those.

Shaw (1997) and McCabe (2015) identified similar difficulties and issues for families spending time together when different leisure activities mean different things to members of the family. While all our participants considered time as an important element of enjoying experiences together as a family, the meanings and value attached to specific family activities experienced within specific spaces can be different for individual family members, which often leads to conflict or constraints.

Money/wealth

Monetary wealth was identified within our focus groups as another key element which improved their family's QOL. This conforms to Rapley's (2003) definition of QOL, which highlights the need for opportunities to participate in recreation or leisure and, furthermore, Sheldon's (2000) definition highlighting the need for prosperity and high GDP in order to participate. Many participants discussed festivals and events in relation to their size and categorised events as 'big and small events', where 'big and more expensive events' were usually considered a treat and not a regular occurrence. Participants also agreed that they would rather pay an up-front entrance fee, with everything within the event included in the admission price.

FG1 Do ticket prices influence your decision to attend different types of festivals and events?
A: I wouldn't necessarily say that if you pay more for a festival, you'll get a better time.

B+C+D: No, no, not at all.

B: Actually sometimes you get a better time when you pay less!

A: And it doesn't have to be loads of stuff either. It's just… having a theme and sticking to it! Sometimes there's so much going on that you're quite overwhelmed and the kids get a bit confused.

The focus groups revealed that admission price was not a defining factor in regard to quality of experience and family happiness during the event visit, and that, actually, less stimulation within the event environment enabled greater family bonding and socialisation to take place. Particularly with 'big events', participants expressed concerns in regard to the perceptual quality gap and whether the event would be over-commercialised. A clear message of 'less is more' was coming through in terms of event organisers providing a space for families to engage in meaningful experiences that enhance socialising and bonding and thus re-emphasising values within the family unit as well as with other families and members of the community.

Rest, health and happiness

A third element contributing to a family's overall QOL as identified by our focus group participants was rest, health and individual and family happiness. Respondents further highlighted that both dimensions also need to be considered in relation to the family's attachment to their local community, an element discussed below as 'environmental happiness', which, in turn, enhances social value.

Individual happiness was defined by the family focus groups as making time for oneself and engaging in individual activities. These contribute to their individual QOL, such as:

F: locking the door and having a shower [laughs]!

E: … or drinking coffee while it's still hot.

F: … just head space and getting out of the house occasionally.

E: Well, I find, going food shopping on my own is a treat! I know that sounds really silly, but wandering down the aisle calmly… without anyone going, "I want this, I want that… I need a wee!"

Second, *family happiness* was discussed in many different dimensions, the most important one being individual happiness in the sense that, 'if I'm not happy as an individual, my family won't be happy either'. The focus groups also revealed a clear relationship between physical health and happiness ('healthy family = happy family'), with many participants describing a state of paralysis if members of the family suffered from illness as a result of the family being at full stretch to look after another. However, 'happy children' was the single most important factor contributing to family happiness overall. This fits well with the early definitions of QOL: "a state of complete physical, mental and social well-being not merely the absence of disease" (WHO, 1997, p. 1) and, similarly, Sheldon (2000), who identifies psychological well-being as a major component of QOL.

Focus groups revealed that festivals and events can act as a unique platform for families to share experiences and generate very powerful bonding memories. These, in turn, enhanced individual (both children's and parents') happiness, as well as overall family happiness. According to our participants, they last for a week or longer – an interesting observation which also links to the previously discussed importance of 'time' as a frame condition for QOL. Examples for these 'memorable' bonding experiences include:

F: It's usually something totally random. Like at the Farmers' Market last weekend, there was the jazz band and they were playing. The toddlers… I was just standing there waiting for my husband, but the toddlers were absolutely fixated and that's just where I knew that was one of those magic moments. But it's usually something completely random, it's not the main point of the event.

E: I'd say for us, it really depends on how the event goes and how the day goes. But especially the church [events], because there's more adults, and with the church events, there's a lot of volunteers. The volunteers help look after our children, so there's more hands and then we relax more and it's a really nice day out. But there are days where you don't really know what to expect until you get there and that can be quite stressful, because you don't know where you're heading, where the facilities are. But when it works, it's a lovely day and you do catch up. You spend quality time, as you said, rather than arguing about the bins and what's for dinner and who's putting them to bed…?

The above discussed examples of both individual and family happiness are closely related to the third element of happiness, *environmental happiness*, in the sense that the right facilities and the creation of a perceived safe 'space' need to be in place in order to be able to relax and 'be happy' as a family. Participants further discussed the importance of a positive engagement with their local community, which acts as another bonding agent between individuals, families and events, and enhances social values. They expressed this in terms of event activities that showcase the local community, local food, or other local themes, and therefore provide a sense of place (see Derrett, 2003) for all members of the family. In turn, these 'simple things' contribute to the family's overall happiness and QOL. It should be understood, though, that the social cultural values of community festivals will only be widely understood if the event planning process has engaged local communities and been inclusive to include all communities within the area (see Jepson and Clarke, 2005, 2013; Jepson *et al.*, 2014; Jepson *et al.*, 2008; Jepson, 2009; Clarke and Jepson, 2011; Jepson *et al.*, 2013; Stadler, 2013; Ragsdell and Jepson, 2014).

Conclusions

This chapter has demonstrated that there are very real practical benefits associated with understanding social values that are created or reinforced through attending events and, in particular, to local government, event organisers and families. Event organisers and other stakeholders, such as local government, through a greater understanding of social values, themes and frame conditions of QOL, would be better placed to tailor event programmes to families' specific needs and expectations, which will ensure families attend events on a regular basis, and hence feel a stronger sense of belonging and pride for their local community. Through creating safe spaces and affordable events with a focus on local themes, families can engage in activities that are meaningful to all members of the family and hence enhance their overall event experience. Families would also benefit from understanding the frame conditions of QOL, which enable or restrict their ability to attend events; from this, an appreciation as to how events can foster social bonding, belonging, attachment to place and create happiness in the family through the creation of positive memories and values.

This chapter has presented Phase 1 of our research. It has concentrated on festival and event consumption by families – in particular, families with young children. Following detailed focus group analysis, a number of important themes and frame conditions (see Figure 10.2) have emerged that demonstrate the creation of social values and the potential for QOL benefits which families can gain from event attendance. We remain reflexive about this research and have no doubt that QOL could be analysed from other event stakeholder perspectives, such as the event producers themselves, local government and other major stakeholders.

The chapter is unique in that it has begun to unravel some of the complexity surrounding QOL and to contextualise this within festival and event settings, where the major motivation for attendance is documented as: socialisation, family togetherness, or spending time with family and friends. It seemed a natural progression to begin to investigate the social values that events create and the potential they have to enhance families' QOL. Due to the complexities of research within QOL domains and events, we see this research as ongoing – especially as, thus far, research has been concentrated upon an individual's QOL, with very limited focus on understanding families and groups and how they experience, understand and create value through event attendance. Festivals and events are value driven and, as such, values are identified and consumed. This is particularly significant to families who seek to reinforce positive social values and relationships between their members for the good of the family unit. The next phases of this research will include: collecting further datasets so that we may measure and understand the meaning of social values that families associate with attendance at festivals and events. Following this, a framework to measure and enhance family QOL in events can be developed.

Appendix

Table 10.A1 Example questions to stimulate focus group discussions and test theory to better understand the relationship between festivals/events and QOL

Focus group question/discussion statement	Researcher focus
When you hear the words 'family quality of life', what first comes to your mind?	Poston *et al.* (2003)
Tell us about times when things have gone really well in your family. What helps things go well?	
Tell us about times that have been especially tough in your family. What are the things that usually create tough times?	
What do you value most about visiting festivals? Why is this important to you?	Packer and Ballatyne (2010)
Why do you usually go to festivals?	
Do you feel more connected with your local community when you attend events?	
What do you enjoy the most about attending festivals/events?	
What do you feel you have gained from attending festivals/events?	
Has it changed the way you feel or think about yourself or about the world?	
Has it changed the way you feel or think about your family?	Jepson and Stadler (2017)
Do you feel more connected to your family when you attend events?	
Do you feel a stronger connection with your local community after attending festivals and events?	
Do you feel proud of where you live after attending festivals/events?	
Do you feel proud of your family after attending festivals/events?	
How often do you and your family attend festivals/events?	Ragheb and Tate (1993)
How do you feel when you attend festivals/events?	
Were you and your family satisfied with the overall festival/event experience?	

Source: Authors, 2016

References

Abrahams, R.D. (1982). The language of festivals: celebrating the economy. In V. Turner (ed.), *Celebration: Studies in Festivity and Ritual*. Washington, DC: Smithsonian Institution Press, pp. 161–77.

Abrahams, R.D. (1987). An American vocabulary of celebrations. In A. Falassi (ed.), *Time Out of Time: Essays on the Festival*. Albuquerque: University of New Mexico Press, pp. 173–83.

Agate, J.R., Zabriskie, R.B., Agate, S.T. and Poff, R. (2009). Family leisure satisfaction and satisfaction with family life. *Journal of Leisure Research*, 41(2), 205–23.

Andereck, K., Valentine, K.M., Vogt, C.M., and Knopf, R.C. (2007). A cross-cultural analysis of quality of life perceptions. *Journal of Sustainable Tourism*, 15(5), 483–502.

Andrews, F.M. and Withey, S.B. (1976). *Social Indicators of Well-being: America's Perception of Life Quality*. New York: Plenum.

Backman, K.F., Backman, S.J., Uysal, M. and Sunshine, K.M. (1995). Event tourism: an examination of motivations and activities. *Festival Management and Event Tourism*, 3(1), 15–24.

Bell, R., Sundel, M., Ponte, J.A., Murrell, S. and Lin, E. (eds) (1983). *Assessing Health and Human Service Needs: Concepts, Methods and Applications*. New York: Human Sciences Press.

Bowen, H.E. and Daniels, M. J. (2005). Does the music matter? Motivations for attending a music festival. *Event Management*, 9(3), 155–64.

Bubloz, M., Eicher, J., Evers, J. and Sontag, M. (1980). A human ecological approach to quality of life: conceptual framework and results of a preliminary study. *Social Indicators Research*, 7, 103–16.

Campbell, A., Converse, P.E. and Rodgers, W.L. (1976). *The Quality of American Life: Perceptions, Evaluations, and Satisfactions*. New York: Russell Sage Foundation.

Clarke, A. and Jepson, A. (2011). Power and hegemony within a community festival. *International Journal of Event and Festival Management*, 2(1), 7–19.

Collier, A. (1994). *Critical Realism: An Introduction to Roy Bhaskar's Philosophy*. London: Verso.

Crompton, J. and McKay, S.L. (1997). Motives of visitors attending festival events. *Annals of Tourism Research*, 24(2), 425–39.

Day, R.L. (1978). Beyond social indicators: quality of life at the individual level. In F.D. Reynolds and H.C. Barksdale (eds), *Marketing and the Quality of Life*. Chicago: American Marketing Association, pp. 11–18.

Day, R.L. (1987). Relationship between life satisfaction and consumer satisfaction. In A.C. Samli (ed.), *Marketing and Quality-of-Life Interface*. Westport, CT: Greenwood, pp. 289–311.

Derrett, R. (2003) Making sense of how festivals demonstrate a community's sense of place. *Event Management*, 8, 49–58.

Diener, E. (1984). Subjective well-being. *Psychological Bulletin*, 95, 542–75.

Diener, E., Emmons, R.A., Larson, R.J. and Griffin, S. (1985). The satisfaction with life scale. *Journal of Personality Assessment*, 49(1), 71–5.

Eckersley, R. (1999). Quality of life in Australia: an analysis of public perceptions, Discussion Paper Number 23. Lyneham, ACT: Australia Institute.

Fairclough, N. (2003). *Analysing Discourse: Textual Analysis for Social Research*. London: Routledge.

Falassi, A. (1987). *Time Out of Time: Essays on the Festival*. Albuquerque: University of New Mexico Press.

Faulkner, B., Fredline, E., Larson, M. and Tomljenovic, R. (1999). A marketing analysis of Sweden's Storsjoyran music festival. *Tourism Analysis*, 4, 157–71.

Formica, S. and Uysal, M. (1996). A market segmentation of festival visitors: Umbria Jazz Festival in Italy. *Festival Management and Event Tourism*, 3, 175–82.

Formica, S. and Uysal, M. (1998). Market segmentation of an international cultural-historical event in Italy. *Journal of Travel Research*, 36(4), 16–24.

Foster, K. and Robinson, P. (2010). A critical analysis of the motivational factors that influence event attendance in family groups. *Event Management*, 14, 107–25.

Fox, K.S. (1974). *Social Indicators and Social Theory: Elements of an Operational System*. New York: Wiley.

Geertz, C. (1973). *The Interpretation of Cultures: Selected Essays*. New York: Basic.

Getz, D. (2010). The nature and scope of festival studies. *International Journal of Event Management Research*, 5, 1–47.

Glaser, B. and Strauss, A.L. (1967). *The Discovery of Grounded Theory: Strategies for Qualitative Research.* Chicago: Aldine.

Harrington, M. (2015). Practices and meaning of purposive family leisure among working- and middle-class families. *Leisure Studies*, 34(4), 471–86.

Hinch, T., Jackson, E.L., Hudson, S. and Walker, G. (2005) Leisure constraint theory and sport tourism. *Sport in Society*, 8(2), 142–63.

Hirsch, B. (1980). Natural support systems and coping with major life changes. *American Journal of Community Psychology*, 8, 159–72.

Jepson, A. and Clarke, A. (2005). The Jubilee Festival in Derby: involving the local community. 3rd DeHann Tourism Management Conference: The Impact and Management of Tourism Related Events, Nottingham University Business School. ISSN: 1471–1427

Jepson, A. and Clarke, A. (2009). Cultural festivals and cultures of communities. In C. Cooper (ed.), *Proceedings of the EUTO Conference 2008 Attractions and Events as Catalysts for Regeneration and Social Change.* Christel DeHaan Tourism and Travel Research Institute, University of Nottingham and Centre for Tourism and Cultural Change, Leeds Metropolitan University, September 2008, pp. 68–88. 2008/1 ISSN 1471–1427

Jepson, A. and Clarke, A. (2013). Community festivals. In R. Finkel, D. McGillivray, G. McPherson and P. Robinson (eds), *Research Themes in Events Management*. Oxford: CAB International, pp. 6–18.

Jepson, A. and Stadler, R. (2017). Conceptualising the impact of festival and event attendance upon family quality of life (QOL). *Event Management*, 21(1).

Jepson, A.S., Wiltshire, P. and Clarke, A. (2008). Community festivals: involvement and inclusion. Paper presentation and publication. *CHME International Research Conference*. ISBN: 0-9548039-1-4

Jepson, A., Clarke, A. and Ragsdell G. (2013). Applying the motivation–opportunity–ability (MOA) model to reveal factors that influence inclusive engagement within local community festivals: the case of UtcaZene 2012. *International Journal of Events and Festival Management*, 4(3), 186–205.

Jepson, A., Clarke, A. and Ragsdell, G. (2014). Investigating the application of the motivation–opportunity–ability (MOA) model to reveal factors which facilitate or inhibit inclusive engagement within local community festivals. *Scandinavian Journal of Hospitality and Tourism*, 14(3), 331–48.

Kant, I. (1978). Anthropology from a pragmatic point of view. In M. Rapley (ed., 2003), *Quality of Life Research: A Critical Introduction*, London: Sage.

Keyes, C.L.M. (1998). Social well-being. *Social Psychology Quarterly*, 61, 121–40.

Keyes, C.L.M. Shmotkin, D. and Ryff, C.D. (2002). Optimising well-being: the empirical encounter of two traditions. *Journal of Personality and Social Psychology*, 82, 1007–22.

Kimmel, W. (1977). *Needs Assessment: A Critical Perspective*. Washington, DC: Department of Health, Educational, and Welfare, Office of Program Systems.

Krueger, R.A. (1994). *Focus Groups: A Practical Guide for Applied Research* (2nd edn). Newbury Park, CA: Sage.

Kuyken (1995). The World Health Organization quality of life assessment (WHOQOL): position paper from the World Health Organization. *Social Science and Medicine*, 41, 1403–9.

Laiho, S. (2004). The psychological functions of music in adolescence. *Nordic Journal of Music Therapy*, 13(1), 47–63.

Lee, C.K. (2000). A comparative study of Caucasian and Asian visitors to a cultural expo in an Asian setting. *Tourism Management*, 21(2), 169–76.

Lee, C.K., Lee, Y.K. and Wicks, B.E. (2004). Segmentation of festival motivation by nationality and satisfaction. *Tourism Management*, 25, 61–70.

Liburd, J.J. and Hergesell, A. (2008). Enhancing the quality of life through cultural events: the case of the Danish Wadden Sea Festival. Retrieved from: http://www.besteducation-network.org/Papers_Presentations/2439, accessed 6 November 2014.

Light, D. (1996). Characteristics of the audience for festivals at a heritage site. *Tourism Management*, 17(3), 183–90.

Lincoln, Y.S. (1995). Emerging criteria for quality in qualitative and interpretive research. *Qualitative Inquiry*, 1, 275–89.

Lincoln, Y.S. and Guba, E.G. (1985). *Naturalistic Inquiry.* Beverly Hills, CA: Sage.

Lloyd, K.M. and Auld, C.J. (2002). The role of leisure in determining quality of life: issues of content and measurement. *Social Indicators Research*, 57(1), 43–71.

Maslow, A. (1954). *Motivation and Personality.* New York: Harper and Row.

Manning, F. (ed.) (1983). *The Celebration of Society: Perspectives on Contemporary Cultural Performance.* Bowling Green, OH: Bowling Green University Popular Press.

McCabe, S. (2015). Family leisure, opening a new window on the meaning of family. *Annals of Leisure Research*, 18(2), 175–9.

Mercer, C. (1994). Assessing liveability: from statistical indicators to policy benchmarks. In C. Mercer (ed.), *Urban and Regional Quality of Life Indicators.* Brisbane: Institute for Cultural Policy Studies, Griffith University, pp. 3–12.

Michalos, A.C. (1980). Satisfaction and happiness. *Social Indicators Research*, 8, 385–422.

Mintel Marketing Intelligence (2004). *Family Holidays UK.* London: Mintel.

Mintel Marketing Intelligence (2005). *Children's Leisure Festival and Special Events Management* (4th edn). London: Mintel.

Mitchell, R., Babarim, O. and Hurley, D. (1981). Problem-solving, resource utilization, and community involvement in a black and white community. *American Journal of Community Psychology*, 9, 233–46.

Mohr, K., Backman, K.F., Gahan, L.W. and Backman, S.J. (1993). An investigation of festival motivations and event satisfaction by visitor type. *Festival Management and Event Tourism*, 1(3), 89–97.

Murrell, S. (1973). *Community Psychology and Social Systems.* New York: Behavioral.

Murrell, S.A. and Norris, F.H. (1983). Quality of life as the criterion for need assessment. *Journal of Community Psychology*, 11, 88–97.

Murrell, S.A., Brockway, J. and Schultz, P. (1982). The Kentucky Elderly Need Assessment: concurrent validity of different measures of unmet need. *American Journal of Community Psychology*, 10, 117–32.

Nguyen, T., Atkisson, C. and Bottino, M. (1983). The definition and identification of human service needs in a community. In R. Bell, M. Sundel, J. Aponte, S. Murrell and E. Lin (eds), *Assessing Health and Human Service Needs: Concepts, Methods and Applications.* New York: Human Sciences Press.

Nicholson, R.E. and Pearce, D.G. (2001). Why do people attend events? A comparative analysis of visitor motivations at four South Island events. *Journal of Travel Research*, 39, 449–60.

Nordvall, A., Pettersson, R., Svensson, B. and Brown, S. (2014). Designing events for social interaction. *Event Management*, 18(2), 127–40.

O'Shea, E. and Leime, Á.N. (2012). The impact of the Bealtaine arts programme on the quality of life, wellbeing and social interaction of older people in Ireland. *Ageing and Society*, 32, 851–72.

Packer, J. and Ballantyne, J. (2010). The impact of music festival attendance on young people's psychological and social well-being. *Psychology of Music*, 39, 164–81.

Pasquier, E. (1555). *Le Monophile*, 20a, cité par Vaganay dans R. Et. Rab., T. 9, 301.

Poria, Y., Butler, R. and Airey, D. (2003). Classifying heritage tourism. *Annals of Tourism Research*, 28(4), 1047–9.

Poston, D., Turnbull, A., Park, J., Mannan, H., Marquis, J. and Wang, M. (2003). Family quality of life: a qualitative inquiry. *Journal Information*, 41, 313–28.

Ragheb, M. and Tate, R. (1993). A behavioural model of leisure participation, based on leisure attitude, motivation and satisfaction. *Leisure Studies*, 12, 61–70.

Ragsdell, G. and Jepson, A.S. (2014). Knowledge sharing: insights from Campaign for Real Ale (CAMRA) festival volunteers. *International Journal of Event and Festival Management*, 5(3), 279–96.

Rapley, M. (2003). *Quality of Life Research: A Critical Introduction*. London: Sage.

Riger, S. and Lavrakas, P. (1981). Community ties: patterns of attachment and social interaction in urban neighborhoods. *American Journal of Community Psychology*, 9, 55–66.

Robinson, P. (2008). Holiday decision-making: the family perspective. In K. Foster and P. Robinson (2010). A critical analysis of the motivational factors that influence event attendance in family groups. *Event Management*, 14, 107–25.

Rubin, H.J., and Rubin, I.S. (1995). *Qualitative Interviewing: The Art of Hearing Data*. Thousand Oaks, CA: Sage.

Ryff, C.D. and Keyes, C.L.M. (1995). The structure of psychological well-being revisited. *Journal of Personality and Social Psychology*, 69, 719–27.

Scott, D. (1996). A comparison of visitors' motivations to attend three urban festivals. *Festival Management and Event Tourism*, 3(3), 121–8.

Schneider, I.E. and Backman, S.J. (1996). Cross-cultural equivalence of festival motivations: a study in Jordan. *Festival Management and Event Tourism*, 4(3/4), 139–144.

Seligman, M. and Csikszentmihalyi, M. (2000). Positive psychology: an introduction. *American Psychologist*, 55(1), 5–14.

Shaw, S.S. (1997). Controversies and contradictions in family leisure: an analysis of conflicting paradigms. *Journal of Leisure Research*, 29(1), 98–112.

Sheldon, T. (2000). Dutch GP cleared after helping to end man's "hopeless existence". *British Medical Journal*, 321, 1174.

Siegel, L., Atkisson, C. and Carson, L. (1978). Need identification and program planning in the community context. In C. Atkisson, W. Horowitz and J. Sorensen (eds), *Evaluation of Human Service Programs*. New York: Academic Press, pp. 215–52.

Sirgy, M.J. (1986). A quality-of-life theory derived from Maslow's developmental perspective: "quality" is related to progressive satisfaction of a hierarchy of needs, lower order and higher. *American Journal of Economics and Sociology*, 45(3), 329–42.

Sirgy, M.J., Samli, A.C. and Meadow, H.L. (1982). Interface between quality of life and marketing: a theoretical framework. *Journal of Marketing and Public Policy* (now *Journal of Public Policy and Marketing*), 1, 69–84.

Sirgy, M.J., Morris, M. and Samli, A.C. (1985). The question of value in social marketing. *American Journal of Economics and Sociology*, 44, 215–28.

Small, K., Edwards, D. and Sheridan, L. (2005). A flexible framework for evaluating the socio-cultural impacts of a (small) festival. *International Journal of Event Management Research*, 1, 66–77.

Stadler, R. (2013). Power relations and the production of new knowledge within a Queensland Music Festival community cultural development project. *Annals of Leisure Research*, 16(1), 87–102.

Tayler, C., McArdle, F., Richer, S., Brennan, C. and Weier, K. (2006). Learning partnerships with parents of young children: studying the impact of a major festival of early childhood in Australia. *European Early Childhood Education Research Journal*, 14(2), 7–19.

Tomljenovic, R., Larsson, M. and Faulkner, B. (2001). Predictors of satisfaction with festival attendance: a case of Storsjoyran Rock Music Festival. *Tourism (Zagreb)*, 49(2), 123–32.

Turner, V. (1969). *The Ritual Process: Structure and Anti-Structure*. New York: Aldine de Gruyter.

Turner, V. (1974). Liminal to liminoid, in play, flow and ritual: an essay in comparative symbology. In E. Norbeck (ed.), *The Anthropological Study of Human Play*. Houston, TX: Rice University Studies, pp. 53–92.

Turner, V. (ed.) (1982). *Celebration: Studies in Festivity and Ritual*. Washington, DC: Smithsonian Institution Press.

Uysal, M., Gahan, L. and Martin, B. (1993). An examination of event motivations: a case study. *Festival Management and Event Tourism*, 1(1), 5–10.

Van Gennep, A. (1909). *The Rites of Passage* (1960 translation by M. Vizedom and G. Coffee). London: Routledge and Kegan Paul.

WHO (World Health Organization) (1997). *WHOQOL: Measuring Quality of Life*. Geneva: WHO.

Part III

Conclusions

11 A synthesis, summaries and some ontological propositions

Donald Getz, Tommy D. Andersson,
John Armbrecht and Erik Lundberg

Introduction

An objective in editing this book was to cover aspects of value creation, assessment and measurement related to planned events, from multiple perspectives. It was a difficult task and, although the results are comprehensive, there is undoubtedly room to continue expanding this discourse. Why is it important?

Almost everyone understands why 'evaluations' are done by event managers, and why external agencies evaluate events and assess their impacts, but when it comes to defining and measuring 'value' or 'worth' the conversation can become very confusing. Technical evaluation focuses on how well goals are met (i.e. effectiveness measures) and problem solving, including improving efficiency. But are any events assigned a value or worth? Who would do that?

Within portfolio theory events can be considered assets and various return on investment measures can be used to assign value. But what about assessments at the city or country levels? What measures of value or worth are to be employed when both the 'extrinsic' and 'intrinsic' values of events are considered? The literature on event impacts is dominated by extrinsic measures such as return on investment (ROI), economic impact and image effects. But many stakeholders, not to say all, also value events intrinsically, without reference to quantitative measures.

One starting point in any discussion of value creation is to stress that economic impacts do not equal value or worth. Economic impact assessments are but one possible input to establishing a value. In the arts or cultural communities, festivals, concerts, plays or other events are considered to be expressions of art and culture and they have intrinsic value regardless of economic impact or ROI. In sport, participation and competition might be valued with no regard to economic impact. Meetings and expositions can have intrinsic value just because people are social and want to get together. Therefore extrinsic measures of value are not always necessary or desired.

We do live in an age when events have become instruments of diverse policy fields, corporate and industry strategies, therefore the quantitative, extrinsic measures of value are constantly on the table, in the media and put forward as justifications for involvement in the events sector. But even here there are serious problems when it comes to establishing value.

Far too many events have been bid on, produced and evaluated on the basis of simple, uni-dimensional value measures. The dominant mode has always been that of forecasting and post-event estimation of economic impact. Mega events might generate economic changes but they are seldom accompanied by full benefit to cost evaluations, taking a long-term perspective. Often the main legacy has been debt passed on to future generations. Politics, the power exerted by elite groups in society and a failure to be comprehensive and inclusive can explain these problems.

Value is, in large part, a matter of perspective. What makes perfect sense to tourism and economic development agencies can be anathema to social and cultural groups. While certain segments can benefit, others pay a price. Ideally, it all gets sorted out in a full, open discourse on strategies, means, impacts and goals – but that can only happen when everyone understands the language, the methods and measures and the lessons from experience.

While there are many negatives associated with past and current practice, there is also the promise of utilising events to achieve broad sustainability goals. Long-term, cumulative value creation across the multiple dimensions of sustainable development should be the aim. Our knowledge of this process is weak, as most research has been conducted on single events, frozen in time. This is an area in need of considerable attention.

The editors believe that the primary objective has been met and the most comprehensive overview of event value to date has been presented, both in terms of theory and the research findings. Obviously, the number of contributed chapters and the contributions of authors in themselves could not illustrate every point, but, as will be seen in this chapter, the coverage has been very wide indeed.

The second objective has been to challenge the industry, students, policy-makers and strategists with new perspectives on value, with implications for impact forecasting and assessment. Here are the main elements of the challenge:

- do not equate economic impact assessment with assigning value or worth to events
- do not accept the dominant approaches to ROI and economic impact assessment as givens, but be critical
- think comprehensively, as value creation is a multi-stakeholder exercise; it can only be carried out in an open, democratic forum
- diverse methods and measures are required, reflecting both extrinsic and intrinsic approaches to value creation.

Objective three was to employ literature reviews, expert reflection, research data and case studies to illustrate all the main aspects of value creation and measurement related to events, including related political, management and methodological challenges. As noted above, the contributions cover a very wide range of issues, methods and measures. The literature cited, including foundation theories, examples and the conclusions of contributors, is vitally important to anyone engaged in this field. In the next section each chapter is summarised as to its main points, reflecting both the authors' and the editors' conclusions. In the final part of this concluding chapter we try to wrap it all up in the context of ontological mapping – that is, an analysis of the main concepts and terms being employed.

Chapter summaries

Chapter 1: Definitions and meanings of value

By the editors: Donald Getz, Tommy D. Andersson, John Armbrecht and Erik Lundberg

Value is a complex subject; even the language we use in English to talk about value can be confusing. That is why so much attention was given in Chapter 1 to definitions. Perhaps the most important distinction to draw is the difference between event 'evaluation' as a technical process (both problem solving and related to goal attainment) and placing a value on an event. Impact forecasting and assessment falls into the technical evaluation category, with impacts being one input to determining value or worth.

Also emphasised in the first chapter is the important difference being extrinsic and intrinsic values. Extrinsic valuation dominates the event literature, stressing quantitative measures of impact and ROI, or seeking 'proof' that events cause certain desired impacts. Events have become legitimate tools of diverse policy goals, although an over-emphasis on economic impacts has left the other dimensions – social, cultural and environmental – less developed in terms of theory, methods and measures.

The intrinsic worth of events is accepted by many people who believe that events are, in themselves important, without reference to their impacts or ROI. Festivals can be valued as art, sport events as embodying certain ideals of fair play or healthful exercise and business meetings can be valued simply as social occasions. At the community level, many people will accept the value of having a diverse portfolio of events even without attending them (i.e. non-use values based on choice or legacy) even if they do not know their value to place marketing or tourism. In the modern world, most people expect their cities and countries to be full of events (i.e. the 'eventful city') and this can be thought of as the popular 'legitimation' of events.

Chapter 2: The value of events and festivals in the age of austerity

By Emma Wood

This chapter picks up the theme of the changing approach to the value of festivals and events and focuses on how these activities are perceived at the level of local government. Emma's discussion is supported by data gathered from three national (UK) surveys sent to identified local authority employees involved with events at both a strategic and operational level and taken at different points in time over the last eight turbulent years (2004, 2009 and 2012). She found the most pronounced changes relate to funding models and the changing rhetoric – with an even greater tension emerging between the economic and social benefits arguments.

The challenges for event evaluation stem from greater austerity, creating a more compelling need for evidence to prove event value and justify expenditure. At the same time, fewer resources are being provided for that evaluation to take place! Emma Wood reflects on a substantial body of personal research to provide advice on what event impact evaluation needs:

- to be tailored to realistic objectives and the resources available
- to include a comparison with other approaches that could be used to achieve the same objectives
- to be conducted over a longer period of time than tends to be the case now
- to incorporate discussion forums, focus groups and ethnographic research tools alongside, or even instead of, surveys
- to take into account the combined effect of all influences on the effect being evaluated
- to develop more robust methods for showing attribution to the event.

She also notes that there is a lack of meaningful longitudinal research, and events still seem to be evaluated in isolation from other activities or interventions. We therefore ignore the cumulative impact of events, even though it is more realistic to do so – given that is impossible to tease out individual elements for attribution. There is also a growing mistrust of the value of survey responses – what people say is not how they behave/d or how they felt; this is even truer of stated behavioural intention. Future challenges lie in the changing and increasing funder demands, with even more emphasis on public relations outcomes. Continuing austerity measures will squeeze evaluation in two ways: by creating a need for greater evidence to justify expenditure and in providing fewer resources for that evaluation to take place.

Chapter 3: Exploring consumers' value co-creation in a festival context using a socio-cultural lens

By Sandhiya Goolaup and Lena Mossberg

Sandhiya Goolaup and Lena Mossberg explore the various concepts related to consumer value, with specific reference to food events. They articulate, in some detail, a socio-cultural conceptualisation of studying event value, and have elaborated upon three holistic and inter-related ways of talking about social, semiotic and economic value.

It is argued that, for consumer value to emerge, the consumer has to interact with the product/service in ways that it generates a positive experience and satisfies personal preference. From the consumer culture perspective, value is a relativistic preference characteristic of consumer experience that may result from fun and playfulness, so the challenge to event organisers is to create places where exceptional experiences can be enjoyed. If the producer can create an attractive environment, then the perceived value that arises is likely to improve the quality of experiences and contribute to the consumer's well-being.

Chapter 4: Successful event–destination collaboration through superior experience value for visitors

By Nina K. Prebensen

Destinations and events collaborate to create value for their customers and this reciprocally also creates value for the destinations and the events. These effects are reinforced when organisations get access to each other's resources and information. Collaboration between destinations and events will benefit tourists and eventgoers in terms of experience values – that is, emotional, social, epistemic value, in addition to various functional values including certain physical qualities and value for money. A fit between the event and the destination will augment potential for collaboration.

This chapter is grounded in literature on experience value and collaboration value and argues that the success of collaboration will result in enhanced attraction value for the collaborative partners. Destinations and events are viewed as value-creating entities through co-creating experience value with their customers; literature regarding collaborative networks is tapped. This is followed by a discussion of potential synergies of collaborative networks between destinations and events.

Event and destination managers have not yet learned how to synergise their efforts; one objective of this chapter is to show how this collaboration may become successful. Successful events and destinations need to create a reputation, providing awareness and visitation for themselves and the collaborative partners. Finally, impacts of collaboration between the destination and events, in enhancing visitors experience value, are demonstrated.

It is suggested that future research should explore success factors such as visitation and sustainability (economic, ecological and social) of destination–events collaborations. Case studies of best–worst practices could be undertaken.

Chapter 5: Creating network value: the Barcelona Sónar Festival as a global events hub

By Greg Richards and Alba Colombo

Through a case study of a music festival, this chapter focuses on the relationship between a festival and the host city. Reviewing the effects generated by the Sónar Festival in Barcelona over a 20-year period, the authors' research identifies how the event generates different forms of value for the host society, including economic development, tourism, animation of static facilities, image making, revitalisation of infrastructure and city branding. But the intrinsic value that the public sector wants to generate through festivals also has to be evaluated.

The chapter specifically analyses value relationships between the city and the festival on three different levels: the role of the festival in generating urban development, related to the economic and tourism effects; the role of the festival in supporting the local music sector and its value for the creative industries, particularly in terms of its ability to become a 'field-configuring event'; and the cultural effect generated for the host society.

One important conclusion is that a mutual dependence emerged between the event and its urban context, producing value in three basic areas: first, in urban regeneration; second, by strengthening the position of the city as a hub for the global music sector; and, finally, increasing its capacity to develop local cultural value.

Chapter 6: The use and non-use values of events: a conceptual framework

By Tommy D. Andersson, John Armbrecht and Erik Lundberg

The concept of utility is rooted in the origins of economic thinking. It describes value created in a very wide sense of the word. In this chapter, the concept of utility is traced from its origins in the eighteenth century to present-day research via cost–benefit analysis to evaluations of use and non-use values, which were developed within environmental economics. Use value, then, describes the use we tap from natural resources in terms of recreation and economic activity. Non-use values refer to intrinsic values related to preserving nature in terms of beauty, quality of life, pride, options for leisure and resources for future generations. These concepts were developed in environmental economics, but the values are easily translated into values related to culture, festivals and events; during the latest two decades, a number of empirical studies have been made in these areas. The chapter reviews empirical studies and conceptual development, with specific reference to festivals and events. Ways to measure the value of events and festivals are suggested, which include not only the value experienced by event participants, but also other values created in the hosting society, both for event participants and other members of the society – that is, the 'non-users'.

Chapter 7: Event evaluation: approaches and new challenges

By Larry Dwyer and Peter Forsyth

This is a must read chapter; for even greater detail, see the book by Dwyer, Forsyth and Dwyer entitled *Tourism Economics and Policy* (2010). It addresses economic impact measurement and its role in policy decisions pertaining to events, and examines various meanings of value in this context. A starting point is the major proviso that "The success or contribution of a particular event should not be measured only by its financial contribution" (ibid., p. 406). Unfortunately, economics have dominated – and, in many cases, remain the sole measure of – an event's purported worth, and this leads policy-makers astray, rendering them out of touch with important segments in society and unable to create a sustainable event or event sector. A second major caution is this: "The economic impacts of an event are not the same thing as the economic benefits which arise" (this volume, p. 106). Too many bids and too much support has been given to events based on forecasted benefits, often using flawed economic impact assessment (EIA) methods that exaggerate benefits and ignore or downplay costs. Dwyer and Forsyth add, in this volume (p.106), "One criticism is that EIA alone usually cannot decide which is the best allocation of public resources in support of events since society has goals other than efficiency."

The typical approach to EIA employing multipliers based on input–output (I–O) tables is not as accurate as computable general equilibrium (CGE) models, and purported economic benefits are often exaggerated. Furthermore, it has to be remembered that one event is unlikely in itself to actually change an economy (perhaps excepting mega events), so it is often better to more simply estimate the direct expenditure of event tourists or a broader direct economic contribution – that is, tourist expenditure attributed to the event alone, plus other income that is in-scope, such as grants, sponsorship revenue or media sales. The authors argue that:

> using a simple direct economic impact estimate will avoid debates on complex methodologies and debates on the inclusion or exclusion of multipliers and that direct economic impact ("in-scope expenditure") works well as a basis for straightforward comparisons to other events.
>
> Ibid., chapter 7, p.113

Dwyer and Forsyth go on to argue that: "Event researchers typically have taken a piecemeal approach to evaluation – much of the impact assessment literature ignores any serious effort to value the social, cultural, environmental and other impacts of events, even though techniques are available to do so" (ibid., chapter 7, p.106). Cost–benefit assessment (CBA) aims to be comprehensive: "By quantifying the net benefits of projects, programs and policies in a standard manner, CBA improves the information base for public sector decision-making, thereby assisting in the assessment of relative priorities... It is designed specifically to answer public policy questions" (ibid., chapter 7, p.110). There remains a major hurdle: that of various intangible costs and benefits that cannot be given surrogate monetary value (or resistance exists to this practice).

Total economic value (TEV) estimation requires consideration of both use and non-use values. Direct use value is the benefit of attending or otherwise participating in events and can be equated with admission prices, whereas indirect use value can be included by adding willingness to pay (WTP, a way to estimate consumer surplus). Non-use values might also be considered, as people are sometimes willing to pay for an event because of its value to others (so-called altruism or vicarious value), the choice it provides for possible future use (option value) and a bequest or legacy value related to a desire to have the event preserved for future generations. All of these can be balanced against environmental and social costs and benefits if appropriate measures can be found, such as giving monetary value to ecological or carbon footprints.

For most events of modest proportions, the simplest approach to forecasting and estimating direct economic contribution is undoubtedly all that is required – so long as this estimate is but one input in determining the overall value or worth of the event within a given context. Only an open, multi-stakeholder approach can assure that this occurs. But when it comes to the really big questions, politics often subsumes logic.

The editors would encourage further reading on the subject of mega events, in particular, as that is where opportunity costs (also discussed in this chapter) become a major issue. Can a city or country really afford to allocate enormous resources and create huge debt in order to host the Olympics or a comparably ambitious event? Do the imputed benefits, often said to be more about legacy than direct economic benefits, really balance the costs? Most experts say no. Economist Andrew Zimbalist (2015a) authored the book *Circus Maximus: The Economic Gamble Behind Hosting the Olympics and the World Cup*. In an article in *World Economics* (2015b), Zimbalist argues that "Scholarly evidence suggests that hosting either the IOC's Olympic Games or FIFA's World Cup event is no economic bargain for the host city or country" (ibid., p. 35). As an example, Zimbalist points to the London Olympics of 2012, citing official reports, as having yielded "a negative balance of $14 billion plus" (ibid., p. 36). As to legacy, he says: "And once again, the independent scholarship has not corroborated any long-term gains in tourism, trade or foreign investment from hosting" (ibid.).

One must assume the gains are all political, or that they accrue to elite groups within society. The opportunity costs are very high indeed, and especially in poor countries that really need housing and hospitals rather than white-elephant stadia or arenas.

Another observation of Zimbalist is that "Political systems in both democratic and authoritarian countries have shown themselves increasingly unwilling or unable to engage in effective long-term event planning" (ibid., p. 35). Certainly one of the problems is that politics often trumps rational planning.

The really big events hold a monopoly and have become very effective at getting what they want by auctioning the rights to host their events. Value is assured to the owners of auctioned events (when there is active bidding), but value creation to the purchasers is a dubious proposition. It is worth emphasising here the claim of Getz (2013), in *Event Tourism: Concepts, International Case Studies, and Research*, that investment in hallmark and iconic events owned by cities and destinations provides the best long-term, sustainable value within all event portfolios.

Chapter 8: Economic valuation of events: combining methods based on revealed, stated and subjective preference data

By Reza Mortazavi and Tobias Heldt

Two methods for the economic valuation of events are discussed, being the travel cost method and a choice experiment. The former is based on revealed preferences and the latter on visitors' stated preferences. Also considered is an intangible value of events using individuals' subjective well-being (SWB) or happiness. The Swedish music festival Peace and Love is the case study, from which survey data were collected from 716 visitors. The survey contained questions about the actual behaviour of the respondents, such as expenditure patterns and travel behaviour. It also had questions on SWB and WTP for certain features of the festival like "other people attending" and "length of the festival". From the data collected, the authors estimated a consumer surplus for the event by applying the travel cost method, plus average and individual measures of SWB. The latter can be used to explore correlations between individuals' SWB and individual socio-economic characteristics, or consumer behaviour patterns.

The chapter ends by discussing the relevance of the approach for policy purposes. It contributes to the literature on value creation by highlighting the potential for using measures of consumer surplus in combination with actual visitor data on preferences to understand current and future impacts and values of an event.

Chapter 9: Valuing the inspirational impacts of major sports events

By Girish Ramchandani, Richard Coleman, Larissa Davies, Simon Shibli and Jerry Bingham

These authors tackle a thorny issue: that of valuing sport events extrinsically, or for what they can do for society. They say:

> Historically the 'value' of sporting events has been judged based on their ability to deliver direct economic/tourism benefits for the communities in which they are held. However, there is a growing acceptance that not all events that are 'major' in sporting terms are also 'major' in economic terms. Hence it is important to consider different types of value for which events can serve as a catalyst, including but not limited to social and environmental outcomes.
>
> This volume, Chapter 9, p.155,

The particular value creation claim they investigated is that sport events have an inspirational value, change attitudes and promote sport participation among attendees. This is often heard when justifying public sector involvement, as no one could argue with the goal of getting more people active and fostering a healthier population.

As with many evaluation studies designed to determine if policies and programmes achieve their aims, demonstrating causality is often illusive. The researchers had to rely on specific examples, plus the weight of available research findings, to draw conclusions.

> The results demonstrate that attendance at non-mega sports events can, to some extent, stimulate increases in participation at grassroots level. While these findings imply that there appears to be an inspiration effect, it is too

simplistic to expose people to an event in the hope of changing their activity behaviour as they are inspired in different ways.

Ibid., chapter 9, p.156

The fact is, many of the people who attend sport events are already active and, while the inspirational effects might encourage them to participate more, this is not the main desired benefit. The authors suggest "There is, therefore, a need for greater cohesive working between the various event stakeholders (e.g. organisers, funders, sport development agencies and national governing bodies) and to build sport participation strategies well in advance of hosting an event" (ibid., chapter 9, p.156). Event organisers/stakeholders should devise strategies to alleviate any barriers that prevent inactive people from attending events and actively encourage inactive people to attend events in order to leverage increased participation in the future.

Chapter 10: Understanding the value of events for families, and their impacts upon quality of life

By Raphaela Stadler and Allan Jepson

The chapter contextualises the potential to increase a family's overall quality of life (QOL) though festival and event attendance, where the major motivation for attendance is documented as enhancing social values through socialisation, family togetherness, or spending time with family and friends. Findings suggest three interconnected themes as being important conditions for family QOL: time and space, money/wealth and rest, health and happiness. These need to be positive, and taken into consideration by event organisers and stakeholders, in order to achieve family QOL through festival attendance.

QOL research has received very little attention within the field of festival and event studies. Researchers generally agree that leisure contributes to well-being and QOL, but that this inter-relationship is a complex one. It is not necessarily the amount of time that families spend together engaging in leisure activities, but how meaningful they are to individual family members and the family as a whole. Life satisfaction is also closely related to leisure satisfaction, particularly when participating with other people with whom one has more intimate relationships, such as families or close friends (Cummins, 1996). Socialisation and family togetherness have been identified in numerous festival studies, but no study has connected QOL.

Ontological 'mapping' of key concepts and terms

When developing a field of study it is always useful to examine terms and concepts, and then move on to assess what we know and do not know, or claims about knowledge. By way of summarising the contents, we have constructed a simple ontological 'map' of the major terms and concepts used in this book – by all authors, including the editors. This has been done in tabular form, first isolating the core concept and terms, then examining the various 'domains' or specific topics considered in the book related to events: meanings of value, methods and measures.

Potentially, this ontological mapping can be extended and detailed in many ways. A thorough search and analysis of the research literature pertaining to claims of knowledge is the main gap. Contributors and editors have made a number of claims of knowledge, but the literature is vast and we do not have a complete synthesis to draw upon. More importantly, the field is not well enough developed to expect any consensus on impacts, let alone value creation. This is emerging, with our ontological mapping being part of the foundation work.

Establishing the core concept(s) of any field of enquiry cannot be done without reference to the literature. Is the subject matter unique? Are there enough people interested in this field or sub-field to warrant elaboration and synthesis? Through this book, we hope to encourage wider discourse and research on valuing events, thereby expanding the scope of event studies and related fields.

A major aim of ontological mapping is to establish a common lexicon, a task that requires everyone to understand the key terms and then to agree upon how they will be used. Some of the terms are essential to understanding the core concept, and many are shared with other fields. Some are linguistically common, but take on nuances when attached to this particular sub-field.

As shown in the box below, the concept 'value of events' is at the core, with closely related terms (like worth, benefit) being essential to understanding value. We also want to consider value concepts for portfolios and whole populations of events, which introduces terms like 'asset value' and 'healthy populations'. Whether planned events are valued for what they are – intrinsically – or what they can do – extrinsically – this book has revealed there is a large and presumably growing number of 'domains' or areas of application within which the assignment of value or worth is important. While the ensuing list might extend the content beyond our contributions, and it is undoubtedly not fully comprehensive, we can identify many domains and consider the key concepts and terms associated with each. These are not mutually exclusive, and an integrative approach to their evaluation is highly desirable.

CORE CONCEPT

- **value of events**
- **value of event portfolios**
- **value of event populations**

Synonyms of value: *worth, utility, profit, benefit, advantage, merit, usefulness*

- intrinsic versus extrinsic value
- healthy event populations
- healthy event portfolios

DOMAINS

- value for the built environment
- value for business
- value for the environment
- value for the economy
- value for consumers
- value for the community
- value for politics
- value for the individual
- value for the society

The first is the built environment, with events singly and as a sector contributing to the form, functioning and 'liveability' of communities and cities. Being a major factor in 'creative' cities and economies it is also a fairly recent theme. Events animate spaces, form part of the strategy for culture-led development (or repositioning) and have an impact on design – as with festival places and other event venues. The term 'festivalisation' has been used to describe the widespread adaption of festivals as instruments of urban policy, perhaps leading to sameness and over-supply.

BUILT ENVIRONMENT

- the value of planned events to the form, functioning and liveability of our built environments
- liveable cities; creative cities; urban design; animation of spaces
- festivalisation (too many events? too much sameness?)

Business, or the private sector and various corporations are heavily involved with events as owners, managers and sponsors. Some not-for-profits also take a business approach to events, looking for specific returns on investment such as fundraising and social marketing. While 'opportunity costs' should always be considered, the private sector, in particular, has to be aware of how its investment in events might preclude or complement other ways to generate ROI. Increasingly, corporate social responsibility is a factor to consider, and this might introduce altruism to the list of values created by and for corporations.

BUSINESS AND CORPORATIONS

- value created for owners, shareholders, directors of event companies, agencies or not-for-profits
- value created for corporations related to producing events; profit/ revenue; ROI
- value created by sponsoring events; marketing; sales; live communications; branding
- corporate social responsibility (CSR) and altruism

Ecological or natural-environment impacts are considered within the framework of 'green' and 'sustainable' events, with emphasis on reducing carbon and ecological footprints. But what value is created by events in this domain? More attention is required to address the positive roles planned events can have in fostering sustainable development and conservation, and this could include social marketing outcomes or actual monetary investments made by events.

ECOLOGY (NATURAL ENVIRONMENT)

- create value for ecological systems or aid in conserving the natural environment
- producing green events; sustainable development; ecological and carbon footprints
- investment in the environment; social marketing impact

The literature on economic impacts is vast, with numerous impact assessments demonstrating how value is created by attracting tourist expenditure, sponsorships, grants and other revenue to particular host areas. Less well understood is the process by which events singly or cumulatively might change economies, although in the context of mega events many experts have concluded that benefits seldom outweigh costs. Those investing in events for purposes of economic development or place marketing need to establish the ROI in quantitative terms, and this has often led to exaggeration through inappropriate methods or incomplete cost–benefit evaluation.

ECONOMY (including tourism and place marketing)

- events make a direct economic contribution
- changes to economies
- tourism, place marketing, economic development, media value
- economic impact forecasting and assessment; ROI
- impacts of single events versus long-term, cumulative effects; legacy; cost–benefit evaluation

---

From a consumer perspective, events offer value propositions: you can have satisfying, unique, rewarding experiences, co-created with the organisers. Using WTP methods, a consumer surplus can be estimated; this figure represents value over and above direct user expenditure. Other estimates of consumer value discussed in the book include the travel cost method and the value of time allocated. From a marketing perspective, value is enhanced through satisfying customers, leading to loyalty or positive word-of-mouth recommendations.

CONSUMERS

- values consumers place on event experiences; co-creation of experiences
- WTP; consumer surplus; travel cost; value of time allocated
- satisfaction; loyalty; future intentions

Taking a place or community perspective on events, all forms of value creation can be relevant – from jobs to entertainment, heritage preservation to urban design. 'Hallmark' events are permanent institutions and valued traditions that offer great value to whole communities. Civic pride, community development, identity building and capital formation (especially social and cultural) are related concepts. Events also have special significance to various communities of interest, with 'iconic' events providing symbolic value. When it comes to impact, taking the community perspective demands consideration of the distribution of costs and benefits of events; unfortunately, many impact studies have failed to do this. Longer-term perspectives on cumulative impacts should include evaluation of positive and negative legacies, a topic that covers the catalyst role of events.

COMMUNITY

- events create value for communities (places) and communities of interest; identity and pride
- community development; self-sufficiency; social and cultural capital formation
- the distribution of costs and benefits
- events as catalysts for change; infrastructure, hallmark and iconic events

---

Most events include cultural activities, if culture is understood in a wide sense of the word. This also means that most events have cultural impact, both by preserving traditions and by developing a dynamic cultural environment in a region. On the one hand, food festivals may bring old traditions and recipes to life and create cultural capital, as well as local pride in a region. On the other hand, modern music festivals, as well as theatre and dance festivals, develop the regional culture and introduce multiculturalism and new cultural capital.

CULTURE

- elements of language, religion, customs, rituals, symbols and heritage preservation
- preserving traditions, versus commodification; celebrating cultures and multiculturalism
- intangible effects and cultural capital
- events create value by developing culture and fostering multiculturalism

---

Individuals are not always consumers; the non-use valuation of events takes into account the fact that people value them for providing choices (option value) and because they are perceived to be good for non-personal reasons like community and economic development. Non-use valuation also covers legacy value, being the passing on of traditions or the consideration given to ensuing generations and their needs. We also have a literature on how volunteers and other participants benefit from attending events, ranging from learning, health and self-development to personal identity building. When individuals and families are happy and healthy, QOL increases for the whole community. And we should not forget the fact that many people work in the event sector for wages and profit.

INDIVIDUALS

- personal identity; self-development through participation
- non-use values: entertainment value; choice; existence value; QOL for persons/families
- leisure experiences (intrinsic value); volunteers (experience)
- staff (income)

Political values seem to play a decisive role for events that, according to existing knowledge, will generate large economic deficits. Mega events like the Olympic Games are often examples of this situation, when the only remaining explanation for countries bidding behaviour is the political value of the event. But political value is also present for smaller events that need support either financially or to overcome red tape and local regulations. In fact, some politicians may actively pursue a festivalisation policy to create value in the community.

POLITICS

- festivalisation of policy
- power; the influence of elite groups
- regulation
- conflict resolution

Value creation for the society is a very broad domain. Here we consider value creation for society as a whole; there are overlaps, especially with value for the community and political value. Societies are often heterogeneous and a well-balanced event portfolio meets the needs of the society as a whole, but also of specific sub-groups and communities within the society. This can also give legitimacy to different communities and create pride, identity and inspiration. Social capital is generated, as well as integration. Social capital is also beneficial for the QOL and health in the society. Social marketing may be actively used, related to the event policy, in order to change habits for the betterment of society.

SOCIETY

- values generated for society as a whole and for specific sub-groups or communities of interest – social capital; integration; equality; identity; well-being; civic/national pride; inspiration
- legitimation of groups; legacy; preservation of traditions
- social marketing
- QOL; health

Process, methods and measures

Value cannot normally be considered without bringing 'evaluation' into the mix. What we want to accentuate is that the technical process of evaluation, with its emphasis on problem solving, efficiency and effectiveness in goal attainment – including all aspects of impact forecasting and assessment – provides possible inputs to the matter of assigning value or worth.

'Intrinsic' and 'extrinsic' are two general approaches to assigning value. The planned-events literature has been heavily weighted towards extrinsic measures that assign value by reference to what events can do, or their instrumentalist value. Quantitative measures of costs and benefits and economic impacts are essential in this perspective, whereas it is also possible to stress the inherent or intrinsic value of events without reference to such measures.

There are many concepts and terms closely associated with the process of valuing events and evaluation as a technical process, including impact forecasting and assessment. Here we focus on the methods and measures that form an expanding toolkit for evaluators.

CORE CONCEPT	**DOMAINS**
- **evaluation of events and event portfolios**	- decision-making and synergies
- forecasting and assessment	- impact assessment
- evaluation as a technical process	- qualitative approach
	- quantitative approach

The starting point is to consider decision-making and the synergies that arise when portfolios of events are considered, or through collaborations, and at the whole-population level through interdependencies among events.

DECISION-MAKING AND SYNERGIES

- decisions on support or termination of an event
- goal attainment (effectiveness measures; proving cause and effect)
- who will assess the value of events (e.g., consultants or academics) and by what methods?
- problem solving (including efficiency measures); continuous improvement
- success strategies and factors
- a multi-stakeholder approach (versus single point of view)
- consensus building; political market square; collaboration; networks
- synergistic effects of multiple events and event portfolios that create additional value (e.g. resource and knowledge sharing; critical mass; the city/destination brand)
- events as catalysts for change; asset value and portfolio value

Emphasis has been placed on the fact that evaluation – in practice, and in terms of coverage in the literature – is dominated by technical processes such as problem solving, proving cause and effect (i.e. goal attainment) and efficiency issues. Impact assessments are part of this type of evaluation, providing one possible input to evaluation of event value or worth.

IMPACT ASSESSMENT

- forecasting and estimating post-event impacts as one factor in assigning value
- evidence and attribution challenges
- direct economic contribution
- economic changes
- triple bottom line approach; triple impact assessments
- long-term, cumulative impacts

Numerous possible measures of value are available and many have been illustrated and discussed in this book. We break them down into qualitative and quantitative, recognising that multiple methods and measures will be the norm when evaluation of worth is the challenge. Some measures are tied to specific value domains, such as WTP being one way of measuring consumer surplus or future demand. Others have many possible applications across the value domains.

QUALITATIVE APPROACH

- suitable for evaluating intangible benefits, costs and impacts

Measures

- QOL; individual or SWB; life satisfaction; socialisation
- resident/consumer perceptions of impacts and attitudes towards events/tourism
- social capital; collaborative value; network value; value co-creation
- inspirational effects; feelings
- altruism or vicarious value
- legitimacy; empowerment; engagement
- pride; loyalty; commitment
- public relations outcomes
- capacity development

Methods

- community forums
- content analysis
- observation; participant observation (ethnography)
- netnography

Many measures and methods have been developed for economic impact and marketing assessments, but far fewer are available for other domains. There is, therefore, a great need for development of methods suitable for evaluation across all the domains.

QUANTITATIVE APPROACH

Measures

- direct economic contribution; multiplier effects; CGE
- use value; WTP; consumer surplus
- bequest or legacy value; option value; existence value (all non-use measures)
- attraction value or drawing power
- behavioural change
- media value (advertising equivalence)
- revealed and stated preferences

Methods

- visitor surveys, interviews
- trend analysis (e.g. occupancy rates, business turnover); longitudinal research
- travel cost method
- choice experiment

The next step in ontological mapping in the sub-field of event valuation will be to catalogue and critically examine claims to knowledge – which inevitably identifies gaps. It can be said with some authority that we know a great deal about economic impacts, motivations and satisfaction – given the emphasis on these topics in the literature – but, as demonstrated, there are many other domains to explore.

What do we really know about the processes by which government agencies, companies or individuals determine the worth of an event or the entire planned-event sector? Can we predict who will support events, or oppose bidding on events, and is it a rational process? Recent consideration of event portfolios complicates the issues greatly, demanding real-world evaluations over longer periods of time, including identification of the cumulative impacts and synergistic effects that might lead to greater value creation.

References

Cummins, R.A. (1996). The domains of life satisfaction: an attempt to order chaos. *Social Indicators Research*, 38(3), 303–28.

Dwyer, L., Forsyth P. and Dwyer, W. (2010). *Tourism Economics and Policy*, Bristol: Channel View.

Getz, D. (2013). *Event Tourism: Concepts, International Case Studies, and Research*. New York: Cognizant.

Zimbalist, A. (2015a). *Circus Maximus: The Economic Gamble Behind Hosting the Olympics and the World Cup*. Washington, DC: Brookings Institution Press.

Zimbalist, A. (2015b). The illusory economic gains from hosting the Olympics and World Cup. *World Economics*, 16(1), 35–42.

Index

academic value 5
aesthetic value 5
altruism 115
Ansoff Matrix 137, 138
Arrow, K. and Fisher, A. 92
associational value 65
Austin, J. E. and Seitanidi, M. M. 59–60, 64–5

Bærenholdt, J.O. 75
Barcelona 76–7
Baumol, W. J. 95
Belk, R.W. 47
Bentham, J. 89–90
bequest value 92–3, 115
Blake, A. 107, 109
Boardley, I.D. 139
Boyle, K. and Bishop, R. 90–1, 96
Brown, S. et al. 4
built environment 192
business and corporations 192

Castells, M. 74, 80
Celsi, R. L. et al. 43–4
chapter summaries 183–90
choice experiment 127–31
Civil Exchange 12–13
Clarke, A. 47
Clawson, M. and Knetsch, J. L. 127
collaborative value creation (CVC) 64–8
community 194
community events and festivals 13–15
computable equilibrium modelling 108–9
consumers 193
core concept 191,196
cost-benefit analysis 109–12
Crofts, C. et al. 139
Crompton, J. and McKay, S. L. 161, 167
Crowther, P. and Orefice, C. 75–6

cultural capital 5, 194
culture 194
customer value 61

decision making and synergies 197
direct expenditure 113
domains 191–6
Donaghy, M. et al. 12
Dwyer, L. and Forsyth, P. 186–7
Dwyer, L., Forsyth P., and Dwyer, W. 186

ecology 195
economic impacts 106–9, 120, 181, 193
economic valuation 124–6; of music festivals 126–7
economic value 46–8, 51–2
economy 193
Edvardsson, B., et al. 41
environmental impacts: the cost of 116–19
existence value 91, 115
expectations and blind belief 15–17
extrinsic value 2, 6–7, 99, 181–3, 191, 196

Falassi, A. 160
Ferguson, B. 25
festival studies 159–60
Foley, M., et al. 10
Foster, K. and Robinson, P. 163–4
Frey, B. S. 91–2

Geertz, C. 160
Getz, D. 59, 188
Goodwin, C. et al. 47
Goulding, C. and Saren, M. 45
Graeber, D. 40–2, 47

Hanley, N. and Barbier, E. 90, 92
Hannam, K. and Halewood, C. 45
Harrington, M. 168

Heldt, T. and Mortazavi, R. 127
Hicks, J. R. 94, 98
historical value 5
Hogan, K. and Norton, K. 136
Holbrook, M. B. 39, 95
Hotelling, H. 127
hybrid approach 119–21

impact assessment 1, 197
individuals 195
informational value 5
input-output modelling 107–8
inspiration effect 143–4; attitudinal
  changes and the likely causes of the
  146–9
interaction value 65
intrinsic value 2, 6–7, 74, 91, 99, 115,
  181–3, 185–6, 191, 196

Kaldor, N. 94, 98
Karababa, E. and Kjeldgaard, D. 40, 42,
  52
Kozinets, R. V. 44–5
Krutilla, J. V. 92
Kuyken. 162–3

Laiho, S. 163
Lane, A. et al. 138–9
Levy, S. J. 44
Liburd, J.J. and Hergesell, A. 164
Light, D. 161

Mackellar, J. 46
Maffesoli, M. 45
Mahtani, K. R. et al. 137
Mair, J. and Laing, J.H. 140, 141
market development 137, 138, 140, 146,
  151–3, 155
market penetration 137, 138, 140, 146,
  151–3, 155
Maslow, A. 162
Mason, R. 5
Massey, D. 13, 21
Mauss, M. 47
May, J. 18–19
McCartney, G. et al. 138
McClinchey, K.A. 14
Mermiri, T. 24
Miller, D. 47
Mintel Marketing Intelligence 160
Mules, T. and Dwyer, L. 96
Muniz, A, M. and O'Guinn, T, C. 43
Murray, J.G. 20

network value 73–6; the concept of 74–6;
  methodological approach to 76;
  strategies to increase 80–3
Ng, I. and Smith, I. 2
non-use value 91, 114–16; examples of **93**;
  in a cultural context 95–6; in an event
  context 96–7

ontological mapping 190–9
opportunity cost 114
option value 91–2, 114–15
Østergaard, P. et al. 47
oyster festival 48–9

Packer, J. and Ballantyne, J. 163–4
participation and engagement in sport:
  conceptual models of 139–40;
  methods 141–3
participation behaviour: changes in 149–51
participation legacies of sports events
  137–9
Peace and Love music festival 128
Pearce, D. W. and Turner, R. K. 91–2
Peñaloza, L. and Venkatesh, A. 41
policy and funding 24–8
political context 11–13, 137, 195
political environment *see* political context
population (of events) 2, 191
Poria, Y. et al. 161
portfolio (of events) 2, 181, 183, 191,
  195–7, 199
Poston, D. et al. 166
process, methods and measures 196–9
Prochaska, J.O. et al. 139–41

qualitative (approach) 198
quality of life 161–2; individual 162–4;
  family 162–5; money/wealth 168–9;
  rest, health and happiness 169–70; time
  and space 167–8
quantitative (approach) 198–9
Quinn, B and Wilks, L. 19

Ragheb, M. and Tate, R. 166
Rapley, M. 162–3, 168
religious value 5
revealed preference methods 94
Richards G. and Palmer, R. 75
Rihova et al. 43
Robinson, P. 160–1
Robson, C. 2
Rojek, C. 10
role of children within families 160–1

Sacco, P.L. 75
Schouten, J. W. and McAlexander, J. H. 43
Seligman, M., and Csikszentmihalyi, M. 163
semiotic value 44–6, 51
Shaw, K. and Theobald, K. 11
Shaw, W. D. and Rogers, J. 126
Sheldon, T. 162, 168–70
Sherry, J. F. 47
Sheth, J. N. et al. 61, 66
Sirgy, M.J. 162
social capital 5, 19, 74–5, 196
social value 42–4, 50–1
society 196
socio-cultural value 5, 8
Sónar festival 77–80
spiritual value 3
Stabell, C.B. and Fjeldstad, Ø.D. 74
stated preference methods 94–5
Stebbins, R. A. 63
subjective well-being 131–2
subjects and objects of study 8
symbolic value 5, 47, 51, 83–4
synergistic value 65–6

Taks, M. et al. 156
Tayler, C. et al. 163–4
Throsby, C. D. 5, 91, 96
total economic value 112–16
transferred resource 65
transtheoretical model (TTM) 139–41
Turner, V. 160

use value 90, 112–13; examples of **93**;
  in an event context 96–7
Uysal, M. et al. 161

value **4**, 60–1, 89–90; and evaluation 28–9;
  conceptualisation within an event
  context 3–6; definition 2–3; for events
  and destinations 61; methods used to
  assess 94–5
value co-creation in networks 62–3
value of involvement 17–23
Van Gennep, A. 159–60
Vargo, S. L. and Lusch, R. F. 40
Veblen, T. 67
Venkatesh, A. and Peñaloza, L. 42
Venkatesh et al. 47
vicarious value *see* altruism

Waterman, S. 14, 18
Weed, M. et al. 136, 138–9
Wilkinson, L. 63
Williams, P. and Soutar, G. N. 61
Woodruff, R. B. 61
worth 2–3, 4

Yngfalk, A. 44

Zeithaml, V. A. 60
Zimbalist, A. 188

For Product Safety Concerns and Information please contact our EU
representative GPSR@taylorandfrancis.com
Taylor & Francis Verlag GmbH, Kaufingerstraße 24, 80331 München, Germany